Screen Comedy and Online Audiences

Screen Comedy and Online Audiences is boldly, brilliantly diverse, offering up a multi-text exploration of how different modalities, hybrids and subgenres of screen comedy are valued (or not) by an equally diverse range of audiences. Inger-Lise Kalviknes Bore also adopts a multi-sited approach, deftly analysing responses and reviews across the likes of amazon.com, Facebook, imdb, Pinterest, reddit, Tumblr, Twitter and YouTube. Brimming with insight, this book shows how indispensable fan/audience studies can be for understanding comedy's cultural politics and affective resonances.
—Professor Matt Hills, University of Huddersfield

At last! A detailed, evidence-based study of *the* major gap in the study of media and comedy; audiences. Offering a convincing argument for the specificity of comedy as a mode of popular media, this book artfully explores audience responses to a range of humorous media on TV, in film, and online. With chapters on gender, fandom, romcom, offence and comic failure, Bore's analysis pinpoints the importance of finding out what people do with comedy. As such, it impressively forges an important new direction in the study of media and humour.
—Dr. Brett Mills, University of East Anglia

The question of why we laugh (or don't laugh) has intrigued scholars since antiquity. This book contributes to that debate by exploring how we evaluate screen comedy. What kinds of criteria do we use to judge films and TV shows that are meant to be funny? And what might that have to do with our social and cultural backgrounds, or with wider cultural ideas about film, TV, comedy, quality and entertainment? The book examines these questions through a study of audience responses posted to online facilities such as Twitter, Facebook, review sites, blogs and message boards. Bore's analysis of these responses considers a broad range of issues, including how audiences perceive the idea of "national" comedy; what they think of female comedians; how they evaluate romcoms, sitcoms and web comedy; what they think is acceptable to joke about; what comedy fans get excited about; how fans interact with comedians; and what comedy viewers really despise. The book demonstrates some of the ways in which we can adapt theories of humour and comedy to examine the practices of contemporary screen audiences, while offering new insights into how they negotiate the opportunities and constrictions of different online facilities to share their views and experiences.

Inger-Lise Kalviknes Bore is Senior Lecturer in the Birmingham Centre for Media and Cultural Research at Birmingham City University, UK.

Routledge Research in Cultural and Media Studies

For a full list of titles in this series, please visit www.routledge.com.

Screen Comedy and Online Audiences

Inger-Lise Kalviknes Bore

Routledge
Taylor & Francis Group

LONDON AND NEW YORK

First published 2017 by Routledge

2 Park Square, Milton Park, Abingdon, Oxfordshire OX14 4RN
52 Vanderbilt Avenue, New York, NY 10017

Routledge is an imprint of the Taylor & Francis Group, an informa business

First issued in paperback 2019

Library of Congress Cataloging-in-Publication Data
Names: Bore, Inger-Lise Kalviknes, author.
Title: Screen comedy and online audiences / by Inger-Lise
Kalviknes Bore.
Description: New York: Routledge, 2017. |
Series: Routledge research in cultural and media studies |
Includes bibliographical references and index.
Identifiers: LCCN 2016059205
Subjects: LCSH: Comedy films—History and criticism. | Television
comedies—History and criticism. | Motion picture audiences—Social
aspects. | Television viewers—Social aspects. |
Online social networks—Social aspects.
Classification: LCC PN1995.9.C55 B67 2017 | DDC 791.43/617—dc23
LC record available at https://lccn.loc.gov/2016059205

ISBN: 978-1-138-78066-8 (hbk)
ISBN: 978-0-367-86970-0 (pbk)

Typeset in Sabon
by codeMantra

Contents

Acknowledgements

I would like to thank the Birmingham Centre for Media and Cultural Research for supporting my development of this project. In particular, I appreciate the advice and help I got from Simon "Coach" Barber, Hazel Collie, Gemma Commane, Rajinder Dudrah, Anne Gräfer, Sue Heseltine, Jon Hickman, Paul Long, John Mercer and Nick Webber. Shout out to my School of Media roomies, who provide a steady supply of laughs and coffee. Outside of Birmingham City University, I would like to thank my extended academic network. Matt Hills offered great advice, as always, and many others kindly shared their work with me. I am grateful for my family and friends, who have offered cheerleading and healthy distractions in equal measure. Finally, thank you to the Internet users who generously agreed to let me include their words in this book and to my editors, Felisa Salvago-Keyes and Christina Kowalski, for their patience and guidance.

This book is dedicated to Marc, Axel and Kasper (despite its sad lack of choo choo trains).

1 Introduction

Our attempts at understanding humour can be traced back as far as Plato, but we still don't know exactly what it is that makes something seem funny, rather than just strange or foolish. I think this sense of mystery is what attracts me to this field. I am fascinated by the different permutations of comedy across cinema, TV and other screens, by our different tastes in comedy and by the ability of comedy to delight, disgust and fall flat. As Billig (2005) notes, "Any attempt to find the objectively laughable – the holy grail of comedy that will guarantee to unleash the biological mechanism of laughter – will be doomed to failure" (186). I am also intrigued by how audiences talk about comedy, how they express their feelings of amusement, affection, excitement or disappointment, and how they argue about what's funny and what isn't. Finally, I am interested in what we can learn by exploring how ideas of humour and comedy circulate in and across different cultures. The cultures I am focusing on in this book are online cultures, digital "worlds" situated on social media like message boards, review sites, blogs and social networks. Through such media, audience members around the world can participate in the ongoing debate about what it is that makes us laugh.

So how can we explore the relationship between screen comedy and its online audience cultures? Studies of comedy viewers are surprisingly rare, but we can identify two key, if overlapping, traditions. One strand focuses primarily on audience responses to specific comedic texts. This media-centric approach includes Jhally and Lewis (1992) and Coleman (1998), who examine audience interpretations of *The Cosby Show* (NBC 1984–1992), as well as Gray's (2006) study of fan, non-fan and anti-fan responses to *The Simpsons* (Fox since 1989). The second strand of research is less interested in responses to specific texts and more interested in audience identities, tastes and practices. Key examples here include sociological studies that investigate the relationship between class and comedy consumption (e.g. Friedman 2014 and Kuipers 2006), as well as Phillips's (2011 and 2012) work on comedy fandom. This book is informed by both of these traditions. Like the former, I discuss audience responses to textual elements, such as style, characters, dialogue, narrative and performance, as well as to paratextual elements, such as stardom, promotional material and reviews. And, like the latter tradition, I explore the significance of audience identities and of wider cultural discourses around humour and comedy.

Through my approach to these issues I argue for the value of a multi-text approach, which facilitates identification of commonalities and specificities in audience responses to different screen comedy forms, including film, TV and web comedy. I also emphasise the importance of considering the context of audience engagement with comedy, and I here reflect on the ways in which different online spaces facilitate particular kinds of audience practices and particular ways of talking about comedy. This approach draws on Williams (2015), who emphasises "the comparative potential of multi-site case studies" in research on online audiences.

Humour, Dialogue and Performativity

One of the key motivations behind my multi-text and multi-site approach is to encourage further debate about how we can adapt existing theories of humour and comedy for thinking about the *diversity* of contemporary comedy texts and audience practices. As Medhurst (2007) points out, "comedy theory can seem irredeemably besotted with Comedy – not comedy, the jumble of texts and pleasures, but Comedy, the essence of the thing itself" (10). Humour theory has been central to such inquiries. As a body of work, it comprises three key strands: superiority theory, incongruity theory and relief theory. Although there are overlaps among these approaches, it is useful to think of them as examining different aspects of joking:

> Incongruity Theory analyses joke content; the Superiority Theory analyses the audience's relationship to the butt of the joke; the Relief Theory analyses the audience's physical and mental reactions to the joke content. Thus they examine the text, the context, and the reaction respectively.
>
> (Mills 1998: 44–45)

Superiority theory can be traced back to Plato's argument that laughter expresses a malicious sense of superiority over the "evil and folly" of others (Morreall 1983: 4). Similarly, Hobbes (1651) maintained that it is produced by a sudden sense of self-satisfaction – either because of something *we've* done, or because we see something "deformed" in *others* that makes us look good in comparison (36). Understandably, these perceptions led both Plato and Hobbes to conclude that humour is a character flaw, but later theorists have pointed out that we might feel morally superior without being amused (Palmer 1994) and that we might laugh at something without evaluating ourselves – for example, when we feel surprised and delighted about running into an old friend (Morreall 1983).

Rather than locating humour in the distinction between superiority and inferiority, incongruity theory connects it to the identification of something that is "out of place, mixed up or not quite right" (King 2002: 5). Bergson (1901/2004) suggests that we laugh at rigidity because it appears to be a comical failure to adapt to social change, and this rigidity is represented through textual elements such as inversion, repetition and situations that belong to "independent series of events" and can be simultaneously understood in two different ways (41). Incongruity theory has been developed further by Palmer (1987), who argues that, in order for an incongruity to be *humorous*, it must contradict our expectations in a way that is both surprising and more implausible than plausible. This "comic surprise" (40) creates a sense of absurdity that reassures us "all will be well immediately after" (56).

The third strand of humour theory is relief theory, and the key theorist in this area is Freud, whose psychoanalytic approach tries to explain the instinctual pleasures of word play, jokes, the comic (1905/1991) and gallows humour (1927/1990). Like incongruity theorists, Freud (1905/1991) argues that jokes rely on the ambiguities of language and techniques like condensation and displacement, but he is primarily interested in how this process lifts inhibitions and gives us pleasure by allowing us to express forbidden thoughts. Based on this observation, Freud identifies aggressive jokes as the most pleasurable, because they offer relief by "lifting suppressions and repressions" (188). Bakhtin's (1968) theory of the carnivalesque can also be positioned within the relief theory strand. Examining medieval festivities such as the carnival, he argues that laughter had a central role at such events, which celebrated a process of rebirth symbolised by temporary subversions of hierarchies and a focus on the grotesque body, with its leaking orifices and protruding belly, nose and genitalia. Within this context, Bakhtin sees laughter as liberating: "Laughter demolishes fear and piety before an object, before a world, making of it an object of familiar contact and thus clearing the ground for an absolutely free investigation of it" (23).

Each of these approaches offers insights into specific aspects and instances of humour (for more extensive discussions of humour theory, see Morreall 1983 or Mills 2009), but audience engagement with screen comedy can't be reduced to a string of responses to isolated textual moments. I therefore want to integrate humour theory in a framework that is informed by another of Bakhtin's concepts, which is dialogue. The idea of dialogue has been developed across most of Bakhtin's work (Holquist 2002), and it emphasises the relationships between texts (or "utterances") and their contexts:

> Each utterance is filled with echoes and reverberations of other utterances to which it is related by the communality of the sphere of speech communication. Every utterance must be regarded primarily

as a *response* to preceding utterances of the given sphere (we understand the word "response" here in the broadest sense). Each utterance
refutes, affirms, supplements, and relies on the others, presupposes
them to be known, and somehow takes them into account.
(Bakhtin 1992: 91)

I want to use the concept of dialogue to draw attention to the relationships between different textual elements, between individual texts and
among texts, audiences and wider cultural discourses. A useful way of
conceptualising this dialogue is to consider how screen comedies and
their audiences are situated within "culturally figured worlds" (Holland
et al. 1998: 52) that have their own narratives and value systems and
that provide "the frames of meaning in which interpretations of human
actions are negotiated" (271).

Within this Bakhtinian framework I want to combine humour theory
with the semiotic concept of "modality", which "concerns the reality
attributed to a message" by a speaker and a listener (Hodge and Tripp
1986: 104). I think comedy's perceived distance from "reality" is key
to making sense of audience responses, because it can make comedy
seem like a "safe" space to explore ambiguities, transgressions and "loss
of control" (Neale and Krutnik 1990: 69). As Hodge and Tripp (1986)
note, different "markers" can strengthen or weaken modality (104). For
example, in the U.S. sitcom *Parks and Recreation* (NBC 2009–2015),
which I discuss in chapter 2, the documentary shooting style is a marker
of a strong modality, while the opening credits that identify the actors is
a marker that weakens the modality. However, both of those evaluations
rely on my understanding of the conventions of screen documentary and
screen fiction. This demonstrates that our modality judgements of screen
comedy are informed by our "modality systems" (130), which have been
developed from our experiences of media conventions *and* our experiences of "the real world". So, in my reading, the contrast between events
in *Parks and Recreation* and what I believe is likely to happen in local
government in the U.S. weakens the modality of the show. As Hodge
and Tripp conclude, "judgements about 'reality' are complex, fluid and
subjective". Importantly, they are also rooted in "ideological struggles"
over "[t]he definition of reality" (130). My particular beliefs about gender roles, government and politics will inform the extent to which I read
certain aspects of the show as making more "serious" comments about
the world and the extent to which I consider those messages as being
close to reality. Our modality judgements, then, are situated within ideological structures.

Integrating this semiotic concept with Mills' (2009) "cue theory" enables us to consider how audiences interpret texts as having a *comedic*
modality, rather than a fantasy modality, for example. Mills argues that
"comedy's primary marker is the *intention* to be funny, for we know that

something is a comedy even if it doesn't make us laugh at all" (94). As Neale and Krutnik (1990) note, "formal comedy" is produced and distributed within the "entertainment" industries, which "designate" such productions as comedy (64–65). This "comic impetus" (Mills 2009: 5) is signalled through "metacues" (95), such as scheduling, opening titles and star personas, that rely on audiences' having specific forms of knowledge that lead them to *expect* a comedy. Comic incongruities, such as jokes, comic situations and comic performances, are also formal features that mark texts as comedic, and they may encourage us to feel superior to representations of foolishness or experience relief at violations of social conventions. So, our previous experiences of watching comedy can help us identify the comic intention of such texts and to recognise specific moments as being sources of humour that are intended to make us laugh.

As cue theory indicates, comedic texts are not *inherently* funny. If they were, we would all laugh at the same things, which is clearly not the case. Instead, we learn to identify certain textual properties as being *intended* as funny, and whether or not we accept this invitation to laugh will depend on our relationships with characters, our understanding of the narrative so far, our comprehension of cultural references, our understanding of cultural discourses around comedy, our tastes, our attitudes towards the themes that are represented, our previous experiences of comedy, our moods, who we are watching it with, and so on. I therefore want to think of humour as embodied and performative. This approach draws on Ahmed's (2004) theory of emotions, which argues that: "It is through affective encounters that objects or others are perceived as having attributes, which 'gives' the subject an identity that is apart from others" (52–53). So, when I perceive a comedy film as *being* funny, my performance of amusement *constructs* the film as having the essential quality of being funny, while also constructing my own identity as a comedy viewer with particular experiences and tastes. My *feelings* of amusement are then seen as a sign that the film *is* indeed funny, which confirms the "truth" of my judgement in a powerful "loop" (194). However, my individual experiences of comedy are situated within an "affective economy" (8) of wider cultural discourses around what is funny and what isn't, and within this environment our repetitive performances of amusement reinforce cultural norms by reproducing "past associations" (194). This book tries to unpack some of these inscriptions of "funny" or "not funny" by investigating how audiences articulate their evaluations of screen comedy, while pondering some of the discursive gaps in those accounts. I am also interested in *who* we allow to "be" funny, and so chapter 3 focuses on the marginalised role of women in screen comedy, while chapter 9 examines ideas of comic failure. And, finally, I want to consider some of the complexities of the label "funny". What kinds of qualities does laughter inscribe in those that are deemed amusing? How does it "grab and reorientate bodies" (Graefer 2014: 7) towards or away from each other?

However, amusement is of course not the only possible feeling in responses to comedy. Freud (1905/1991) identifies a sense of relief, while we also often experience a range of other "affective resonances" (Paasonen 2011: 189). Screen comedy can adopt different strategies to encourage viewers to read moments as exciting, sad or romantic, for example, and modality shifts are important mechanisms in such strategies. A weaker modality offers "comic insulation" (Palmer 1987: 45) by reminding us that what we are seeing is not "real", which encourages us to relax and laugh at characters' failures, mishaps and "unlikely triumphs". In contrast, a stronger modality can invite us to "care" about characters and "to follow their fortunes with a degree of emotional investment in the outcome" (King 2002: 9). Many narrative-driven comedies will use subtle and more marked modality shifts to offer viewers comic pleasures while encouraging us to follow the narrative and care about what happens. Across different narrative situations, then, we might inscribe characters with different emotions, so that they might be deemed "laughable" in one scene and "romantic" in another, or we might experience different and sometimes conflicting emotions at the same time.

I think it is also important to interrogate the notion of comic distance or insulation, because viewers are also clearly able to feel closeness to comedy. Although a comedic modality can distance us from a character's foolishness or misfortune, for example, the sense of amusement might make us feel close to those who are perceived to "give" us that jokework or comic situation (the characters, the writers, the director or the performers, for example) through a sense of shared understanding, perhaps, or through a sense of gratitude for the pleasurable experience. While a comedic modality reminds us that the events we see are fictitious, comic moments also draw attention to the "realness" of their performers and other creative practitioners and the "authenticity" of their displays of comedic skills in writing, improvisation, comic timing and physical clowning, for example. So, comedy invites viewers to adopt reading strategies that shift between orientations towards characters and performers (Cook 1982), and the resulting combination of distance and proximity is explored further in my analysis of comedy fandom in chapters 2 and 9, and of responses to sitcom in chapter 6.

Finally, it is important to stress that we don't necessarily fully recognise our own affective responses. Feelings can be vague or fleeting, they might involve a combination of reactions, and we might not be able to identify which object or "other" they are directed against. As Paasonen (2011) notes, "Affect is visceral, multisensory, and untranslatable" (205). She uses the concept of resonance to consider the relationship between porn and its users, and I think it can usefully be adapted to offer insights into audience engagement with comedy, too. As she suggests, "Resonance encompasses the emotional and cognitive as well as the sensory and affective, and it points to the considerable effort involved in separating the two". While the term has different meanings in different disciplines, she defines it as referring "to movements and experiences of being moved, touched, and affected by what is tuned to the 'right frequency'" (16). What I am interested in exploring here, then, is how screen comedy audiences *articulate* affective responses and resonance, and how the *performances* of audience identities are situated within what we might call discursive environments, dialogues or cultural worlds. What kinds of affective registers can we identify by analysing online audience responses to screen comedy, and what can this tell us about our relationships with different kinds of comedic texts? How do different audience groups value different kinds of viewing experiences and different textual elements, and what might that have to do with broader cultural hierarchies? And where are the gaps or contradictions in these narratives of affective resonance and "dissonance" (Paasonen 2011: 16)?

So, to adapt existing theories of humour and comedy for thinking about contemporary screen comedy audiences, I here integrate those concepts into a Bakhtinian framework that facilitates analysis of the dialogic relationship among different textual elements and among texts, viewers and their wider cultural contexts. Within this framework, combining humour theory with the concepts of modality, affect and resonance enables me to consider different emotions in encounters between audiences and texts, while conceptualising humour as performative is key to my examination of the relationship among audience responses, identities, online cultures and wider cultural discourses of comedy.

Multi-Sited Research and Online Audiences

The emphasis on articulations and performativity reflects my interest in the mediation of reality and my affinity with a poststructuralist tradition (Saukko 2003). More specifically, my research sits within the "textual turn" in qualitative audience research, which analyses audience responses as text or discourse. The texts I am focusing on here can be conceptualised as "audience-created paratexts", which Gray (2010) defines as "creative and discursive products" (143) that "position, define and create meaning for film and television" (3).

In designing this research, I have drawn on Saukko's (2003) proposal for dialogic, multi-sited studies that examine "how any given phenomenon takes shape in and across multiple locales and sites" (176). I would like to stress that I am not suggesting that data collected from different online sites are identical pieces of evidence. On the contrary, my approach aims to demonstrate how audience engagement with comedy will appear *differently* depending on perspective and context and to identify links between my object of study "and other social processes or locations" (178). So, while online audience research has tended to focus on single communities, this book examines different audience cultures in each chapter. There is, of course, no privileged site that can provide a "window" on online audience activities. As Hine notes:

> In a contemporary society within which the concept of context appears to have spiralled beyond comprehension with the advent of diverse forms of technologically mediated communication, the challenge of choosing appropriate contexts to study, and reflecting on the consequences of those choices for our ability to theorise adequately, seems greater than ever. (2011: 567)

Graefer (2014) observes that researching audience responses to screen comedy is tricky because "[t]he physical moment of laughter is largely invisible to the researcher as it happens in private, at home and spontaneously" (110). How can we tackle this challenge? My previous work in this area has been based on focus group data, and I have reflected on the tension between the "serious" and analytical talk that I encouraged in the focus groups and the ways in which participants reported that they "normally" talked about comedy (Bore 2012). The focus on "naturally occurring" online data in this book is, in part, a response to this tension. I am interested in exploring some of the different ways in which audiences choose to articulate their responses to comedy when they are not being coaxed by a researcher. *What* do they choose to share with other Internet users? *How* do they choose to share it? Importantly, my multisite approach also enables me to examine audience responses in the form of still and moving imagery in addition to different types of written material, and so I am replacing the challenge of encouraging talk about comedy with the challenge of analysing rather diverse content.

My methodological approach, then, is designed to highlight diversity while examining commonalities, to encourage reflection on how the selection of sites can impact on research findings, and to facilitate investigations of a range of theoretical concerns that have preoccupied studies of comedic texts. This includes the significance of cultural identities and belonging, stability and developments in comedic genres, and the meanings, pleasures and displeasures of transgressive comedy.

Research ethics remains a contested topic in debates on online audience research. It is important to acknowledge that when I quote posts that have been contributed to blogs, review sites, message boards and social networking sites, I shift these audience-produced texts from their intended context into an academic context. I am here only quoting posts from sites that are open to the general public (the sites don't require any log-in details to display content), but this still distributes the texts to a different readership and, if the producer of a post should decide to delete it, the quote will still remain in this book. I am adopting a two-part response to this ethical problem. First, when the sites enable me to do so, I have contacted the posters I am quoting in this book in order to ask for their informed consent to participate in this research by allowing me to use their material. I have chosen not to reproduce posts that included very aggressive or misogynistic content because I did not want to contact the contributors and risk attracting the hostility that is often directed at women who challenge sexism and misogyny in online spaces. I was also concerned about the harm that I might cause by reproducing such material out of its original context, so I have chosen to summarise and describe such posts rather than quote them directly.

Unfortunately, many of the posters I did contact did not respond to my request. In some cases, they may rarely log in to the particular site I used, or they might have left them altogether. As Williams (2015) observes, "permission for use of postings is difficult to attain owing to the transitory nature of online environments in which in which posters often leave communities" (13). Other sites, such as Facebook, make it difficult to get in touch with users who are not in our network. I have therefore decided to quote posts from users even if they did not respond to me. I acknowledge that my approach is problematic, but I am concerned that this stumbling block would otherwise prevent most qualitative research on Internet users or force researchers to eliminate quotes, which leads to other ethical concerns about academic rigour and whose "voices" we get to hear. Therefore, my second response to ethical concerns about context-shifting online quotes is to anonymise users, unless they have explicitly requested that I identify them by a particular name. In some cases, I have also refrained from identifying the site itself. I have ensured that whenever I quote posts that have been made under what appears to be a "real" name, rather than a nickname, it is not possible to track down that post by entering the quote into a search engine. And, finally, I have tried to retain the presentation of quoted material, including unconventional spelling and grammar.

Coming up

I will begin by looking at an example of comedic success, and end with an example of comic failure. In between, I examine a series of issues that complicate audience engagement with comedy. Chapter 2, then, explores *Parks and Recreation* fandom on the microblogging platform Tumblr, and it aims to illuminate some of the specificities of comedy fandom. My analysis highlights a push/pull dynamic facilitated by modality shifts that invite comic distance and emotional investment, as well as by fan attachment to comedies and comedians. I will explore how this tension is articulated through the quotation practices that are central to comedy fandom and consider how such quotations worked to shape the show itself.

The following three chapters explore the significance of cultural identities and belonging for online comedy audiences, through case studies that highlight comedy that is marginalised along the axes of gender, nationality and "race". Across these discussions, I will highlight and problematise the ways in which such comedy can become invested with representational responsibilities because they are seen to lack the contextual continuity afforded to texts that are closer to the centre of comedy culture.

Chapter 3 contributes to the debate around the marginalisation of women in comedy by examining responses to two Hollywood comedies that centre female characters and performers. Analysing blog reviews of *Bridesmaids* (2011), I identify a tendency to celebrate this film as a singular achievement for female-driven comedy and to inscribe it with responsibilities for promoting feminism and showing male audiences that women can be funny. I compare this reception with Twitter responses to Paul Feig's news that he would direct *Ghostbusters* (2016) and cast women in the lead roles. Exploring how Twitter users invoked different paratexts to imagine what this film would be like, I argue that this practice challenged the discourse of isolated achievement by situating *Ghostbusters* within a comedy culture where female-driven comedies and female comedians were visible and interlinked.

Chapter 4 addresses the dominance of Anglophone (and particularly U.S.) comedy by exploring national and transnational responses to the Norwegian comedy show *Lilyhammer* (NRK1/Netflix 2012–2014). Tracing this engagement across three different online spaces, I consider how audiences invoked notions of nationality and invested it with affects. I argue that some Norwegian viewers were initially worried that this rare TV export would implicate them in "national shame" (Ahmed 2004: 101) and contrast this with Norwegians who claimed privileged fan identities within the safe space of the official *Lilyhammer* Facebook page. Transnational fans rarely spoke to the Norwegianness of *Lilyhammer* but instead invoked the nation by positioning their engagement simultaneously within an imagined, international fan community and within their own specific national and regional contexts. This often worked to highlight that the Facebook page structured the fan community around an imagined U.S. audience, while fans on the periphery had delayed access to new episodes and were unable to participate in promotional fan activities.

Chapter 5 provides a bridge between my explorations of cultural identities and genre developments. Analysing YouTube comments in response to the British web comedy *Brothers with No Game* (since 2012), I consider how audience articulations of blackness intersected with identities of gender and nationality in discussions of representations and of investment in romantic relationships. Through this discussion, I reflect on the extent to which *Brothers with No Game*, as amateur media, offered a space to centre black narratives and black audiences. Highlighting that the web comedy genre was seen as an important alternative to (white) television comedy, I argue that the show's observational comedy facilitated experiences of pleasurable recognition, while the comment threads enabled viewers to feel part of an imagined, heterogeneous, diasporic audience laughing together.

Chapters 6 and 7 continue this analysis of audience responses to developments in comedy genres. I begin with a multi-sited study of the three television sitcoms *Everybody Hates Chris* (UPN/The CW, 2005–2009), *Gavin & Stacey* (BBC3/BBC2/BBC1, 2007–2010) and *Miranda* (BBC2/ BBC1, since 2009). While the case studies reflect on how each online site facilitates particular ways of talking about comedy, my discussion will identify a recurring desire for traditional sitcom that could be enjoyed by (nuclear) family audiences or that foregrounded the pleasures associated with established sitcom conventions. I suggest that this resistance to on-going generic developments challenged a critical discourse that foregrounds niche audiences and conflates "quality" with stylistic innovation.

Chapter 7 concludes my exploration of generic developments by shifting attention from web and television comedy to film. Analysing IMDb reviews of the romantic comedy *(500) Days of Summer* (2009), it examines how reviews articulated criteria for "good" romantic comedy and how individual reviewers evaluated the film against those criteria. I argue that, although IMDb and other online spaces offer amateur reviewers opportunities to participate in critical debates around film, these reviews remain preoccupied with a romcom discourse established by professional film critics. The posts revalorise affective experiences that had been dismissed through this dominant discourse, but they also frequently attempt to "rescue" *(500) Days of Summer* from the feminized, commercial romcom genre by constructing it as original and innovative.

Chapter 8 examines audience engagement with transgressive comedy through a case study of Amy Schumer paratexts on the social bookmarking site Pinterest. Returning to the significance of gender in comedy culture, I argue that Schumer here became a flexible symbolic resource within a project of feminine self-improvement, providing inspiration for individual style as well as feminist agency. My analysis problematises this function, arguing that Pinterest practices obscured Schumer's compliance with postfeminist ideals as well as her comedic engagement with the complexities of everyday gendered negotiations.

The book's final chapter is dedicated to unintended comedy and comic failure. It draws attention to some of the tensions and ambiguities of laughter by examining the critical fandom around cult celebrity Tommy Wiseau, his unintentionally funny melodrama *The Room* (2003) and his sitcom *The Neighbors* (Hulu 2016). Analysing fan engagement with Wiseau on reddit, I consider how contributors constructed him as a ridiculed and celebrated other. I return to the push/pull dynamic I explore in chapter 2, which here works to distance fans from Wiseau, while simultaneously reinforcing their attachment to him as a fan object. Examining responses to *The Neighbors,* I demonstrate that fans rejected Wiseau's attempt to position himself as a comedian, rather than as an object of laughter. Emphasising that he had become sticky with the pleasures of unintentional comedy, I argue that he was excluded from the privileged group that is "allowed" to direct laughter and that his failure demonstrates the rigidity of symbolic boundaries in comedy culture.

2 Comedy and Comedian Fandom

Parks and Recreation on Tumblr

In this first case study chapter, I want to focus on comedy fandom in order to explore the relationship between comic distance and audience investment. The introductory chapter reflected on the necessity for comedy to distance viewers from characters and events in order to enable them to laugh at mishaps and misfortunes. In many comedic texts, though, such strategies work alongside attempts to get viewers emotionally invested in characters, relationships and storylines so that they want to see what happens next. However, fandom highlights a second form of investment, which is fans' emotional attachment to their fan objects. How do comedies invite both laughter and affection? And how do fans negotiate this push/pull dynamic? I explore these questions through an analysis of the Tumblr-based fandom of U.S. sitcom *Parks and Recreation*. This show can be positioned within the trend of what Mittell (2015) terms "complex TV". Its combination of episodic and serial narratives facilitates the development of complex characters and the delay of conflict resolution, while its adoption of a mock-documentary aesthetic provides diverse means for character alignment (Smith 1995). Nonetheless, as a sitcom, it remains driven by its "comic impetus" (Mills 2009: 5), and this commitment is signalled by its focus on star comedian Amy Poehler as local government official Leslie Knope. Considering what *Parks and Recreation* fandom on Tumblr might tell us about the specificities of comedy and comedian fandom, I position these fan practices within a wider quotation culture and reflect on which textual elements fans chose to quote, and what the significance of such selections might be.

Researching Tumblr

I collected and coded the top 100 Tumblr posts tagged #Parks and Recreation a week after the show ended in the U.S. The sampling strategy aimed to provide a sense of the dominant discourses around the show that circulated within this particular fan culture at the end of the series. Fans sometimes respond to the endings of TV series by revisiting moments and elements that have particular resonance for them as a way of "intertwining" their self-identities "with the history and narrative of the text" (Williams 2015: 81). This can form part of a "reiteration discourse" that confirms the significance and value of the fandom at a time of disruption (78). The most frequently circulated #Parks and Recreation posts helped "shape" (Ahmed 2004: 4) *Parks and Recreation* by repeatedly inscribing particular elements with value, while marginalising other elements, and I was interested in exploring that "shape" and the affective registers associated with it.

However, while Tumblr users can view specific types of content through the use of hashtags, their Tumblr feed will otherwise be made up of content contributed by users they have chosen to "follow". As Betz (2014) notes, fan screenshots and GIFs can be seen as a "continuous flow of affective images" (para. 2) that enable Tumblr users to align themselves with others who have similar affective interpretations. It is therefore important to stress that the hierarchy of discourses around TV shows will vary across the "loose and informal" (Deller 2015: para. 3: 3) fan networks on Tumblr. In order to include a little of that diversity, I am also exploring some of the Tumblr blogs dedicated to actors and characters from *Parks and Recreation*, and I will consider some of the similarities and differences in how this fandom is articulated across those fan spaces.

Quoting Comedic Dialogue

As previous studies (e.g. Bore 2012, Klinger 2010, Smith 1999) have observed, quoting is one of the key pleasures in comedy fandom. This practice is not confined to comedy, of course. I quote others throughout this book, while we might also quote proverbs, nursery rhymes, religious texts, poetry, friends and relatives, pop songs, films, TV shows, etc. As Finnegan (2011) notes, we aren't always conscious of such habits because they are quite a mundane part of everyday speech (17) and because many (mis)quotes have become so "embedded in the language" (18) that they go unnoticed. The kinds of lines that are appropriated through quotations are often (though certainly not always) humorous or playful, and the practice itself can offer the pleasures of humour. For example, Newman (2014) examines the use of "mashed-up fan creations" in *Pulp Fiction* fandom, and argues that they construct comic incongruities by making the film seem "more gentle" and "domesticating its more transgressive qualities of representation" (10). Finnegan (2011) also notes that respondents in her study said that they used quotes to make people laugh, for sarcasm or for "mischievous provocation", and that they also "played around" with quotations to create new comic incongruities (62):

> People were … skilled in tapping into the occasions where quotations could be deployed, to an extent shared with others but also manipulated in ways personal to the individual. The open-ended but

multiply evocative dimensions of quoting could be turned to many situations. Part of the pleasure lay in bringing out the connections and analogies, building on the capacity of quotation to capture something succinctly and wittily while at the same time introducing an element of distance and perspective.

(Finnegan 2011: 63)

Jenkins (1992) and Finnegan (2011) both connect such appropriation with the dialogue that structures wider patterns of speech and writing. As Bakhtin observes:

Our speech, that is, all our utterances (including creative works), is filled with others' words, varying degrees of awareness and detachment. These words of others carry with them their own expression, their own evaluative tone, which we assimilate, rework, and re-accentuate. (1992: 60)

Quoting makes explicit a practice that is inherent in all our communication. More precisely, it can be described as "reported speech", which "is regarded by the speaker as an utterance belonging to *someone else*, an utterance that was originally totally independent, complete in its construction, and lying outside the given context" (Vološinov 1973: 116).

Writing about film quotation, Klinger (2008) describes it as an "ordinary" and repetitive "immersion in dialogue" that helps the viewer develop a sense of familiarity with a film, making it "a part of the viewer's identity, a unit within a repertoire of elements that he or she may draw upon in diverse circumstances to momentarily or in a more sustained fashion occupy different subjectivities" (para. 9). If we apply this idea to comedy fandom, it demonstrates the dual value of comic surprise *and* familiarity: While we might want a comedy to surprise us when we first watch it, this particular pleasure will be limited during repeat viewings (although we might still discover nuances that we hadn't noticed before). Instead, we may feel an increasing sense of closeness to the text, and we might hone in on moments that resonate with us, and appropriate them for use in performances of fandom or other cultural identities. As Jenkins (1992) argues, such "textual poaching" can "transform the experience of watching television into a rich and complex participatory culture" (23) that extends textual engagement well beyond the moment of reception.

Klinger (2006) examines gendered practices of film quotation and notes that her male respondents tended to appropriate "macho, zany, or antiauthoritarian" lines that provided them with particular ideas of masculinity, "from the supercool to the laughably inept to the rebellious", that they could appropriate through repeated performances (184). In fact, quoting comedy has been associated with masculine culture

(Klinger 2010, Bore 2012), but my Tumblr case study indicates that both male and female fans participate in this particular "quotation culture" (Newman 2014). While Tumblr does not ask participants to state their sex, many contributors perform masculine or feminine user identities through usernames and avatars. I wonder, then, if some male viewers might just be more aware of their quoting practices. Unlike "gossiping" and "sharing" experiences, comedy quotation fits with established ideas of appropriate, playful interactions between male friends. Coates (2003) notes that "having a laugh" is "an important theme of male friendship in adulthood", particularly for both younger men and those who are working-class or lower-middle class (53). Similarly, Hay's (2000) study of friendship groups found that her young, male participants tended to use humour to foster solidarity and to "perform positive work on their personal identity" (738). So, quoting comedy can be a way for male and female friends to reinforce the sense that they have shared tastes, experiences and outlooks, but it can also be a way for individuals to demonstrate that they possess a type of knowledge and performative skill that is valued in their group, whether that is a friendship group or an online fan culture.

#Parks and Recreation Quotes on Tumblr

The practice of quoting comedic dialogue tends to detach spoken lines from most of their visual context, although fans will often pay attention to the original delivery of the lines. As Smith (1999) argues, "fans try to reperform the lines, mustering whatever impersonative vocal skills they have" (65). This emphasis on spoken quotations reinforces the cultural hierarchy that privileges verbal over visual humour. However, the quoting practice in the *Parks and Recreation* fan culture on Tumblr differed from this approach in three key ways: First, the quotations tended to emphasise the visual, rather than the verbal. The most popular posts tagged #Parks and Recreation predominantly consisted of TV screenshots and animated GIF sets that froze or looped particular moments from the show, often "arranged in sequence like the frames of a comic book" (Abbott 2014: 12). These images often included dialogue through superimposed captions, and posts sometimes added brief comments or descriptions, but most of the space was devoted to still or moving images with no sound. This practice challenged the privileging of verbal humour and drew attention to physical performances, costumes and sets.

Second, it tended to lack the spontaneity that we might associate with the quoting of comedic dialogue. While we might suddenly remember and reperform a line that seems to have relevance to a situation in which we find ourselves, creating and posting an animated GIF set takes a bit more time.

Third, such appropriation does not demonstrate fan skills in the reperformance of comedic delivery or body language. Tumblr participation and the production of animated GIFs, for example, require a certain amount of technical skills (Hillman *et al.* 2014), while some posters also demonstrated creative skills by posting their own fan art, fan fiction or mash-ups that inserted *Parks and Recreation* dialogue into screenshots from other shows. However, the most salient skill here was perhaps the ability to select textual moments or paratexts that resonated with other fans. Such resonance was indicated by the number of "notes" a post attracted, which comprised "likes" and reblogging by other users. So, while a spoken comedic quote might lead to the collaborative reperformance of an entire scene, the emphasis here was instead on sharing the same quote with a new audience. As popular posts were shared with a widening audience, this repetition reinforced the salience of particular textual moments within the fan culture.

So, how was this particular quotation practice facilitated by the characteristics of Tumblr? Abbott (2014) argues that Tumblr's focus on "microblogging" rather than blogging foregrounds curation, sharing and annotation "over long-form original content" (12). On Tumblr, this fan-produced content "is easily discovered, available for free and on-demand, shared and collected with trivial effort, and evocative of the wider social structures that make production and sharing pleasurable" (13). As such, #Parks and Recreation quotes can be considered an example of the broader cultural practice associated with "spreadable media", which Jenkins *et al.* (2013) describe as media content that users choose to circulate because it "matters to them" (294).

Since Hillman *et al.* (2014) have observed that fans on Tumblr often use animated GIF sets as a starting point for analysis, the overwhelming focus on *quotation* in my sample did not appear to simply be a result of limitations imposed by the Tumblr platform. I therefore suspect discourses around genre might be another significant factor. Hillman *et al.* primarily interviewed fans of drama series, and analysis is a key feature in online drama fandoms more broadly (see for example Gray and Mittell 2007 on *Lost* fandom or Williams 2011a on *The West Wing* fandom). This can be contrasted with the common-sense ideas that analysis kills jokes, that our responses to humour are gut reactions and that comedy offers simple pleasures that aren't worthy of further examination (Mills 2009: 8). Comedy quotations occupy "the realm of humour" (Mulkay 1988: 21), and so the #Parks and Recreation quotes seemed to reproduce culturally sanctioned ways of talking about comedy.

The emphasis on visual quoting in these posts was facilitated by the characteristics of Tumblr as a microblogging platform and the practices that have developed there. While Tumblr enables users to post messages in the form of text, photo, audio or video, Chang *et al.* (2014) found that

78.11% of posts were photos (2), while the fans interviewed by Hillman *et al.* (2014) reported that animated Gifs and GIF sets have an "integral role in communication" (5):

> Through both our three-month observation and the review of participants' blogs, we found that animated Gifs and GIF sets allowed fandom users to take key scenes of TV shows and post them for discussion, creation, and adaptation. GIF sets were often created for: comparing character development over time, pointing out a specific show detail that might have otherwise been missed by other users, and re-watching key scenes in order to add analysis or express emotion around that scene.
>
> (Hillman *et al.* 2014: 5)

Unlike the verbal quoting of comedic dialogue, screenshots and animated GIF sets maintained more of the televisuality of *Parks and Recreation*, which replaced the pleasure of reperformance with the pleasure of re-watching. And while I saw little analysis in the posts, I think expressions of affect were key to this quotation culture.

Of the 100 posts I examined, 65 articulated amusement, but 35 did not. So, what can the selection of textual moments tell us about the affective registers of the show and about the dominant values of this *Parks and Recreation* fan culture? Amongst the humorous posts, I found an emphasis on moments where Leslie, Andy, April and Ron are behaving in ways that reiterate certain comedic character traits: Leslie is being intense, Andy is acting as a fool, April is resisting social conventions and Ron is giving stern verdicts. For example, there was an animated GIF of a scene where Andy sits in front of the computer, with the caption: "Leslie, I typed your symptoms into the thing up here and it says you could have network connectivity problems". However, across the expressions of amusement in my sample there also seemed to be indications of other affective resonances, such as *admiration* for Leslie's commitment, for April's rebelliousness, for Andy's exuberance and for Ron's snappy authority. In my sample and in blogs dedicated to Ron, posters quoted "inspirational" lines like "Never half ass two things, whole ass one thing" or "I can't go because I don't want to". These compound affective responses suggest that, while fans might sometimes laugh "at" characters and feel superior to them, this sense of superiority is destabilised because they also inscribe those characters with value.

As Mills (2011) notes in his analysis of a Joan Rivers stand-up performance, the comedian's position of power complicates this relationship further. For example, the Tumblr post about Leslie's "network connectivity problems" had 38 "notes", and one of the Tumblr users who reblogged the GIF added the comment "he improvised this line", while another user reblogged that post and added "Really? Just when

I thought he couldn't get any more awesome". These two comments shifted attention from character to performer and inscribed Chris Pratt's perceived improvisation with value. They also demonstrated that the dual reading strategy (Cook 1982) invited by comedic texts can draw attention to the *processes* of comedy, such as the role of improvisation in performance. And, finally, the evaluation of Chris Pratt as "awesome" indicated the paratextual significance of his stardom. There is a marked contrast between Andy as a chubby, sweet-natured fool and Pratt's persona as a buff, accomplished comedic and action star, developed through the blockbusters *Guardians of the Galaxy* and *Jurassic World*. Pratt's stardom complicates readings of Andy as a buffoon, and this incongruity was a recurring focal point in Tumblr blogs dedicated to the actor, with posts frequently expressing bemusement, admiration and affection.

Similarly, while Leslie's intense approach to politics and community service is a source of humour in *Parks and Recreation*, the idea of comic superiority is problematised both by the show's construction of Leslie's work and dedication as valuable and by Amy Poehler's persona as a feminist activist. Her "Amy Poehler's Smart Girls" social media initiative operates across Tumblr, Facebook, Twitter and Instagram, and its output replicates Leslie's optimism by celebrating girls' and women's achievements. Among the posts contributed to #Parks and Recreation, to the "Smart Girls" accounts and to the Amy Poehler fan blogs on Tumblr, several inscribed Leslie with valued attributes like loyalty to her friends, commitment to feminism and passion for her work. This is one example from my #Parks and Recreation sample:

> You know what else I love about the Parks finale? When Garry gets sworn in as mayor the fourth time, Brandi Maxxx is the head of city council, and there's another woman on the council. When he gets sworn in the tenth time, of the five members, four are women. Please don't try to convince me that Leslie didn't have something to do with that.

Newman (2014) emphasises that what is "unquoted" is as important as what is included because the repeated process of selection can help form the meanings of a text to "fit prevailing norms of what ought and ought not to be represented" (16). By circulating posts that focus on specific character traits, fans co-create a hierarchy of characters and inscribe certain traits with value. It is notable that Chris, Tom, Donna and Gerry were peripheral in the #Parks and Recreation posts in my sample, despite the fact that some of them featured prominently in the show. In contrast, Ann and Ben were only occasionally the focus of humorous posts but more frequently included in posts about their relationships with Leslie. I think this indicates the value placed on "shipping" and what we might call "friendshipping" in this *Parks and Recreation* fan culture.

Shipping and Friendshipping

Shipping refers to the fan practice of supporting particular romantic relationships or "ships". Across film and TV fandoms, this often involves conflicts between groups of fans who support different ships, with intense debates over which pairing is most suitable (e.g. Scodari and Felder 2000 on *The X-Files* fandom and Bore and Williams 2010 on *Twilight* fans). However, across the #Parks and Recreation sample, I identified widespread support for the two most stable romances in the show: April/Andy and Leslie/Ben. Both of these couples meet, date, marry and have children over the course of the sitcom, and so the dominant shipping practices within Tumblr-based *Parks and Recreation* fandom can be situated within the stability of the sitcom genre, where viewers expect a happy ending, but they can also be seen as a result of my data collection strategy, which focused on the posts that were most frequently shared at the time of sampling.

Comparing shipping to slash fiction, Williams (2011a) suggests that shipping's focus on romance enables fans to perform affect while distancing themselves from "sexual 'deviance'":

> Identification with female characters and possible accusations of inappropriate (queer) desire for these *and* any association with culturally feminised "drooling" over male characters can be subsumed into the supporting of a ship featuring both characters … It also counteracts the possibility of fan attachments simultaneously being too heterosexual/too queer by neatly converging attractions to both male and female characters into one fan object which is culturally accepted via its validation of normative heterosexual relationships.
> (Williams 2011a: 281)

Thinking about the significance of desire for some shippers might help explain the *absence* of Chris/Ann shipping in my #Parks and Recreation sample. Although these characters date briefly and are later reunited and have a baby, this relationship is usually cued as comedic rather than romantic in the show. While the representations of the Andy/April and Ben/Leslie relationships do function as sources of humour, they also encourage viewers to invest in those romances through occasional shifts to more complex modalities (King 2002: 13) that position them closer to reality and invite "[a]ffective implication" (Purdie 1993: 85). The resonance of such moments was indicated by several posts in my sample, which included quotations of Ben's proposal to Leslie and his suggestion that they start a family, as well as quotations of April expressing her love for Andy and giving him encouragement when he was worried about his job performance. Some posts also shared paratexts, such as interviews and behind-the-scenes photos that constructed the relationship between Chris Pratt and Aubrey Plaza as close and affectionate. Within the affective flow of #Parks and Recreation, these paratexts reinforced the inscribed value of the on-screen relationship between Andy and April.

In contrast, the romance between Ann and Chris is constructed as a comic incongruity in *Parks and Recreation*. While Ann is usually the "straight" character that we see reacting to the comic behaviour of others, Chris is represented through a modality of comic excess. His absurdly exaggerated behaviour and ineffective emotional displays invite audiences to laugh at him rather than desire him. He is obsessed with exercise and healthy eating, he is terrified of ageing and illness, he grieves excessively when he is dumped by his girlfriend and his speech tends to be in the form of clipped, hyperbolic statements that overuse the term "literally". The marked disparity between him and Ann contributes to the comic distance between the couple and the viewers, and this hinders the intense emotional investment or "feels" that is a key pleasure in shipping (Hillman *et al.* 2014: 7).

However, while these characters and their relationship only had a marginal presence in my #Parks and Recreation sample, Tumblr blogs that are dedicated to actors Rashida Jones and Rob Lowe inscribed Ann and Chris with funniness and importance by sharing screenshots and animated GIF sets from their scenes in the show. Here, these characters and performances were contextualised primarily by Jones's and Lowe's celebrity, rather than by *Parks and Recreation*. For example, Rob Lowe blogs presented him variously as an object of desire, as an accomplished actor and as a talented comedic performer. Some posts highlighted the ageing of his (continuously desirable) appearance or the development of his acting career through series of screenshots from different films and TV shows, while others focused in on moments from his comedic performances through animated GIFs and GIF sets. On these Tumblr blogs, then, quotations from *Parks and Recreation* became paratexts that related to other paratexts, such as promotional stills, press photography, screenshots from Jones's and Lowe's performances in other films and TV programmes, and so on, creating a dialogue among discourses of comedy, beauty, ageing, desire, celebrity and achievement.

Alongside support for romantic relationships, support for friendships was also evident in the #Parks and Recreation sample. Such "friendshipping" tended to focus on Leslie/Ron or Leslie/Ann, but these posts were also often open enough to be read as examples of romantic shipping. Leslie and Ron's close relationship is established at the very start of series 1, and while Ron's exaggerated libertarian views and Leslie's over-zealous commitment to local government forms one of the comic incongruities that structure the narrative, they are repeatedly shown to understand, respect, support and care for each other. This togetherness is sometimes highlighted through scenes that focus on their shared and excessive love of breakfast foods, which is a recurring source of humour on the show. Surprisingly, then, the start of the final series (series 7) reveals that the two have somehow fallen out, and their mutual hostility becomes a key plot device that encapsulates the unsettling of the narrative world during the three-year diegetic time lapse between series 6 and 7. The series' fourth episode is largely dedicated to a showdown between the two, when the other characters lock them up in their old office so that they can resolve their differences. While this confrontation is cued as comedic, audiences have been invited to invest in their friendship over the course of the previous 6 series, and the episode frequently uses a complex modality that presents their conflict as mysterious, sad and amusing. The following morning their drunken togetherness is celebrated with a modality of comic excess that showcases Poehler's and Offerman's skills in improvisation and clowning.

Their re-established relationship was the focus of a #Parks and Recreation quotation post that shared a screenshot from the final episode where Leslie and Ron sit on park swings, looking at each other and holding hands. Another post shared screenshots from an earlier series, where Leslie and Ron sit in a diner:

LESLIE: "Why would people ever eat anything besides breakfast foods?"
RON: "People are idiots, Leslie."

These were juxtaposed with screenshots from episode four, after Leslie and Ron's reunification, as they are heading off to the diner:

RON: "Why does anybody in the world ever eat anything but breakfast food?"
LESLIE [PUTTING HER ARMS AROUND RON]: "People are idiots, Ron."

By demonstrating a recognition of the show's self-referentiality, the poster performed fan knowledge, drew attention to a connection other fans might have missed and moved beyond quotation towards fan analysis. The juxtaposition also constructed Ron and Leslie's shared love of breakfast foods as a significant and enduring part of their relationship.

However, these Leslie/Ron posts can also be read as articulations of romantic shipping, which draws attention to the polysemy of the representations of character relationships within *Parks and Recreation*. The show repeatedly emphasises the value of friendship both within ostensibly platonic relationships and within romantic relationships, and Leslie frequently provides excessive displays of affection for Ron and Ann through compliments and gifts, for example. One post in the #Parks and Recreation sample used a series of screenshots to share a scene where Leslie quietly addresses Ann, who is out of earshot:

LESLIE: Oh Ann, you beautiful spinster. I will find you love.
ANN [TURNING AROUND]: What? Did you say something?
LESLIE [SMILES]: Love you.

This, like other Leslie/Ann posts, can be read as an articulation of investment in a Leslie/Ann friendship or in a Leslie/Ann romance, *and* as inscribing their interactions with comedic value. Amy Poehler has reportedly argued that "the real love story [in *Parks and Recreation* was between Leslie and her friend Ann" (Freeman 2015), while co-creator Michael Schur has said:

> To me, Leslie and Ron's relationship is the heart of the show. There's a couple different heartbeats, I guess: One of them is Leslie and Ann's friendship, and one of them that we didn't expect when we started the show is Leslie and Ron. When she needs a shoulder to lean on, she goes to Ann. When she needs just a solid, rock-like moral foundation, she goes to Ron.
>
> (Adams 2012)

The ambiguity of the Leslie/Ron and Leslie/Ann quotation posts highlights the significant challenge that reading poses in the analysis of this data. Without added commentaries or tags that anchor the posts as an articulation of either romantic shipping or friendshipping, they remain open for interpretation by readers following #Parks and Recreation. However, shippers can follow each other's Tumblr blogs, and the meanings of such posts are then framed by the shipping discourses that circulate within and across those blogs.

So, while my analysis of the top #Parks and Recreation posts is intended to shed light on the *dominant* discourses in Tumblr-based *Parks and Recreation* fandom, exploring other hashtags offers insights into more marginal fan discourses. #Leslie x Ron, for example, includes posts that inscribe their relationship with romance and articulate emotional investment in that romance:

> I'm sorry, all I got from that Parks and Rec episode was Leslie saying she loved Ron and would do anything for him. So.

Similarly, posts tagged #Annslie[1] form an affective flow that is characterised by a marked emphasis on animated GIFs from moments where Leslie compliments Ann ("Ann, you're beautiful and you're organized!"), where they look at each other and where they embrace. These moments were queered and inscribed with romantic love through the #Annslie tag, but posts also often articulated fan investment in that love through other tags and captions, such as "too many feelings all over the place" and "but look at how she's smiling at her ahsjkfhdkal". This key sequence resembles "alksjdf;lksfd", which is commonly used in online cultures "to represent a user pressing random keys in uncontrollable excitement" (Hillman *et al.* 2014: 7). Moreover, while the top #Annslie posts at the time of sampling were image based, there were also numerous text-based

#Annslie posts. These included sexually explicit "femslash" fan-fiction, posts that articulated investment in a Leslie/Ann romantic relationship and posts that expressed frustration about the development of that relationship in *Parks and Recreation*, as seen in this extract:

> So tired of *almost* canon lesbians. Tired of the tease, tired of the denial, tired of *almost* enjoying books or t.v. or movies. Tired of loving characters and seeing their lesbian potential and then witnessing the oncoming dick parade.

This post had 4,323 notes and was also tagged #swan queen, which refers to a f/f (female/female) ship in the TV drama *Once upon a Time*. It positioned Leslie/Ann within a wider context of heteronormative fiction, where lesbian desire is invoked but ultimately denied within "heteronormative canon" (Isaksson 2013: 298) narratives and where lesbian audiences are repeatedly disappointed. As Ahmed (2004) notes, the repetition of heterosexual practices is imprinted on the surfaces of social as well as bodily spaces, and this process creates a world that is not noticed "when one has been shaped by that world, and even acquired its shape" but can make the bodies of "queer subjects" feel "out of place, awkward, unsettled" (148).

Post-Object Fandom

Of the 100 #Parks and Recreation posts I coded, 20 focused on the ending of the show. As Todd (2011) notes in her discussion of the *Friends* series finale, "fans participate in the media event" through their online discourse, which enables them to "become active architects of meaning in television discourse" (868). Through their selection and sharing of moments from the final episode and from *Parks and Recreation* as a whole, fans inscribed those moments with significance, while repeating and circulating particular readings of the show. This affective practice contributed to the shaping of the discourses around the show. Reflecting on the series finale of *Sex and the City*, Ross (2005) observes that fans were able to construct it alternately as "a show about romance and dating" and as being "about female bonding and lasting friendships". She suggests that "the key to its continued popularity after its initial run on cable might be its refusal to answer this question in a clear-cut way and its ability to advance epistemic negotiations about its meanings outside of its own narrative boundaries" (122). The identification of such diverging reading strategies and "post-object" (Williams 2015) fan discourses underscores the importance of paying attention to nuance in fan responses to endings.

Within my #Parks and Recreation sample, some posts reinforced the show's position within the sitcom genre and inscribed its comedic modality with value by quoting humorous moments from the series finale. These moments included flash forward segments to Donna phoning "Satan's Niece" through her watch and reaching April and to Jean-Ralphio's funeral, where he is revealed to have faked his own death for insurance money. The flash forward device here works to "detach" *Parks and Recreation* from its audience by showing us a combination of change and sameness in the way characters live beyond the end of the narrative (Savorelli 2010: 29). Mike Schur has constructed the use of this device both in terms of rewarding audience commitment to the show and its characters and in terms of celebrating individual cast members and characters:

> The writers talked a lot about what makes good finales, and one of those things is giving the audience an idea of what happens to the characters in the future. Then it was a very short jump from there to "Why don't we just show it?" And the cast was so strong, I felt it was a good way to give every character a little moment in the sun.
> (Fretts 2015)

In her analysis of survey data, Williams (2015) also identifies "the common sentiment that fans deserve to be rewarded for their devotion and that a finale should privilege the needs of long-term viewers over the less dedicated audience" (37). This sense of fan "needs" was evident in my #Parks and Recreation sample. While some posts stayed within a humorous realm by focusing on comedic moments in the series finale, many articulated a sense of loss. Some celebrated the show by sharing screenshot sets of their favourite moments, some shared photos of the actors being together on set, some shared screenshots or GIFs of the characters' group hug in the final episode (in some cases with the superimposed caption "Pawnee forever") and some wrote about their affective responses:

> Finally watched the last ep of Parks and Rec I'M NOT CRYING I'M NOT CRYING okay I cried the whole time

Unlike posts that emphasised the comedic modality of the *Parks and Recreation* series finale by quoting humorous moments, this post inscribed the episode with sadness. Laughter, normally considered to be the key desired affective response to sitcoms, is entirely absent from this brief account. Instead, the fan articulated a sense of grief that the show had finished. In her discussion of post-object fandom, Williams (2015) argues that TV series fandom can offer fans a sense of ontological security and contribute to their self-identity, for example through the routine of viewing episode after episode and through a sense of belonging to a specific or imagined fan community (25). This sense of stability is threatened by the ending of a favourite TV show (101):

> Actual thought that just went through my head
> All right! Tomorrow's Tuesday! It's Parks and Rec ni–
> *sigh*

> The parks and rec finale was everything the how I met your mother finale was not.

Williams (2015) argues that experiencing the final episode as "successful" enables fans to counter the threat to their ontological security because they still have an "ongoing love for the show" (100). This attachment and sense of belonging was also articulated through several "Pawnee forever" posts, where fan investment was not linked to specific characters or actors, but to the *Parks and Recreation* world, as represented through the fictional setting of Pawnee, Indiana. The significance of setting in post-object fandom is discussed by Todd (2011) in relation to *Friends* fandom, where online fans shared advice on how they could get hold of décor like cushions or posters that had become familiar parts of the *Friends* apartments and could help fans "appropriate the show" and make it part of their "lived experience" (861–62). Such avowals of continued fan commitment forms part of what Williams (2015) terms a "reiteration discourse":

> when fans offer personal anecdotes or stories about their fandom and its importance to them, bid farewell to the show or other fans and when they work to reiterate the importance of a show to their own sense of self-identity, narrative and ontological security via positioning a series as important and as a worthwhile object of their affection.
> (Williams 2015: 81)

Some posts shared paratexts that validated the significance that fans attributed to *Parks and Recreation*, such as an animated GIF set showing Aubrey Plaza and Chris Pratt embracing on set, accompanied by a quote from Plaza:

> *I'm gonna miss Chris Pratt in my life. Because he's my TV husband. And I sometimes forget he's not my real husband.* [italics in original]

This quote valorised the relationship between April and Andy and between Plaza and Pratt. Plaza's articulated sense of loss validated the fans' sense of loss, just like tabloid photos of "a tearful Jennifer Anniston on the set of the final episode" validated the "remorse" of *Friends* fans

(Todd 2011: 865). Another Tumblr post shared a screenshot of a tweet from the FBI that referred to Andy's recurring impersonation of fictional FBI agent Burt Macklin:

@FBI 25.02.2015:
Your ways were unconventional, but you´ll be missed Macklin. #ParksFarewell To learn about a real FBI career, visit FBIjobs.gov.

The Tumblr poster had playfully added the caption "What do you mean REAL?", which continued the tweet's blurring of the boundary between the *Parks and Recreation* diegesis and the real world. The public recognition of Andy's creation by an institution like the FBI reinforced the cultural significance of the show, and at the time of writing their tweet has been retweeted 29.4K times and favourited 28.2K times. Across my #Parks and Recreation sample, then, fans responded to the series ending with a reiteration discourse that alternately celebrated moments from the final episode, curated retrospective celebrations of favourite moments from across character histories or emphasised the continued significance of the show. In doing so, they inscribed *Parks and Recreation* with particular kinds of values, meanings and emotions, and the production and sharing of these posts helped shape the post-object discourse around this sitcom on Tumblr.

Amy Poehler Fandom

For Tumblr users who perform *Parks and Recreation* fandom and Amy Poehler fandom through their posts, the comedian offered a point of both continuity and change after the series ending. On Tumblr blogs that focused on Amy Poehler, moments from *Parks and Recreation* were positioned within affective flows that connected this show to Poehler's other work, such as her comedies, her presenting work, her book *Yes, Please* and her feminist initiative Amy Poehler's Smart Girls, as well as paratextual material like interviews and photographs. For *Parks and Recreation* fans, then, Poehler-as-fan-object could provide a sense of ontological security beyond the final episode, and this security may be reinforced by perceived similarities between Leslie and Poehler. Such blurring is particularly common for comedians, who switch between "acting" and "being" both within and outside of comedic fiction (Mills 2010: 200), and Morreale (2008) notes that *30 Rock* conflates Tina Fey and her character Liz Lemon, encouraging a reading of the comedian/character "as a strong, successful woman who disturbs hierarchies of social and economic power" (486). According to *Yes, Please*, Leslie was specifically written for Poehler, who provides the following description of the character:

> She was an extremely low-level Parks and Recreation Department employee who had big dreams. She was inspired by the "Yes We

Can" spirit of Obama's recent election. She believed that it only took one person to make a difference. She wanted to effect change, she wanted to someday be president, but most importantly, she wanted to turn an empty lot in her town into a park.

(Poehler 2014: "Let's Build a Park")

Later in her book, Schur explains that the writers had "imagined that her relationship to the camera was one of guarded caution" because of her aspirations, but that Poehler stopped looking into the cameras outside of her talking heads:

Amy had made her into a completely consistent, heart-on-her-sleeve character who was not embarrassed or ashamed by anything she ever said or did in any scenario ... It's a pretty badass character trait, I think, and it only works because of the supreme sincerity of the actress who embodies it.

(Schur in Poehler 2014 "Let's Build a Park" note 15)

Sincerity, ambition and a desire to effect social change was also inscribed into Poehler across Tumblr fan blogs. Here, it was connected to her position as a successful comedian and to her promotion of feminist ideas. For example, one reblogged fan post shares a photo in which Poehler appears to adopt a mock-angelic pose, followed by this quote from *Yes, Please*:

I just love bossy women. I could be around them all day. To me, bossy is not a pejorative term at all. It means somebody's passionate and engaged and ambitious and doesn't mind leading, like, "All right, everybody, now we go over here. All right, now this happens." (italics in post)

Another fan reblogged an animated GIF set from an interview in which Poehler was promoting her latest film, the Pixar production *Inside Out*. This is presumably a response to a question about her new, red hair colour:

POEHLER: Well, let me tell you, I changed my hair colour. And that's the whole story. I'm actually playing Black Widow on Broadway.
INTERVIEWER: Are you really?
POEHLER: No.

In this extract, Poehler refused to participate in the dominant media discourse on celebrity, where actresses are asked about their appearance rather than their professional practice, and she then used humour as a discursive strategy to misinform the interviewer. By failing to read her response as humorous, the interviewer appeared uninformed and gullible, and although Poehler's brief "no" was delivered with a smile, she made no other contribution towards remedying the interviewer's loss of power.

Through the production, sharing and curating of such content, fans co-constructed Poehler as a feminist comedian who challenges conventional narratives of femininity through the use of both serious and humorous discourse. They also repeatedly situated her within a community of comedians where female practitioners are prominent, for example, by sharing texts that focus on her friendships and professional collaborations with comedians like Tina Fey, Mindy Kaling, Maya Rudolph and Julia Louis-Dreyfus. These Tumblr posts participated in a wider dialogue around the role of women in comedy and reinforced the significance and value of these comedians by constructing them as stars and fan objects. Within this "uneven terrain of apparent advances and regressions" (Taylor 2015: 64), female comedian *stardom* is significant because it impacts the perception of other women comedians and the work that they are offered (Patterson 2012: 248). However, Lauzen (2014) observes that several high-profile women seem to offer each other work and support. One of her examples is the promotion of *Bridesmaids* by a range of female actresses, producers and screenwriters who were not connected with the film; the reception of this comedy will be discussed further in the next chapter.

While Poehler does not have her own social media accounts, she engages with fans in a carefully managed way through the Amy Poehler's Smart Girls initiative, which has the following description on amysmartgirls.com:

> Smart Girls is the brainchild of Amy Poehler and Meredith Walker, two best friends who support each other and want to share that support with teen girls from around the world. Support that they share with the teen girls who are ready to move against the crowd. Funny, focused, and powerful, Smart Girls seeks to help future women channel their intelligence, imagination, and curiosity into a drive to be their weird and wonderful selves.

Smart Girls has a Tumblr account called "Smart Girls at the Party", with the tagline "Change the world by being yourself". Like their other social media accounts, this Tumblr adopts a discourse that is strikingly similar to that of Leslie. Consistently addressing readers as "smart girls", it places great emphasis on education and citizenship and on being "positive" and creative, taking risks (for example through the tag #getyourhairwet), valuing diversity and celebrating girls' and women's achievements. However, it also voices critique of the marginalisation of women, black Americans, transgender people and other social groups.

As a paratextual frame, then, Smart Girls at the Party encourages us to read Amy Poehler as a champion who invites other "smart girls" to collaborate on reshaping narratives of femininity that limit and devalue girls and women, and reblogged fan-produced content is a key part of their output.

So, through posts to Smart Girls at the Party and through the Amy Poehler fan blogs, Tumblr users circulated discourses that challenged dominant ideas of femininity, including the gendering of comedy as masculine. However, there was also a recurring tension between the idea of Poehler as feminist comedian and a discourse of Poehler as *celebrity*. Fans shared red carpet photos that associate her with beauty, fashion and glamour, while paparazzi shots of her alone or with her children constructed her life as simultaneously ordinary and special (Dyer 1979/1998). Patterson (2012) identifies a similar incongruity in her analysis of Tina Fey's star text, arguing that her stardom "becomes discursively incoherent, and reiterates the contradictory nature of media stardom in a celebrity culture wherein power is unequal and always in flux" (234). Examining industry discourses around female comedians, Taylor (2015) further notes that they are required to have "nailability", while their characters should also be "likeable" (65). So, while women in comedy "are always already gender-inappropriate" (White 2010: 357), gendered industry and celebrity discourses persistently define and evaluate them against heteronormative femininity. By including photographs that inscribe Poehler with glamour and desirability within the wider affective flow of their Tumblr blogs, fans co-created a "fractured" comedian-as-star text, characterised by a dissonance between Poehler's feminist discourse and her "post-feminist cultural context" (Patterson 2012: 239).

Conclusion

This chapter has explored *Parks and Recreation* fandom on Tumblr to shed light on some of the specificities of comedy and comedian fandom. My discussion has identified two key issues: The first is the push/pull dynamic of comic distance, emotional investment in characters and relationships, and fan attachment to the show itself and its performers. The second is the salience of quotation practices for comedy fandom. Examining the most frequently shared Tumblr posts labelled #*Parks and Recreation* at the end of the show, I have discussed how this sitcom was shaped by quotation patterns that marginalised some textual elements while repeatedly inscribing others with value.

Reflecting on the affective registers produced through these patterns of resonance, I emphasised the circulation of compound affective responses that positioned characters as laughable while simultaneously valorising them. I connected this tension to modality shifts within *Parks and Recreation* that invite audiences to admire characters and invest in their friendships and romances. I also connected it to a dual reading strategy (Cook 1982) that enables viewers to follow the narrative while simultaneously evaluating the text. This second form of engagement can draw attention to the processes of production, including performance, and works to rupture the boundary between laughable characters and the performers who make fans laugh. When the show came to an end, this rupture offered some continuity for fans, who could extend their engagement with *Parks and Recreation* by watching Nick Offerman's stand-up comedy or Aziz Ansari's *Master of None* (Netflix since 2015), for example, or by following Amy Poehler's Smart Girls initiative, which promotes attitudes and ideas that are consistent with the Leslie Knope character.

By focusing on comedy fandom, this first case study chapter has foregrounded ways in which comedy was seen to be successful. The next chapters will examine different factors that might complicate this potential for success, and I turn now to the affective-discursive reception of Hollywood comedies that centre on female performers.

Note

1 Thank you to Nicolle Lamerichs who drew my attention to Leslie/Ann shipping when I presented parts of my findings from this chapter at the 2015 Fan Studies Network Conference.

3 Women in Hollywood Comedy
P/reviewing *Bridesmaids* and *Ghostbusters*

Upon its release, *Bridesmaids* received a lot of media attention for featuring female comedians in all the central roles. This media "hype" (Austin 2002) framed *Bridesmaids* in gendered terms and distinguished it from the masculine comedic "norm" in much the same way that my chapter title does. As Warner and Savigny (2015) point out, film journalists have repeatedly heralded the dawn of gender equality in comedy. However, they argue that critical reception discourse often hinders the "momentum" of this development by treating successful female-driven comedies as isolated incidents or competitors, rather than seeing them as building on each other's successes (115). While this focus on competition is certainly prevalent in film review culture more broadly (Gray 2010), within the context of female-driven comedy this narrative excludes the possibility of more than one "success story" (Warner and Savigny 2015: 115).

This is the first of three chapters that explore the significance of cultural identities for online audience engagement with screen comedy. I here want to contribute to the ongoing feminist debate around the marginalisation of women in comedy (e.g. Lockyer 2011 and Sutherland 2013) by examining blog reviews of *Bridesmaids* and Twitter "previews" (Chin and Gray 2002) of *Ghostbusters*. This dual focus draws attention to the ways in which audience-produced "paratexts" can enter the dialogue surrounding films or TV shows at different points and enables me to examine how these audience paratexts respond to the comedies themselves, as well as to other paratexts (Hills 2015). Examining the themes that emerged through my analysis, this chapter will identify a recurring discourse of responsibility that was articulated in two distinct ways: *Bridesmaids'* responsibility to women for promoting feminism and for convincing a broad audience that women can "carry" comedies and *Ghostbusters'* responsibility to (predominantly male) *Ghostbusters* fans for maintaining the cultural value of their fan object.

Bridesmaids in the "Blogosphere"

The R-rated *Bridesmaids* was written by Annie Mumolo and Kirsten Wiig, directed by Paul Feig and produced by Judd Apatow and stars Wiig alongside Maya Rudolph, Rose Byrne, Melissa McCarthy, Wendi

McLendon-Covey and Ellie Kemper. One narrative strand focuses on single and unemployed Annie's (Wiig) deteriorating behaviour, as she competes for the position of bride's (Rudolph) best friend with fellow bridesmaid Helen (Byrne). A second narrative strand follows Annie's developing romantic relationship with police officer Rhodes (Chris O'Dowd). The film received an "overwhelmingly positive" press reception (Warner 2013: 222) and over-performed at the U.S. box office. Opening second only to the Marvel movie *Thor* (2011), it reportedly grossed $24.6 million in its U.S. opening weekend, rather than "the anticipated $15 million to $17 million, a result of getting a reasonable number of males (who made up 33 percent of the audience)" (McClintock 2011). In addition to a total domestic gross of $169 million, it also made $119 million abroad (Box Office Mojo), despite its lack of international stars. The film's pre-release hype was in part associated with "the blogosphere", which "dubbed 'Bridesmaids' a ladies' take on 'The Hangover,' a film that won a Golden Globe, sparked a cache of catch-phrases and grossed $462 million worldwide" (Angelo 2011). So, what did bloggers make of it?

According to Rettberg (2013: 28), "there is a fairly even gender balance" in blogging, and my analysis examines 15 reviews by female bloggers and 15 reviews by male bloggers. This sampling strategy enables my study to complement Boyle's (2014) analysis of *Bridesmaids* reviews on IMDb, where she found that 65% of those giving the film a numerical rating were men, while only 35% were women. And while most of the users who contributed written reviews did not identify themselves as male or female, 72.5% of those who *did* so identified as male. As Boyle notes, this genders IMDb as a masculine space, and she found that its debate about *Bridesmaids* focused on whether it "works for men" (46). I suspect that this pre-occupation with male viewers is a result not only of the masculine culture on IMDb but also of a wider, gendered discourse of comedy where masculinity is the norm in both production and reception. So, while my sampling strategy ensured that I gathered views from male and female viewers, I did not assume that this would lead to radically different findings. I asked all bloggers for permission before quoting their material, and they decided whether those quotes should be anonymous or attributed to them in a particular way. However, some bloggers did not respond to my enquiries, and in those cases I have chosen to quote their work anonymously.

Film reviews on blogs (or "weblogs") might be seen to occupy a space between the IMDb reviews I examine in chapter 7 and the reviews that professional film critics have traditionally published in newspapers and magazines. As Fricker (2015) notes, blogs have a "liminal status" as simultaneously "personal and public" and as self-published work operating outside "systems of legitimation such as the mainstream media" (39). Unlike professional critics, their word count is unlimited, they are not obliged to abide by the conventions of the review genre and they can foreground the subjective nature of their responses (41). The blog also positions each post within an overarching narrative that "foregrounds the blogger's perspective and personality" and distinguishes it from other blogs (Meyers 2010: 44). Through links, "critical engagement" and frequent updates (Tryon 2009: 130), blogs might be thought of as connected authoring. They are able to engage with readers and fellow bloggers through links and comments, participating in blogging networks that develop "conversations across blogs" (131).

However, the blogs in my sample were clearly side projects, which means that the writers had to juggle their blogging labour with paid jobs, studies, childcare, chores or other commitments (Lopez 2014). So even when the responsibility was shared among two or three contributors, it would still be challenging for them to maintain the post frequency and engagement associated with more prominent blogs, and the posts in my sample had received few, if any, comments. The 2005 analysis by Herring *et al.* of blog connections indicates that such "minimally connected" or "free-floating" blogs actually represent the norm and that the "much-touted textual conversation that all of the blogosphere is supposed to be engaged in involves a minority of blogs" (10). In fact, Chang *et al.* (2014) found that only 3% of bloggers were reciprocal followers. This suggests that, while film and TV blogging offers viewers opportunities to contribute to critical reception discourse, most bloggers' participation in paratextual dialogue may be constrained by their limited connections and readership.

My analysis of the 30 blog reviews of *Bridesmaids* identified two key themes, and the first of these was the evaluation of *Bridesmaids* as a comedy. While a minority shrugged it off as "average" or "overrated", most male and female bloggers praised the film for being "funny" or "hilarious" or for making them "laugh out loud". This centred laughter as the key desired response to comedy, and many bloggers foregrounded the film's use of broad or gross-out modalities by describing it as an "over-the-top" comedy with "vulgar" or "filthy" humour. The characters' incongruous onset of vomiting and diarrhoea in a bridal shop was a frequent reference point for such descriptions, which illustrates King's (2002) observation that "Gross-out comedy is often sold in publicity material, and discussed in media coverage and more informal discourses, on the basis of these sometimes isolated moments of transgression" (63). However, the transgressive humour in *Bridesmaids* was also frequently located in the dialogue, as in this post by a male blogger:

> What's more Wiig is not afraid of a little raunch. Check that. She's got a potty mouth on her that would make a sailor on shore leave blanch. It's put to especially good use during a flight to Las Vegas that's rerouted thanks to her white-knuckle flyer's drunken hallucinations.[1]

Across the reviews, laughter was first and foremost constructed as a response to comedic performances. Many bloggers commended the cast in general, but Wiig's portrayal of Annie was frequently singled out for further discussion. Some emphasised her command of physical comedy, with an "elastic face and ever more elastic body" (Glenn Lovell at CinemaDope.com), or her willingness to "get ugly": "Her chin turtles back into her neck, her eyes roll, her nose scrunches, and the venom flies". This pleasure in watching female comedic characters flinging profanities or contorting their faces may be linked to the carnivalesque potential of the "unruly woman" (Rowe 1995), though I would argue that this "topos ... of female outrageousness and transgression" (30) was most clearly articulated in Megan, the bride's butch future sister-in-law.

McCarthy's performance as Megan was repeatedly praised by both male and female bloggers, with some constructing her as "standout" or arguing that "she steals every scene she's in". However, two commenters who identified themselves as McCarthy fans described her character as "borderline obnoxious" and "fodder for fat jokes", which articulates a concern that McCarthy's feminine star image was undermined or even degraded by this particular performance. A slightly different reading dismissed Megan as stereotypical, with a male blogger reproducing traditional sexist discourse by citing "the stock type of the overly confident fat chick" and a female blogger contextualising Megan within Hollywood casting conventions as "the token chubby-but-good humoured sister of the groom".[2] Here, Megan was defined primarily in terms of her fat body, while a second female blogger focused on her intersection of androgyny and sexual appetite, arguing that she "wasn't believable as a sex crazed person chasing after all these men. She was not giving off a heterosexual vibe at all".[3] Such maintenance of the boundaries of heterosexual femininity was challenged by one female blogger through an exchange with a reader:

> in a way, the Melissa McCarthy character is kind of defying a stereotype. She's depicted as not stereotypically feminine, BUT also super sexual and confident. It seems almost like a way of saying "screw you" to the stereotype of who gets to be sexual.[4]

The diverging readings of Megan reflected the "ambivalence" that the unruly woman "evokes": "on the one hand, delight; on the other, unease, derision, or fear" (Rowe 1995: 30). The continued prevalence of this response is demonstrated by Warner and Savigny's (2015) analysis of the press reception of McCarthy's next Feig movie, *The Heat* (2013), where her body was again subjected to "intense" scrutiny (120).

Alongside the reading of *Bridesmaids* as broad comedy, a second recurring interpretation identified a combination of broad humour with a "less comic" modality (King 2002: 10). This reading was primarily made by female bloggers, who described the film as "heartwarming", "emotional" or "meaningful":

> The balancing act between comedy and drama is a difficult one, and although Bridesmaids is very firmly one of the former ... it's the sensitive, intelligent way that the latter is intertwined into the comedy that makes Bridesmaids such a winner ... We come to care for Annie and her plight; this film isn't just about her failings as a bridesmaid-in-chief, they are purely a microcosm of her problems in life as a whole.[5]

Although our enjoyment of slapstick will often require a certain comic distance, a broad comedic modality can be combined with devices that encourage us to form "allegiances" (Smith 1995) with characters and "follow their fortunes with a degree of emotional investment in the outcome" (King 2002: 9). So, while Annie's unstable identity is a traditional comic device (Jenkins and Karnick 1995) and functions as an impetus for many of the film's comic moments, many bloggers described their allegiance with Annie, their investment in her gradual unravelling and recovery and their affective responses to this narrative. This audience investment was constructed as a result of the film's "true to life", "honest" or "heartfelt" representations of "complex" and "relatable" female characters and their interactions with each other:

> Everything about these female characters is spot on. Annie's forced enthusiasm and feelings of inferiority during Lillian's wedding preparations is a feeling I know many women can identify with, and Wiig's chemistry with Rudolph perfect. The script, co-written by Wiig, is impressively sharp and the dialogue between the friends is genuinely heartfelt and comedic at the same time.

There was a recurring excitement about *Bridesmaids'* perceived portrayal of women who were funny *and* complex, and this discussion was closely connected to the second key theme identified in my analysis: The centrality of women as characters and as comedians.

Across the blogs, some posts referred to the gendered significance bestowed upon *Bridesmaids* by its hype, some identified the film as a rare and welcome opportunity for female comedians in the industry, and one male blogger asked: "How is it that this movie didn't exist before now?" So although the bloggers tended to be very enthusiastic about *Bridesmaids'* focus on women, they also tended to reproduce the discursive isolation of successful female-driven comedy that Warner and

Savigny (2015) noted in their analysis of *The Heat*'s press reception. The narrative of competing women was most clearly articulated by this male blogger:

> Move over, Tina Fey. Step aside, Jennifer Aniston. There's room for only one funny girl at the top and that spot has just been claimed by the devilishly disarming Kristen Wiig. ...[6]

Within this discourse of *Bridesmaids* as exception, posters often constructed it as a rare representation of women that was not created *for* male viewers or *in relation to* male characters: The women are funny, rather than sexy, and the narrative focuses on female friendship rather than romance. Several bloggers noted that the male actors have little screen time in the film, while the groom is barely seen at all, and some contrasted this with producer Apatow's previous output:

> 'Bridesmaids' is a rare comedy that gives women permission to be funny, to pull ugly faces and to fart in public. Unlike the majority of comedies which relegate female characters to disapproving shrews and the perennial, sighing babysitters of giant man-children, this is a film in which the few male characters play it relatively straight whilst a female ensemble carries all the crass, sweary jokes. In this way it both subverts and conforms to the lucrative Apatow comedy model.

Alongside Wiig's background on *Saturday Night Live*, it was producer Apatow's films, rather than director Feig's work that tended to be invoked as significant paratexts for *Bridesmaids*. However, Apatow's output was used to frame this comedy in quite different ways. Some located *Bridesmaids* within his string of box office successes, and one male blogger argued that Wiig and Mumolo had tried "really hard to ape the male-oriented Apatow films".[7] Some identified him as the source of *Bridesmaids'* gross-out humour, and some feminist bloggers constructed him as a producer of "dude" comedies with sexist or even misogynistic representations of women that were fortunately avoided here. Such diverging readings of Apatow demonstrate the importance of considering the polysemia of paratexts (Hills 2015).

Warner (2013) has argued that *Bridesmaids'* feminist potential was contained in its Anglo-American press reception, where reviews tended to locate this debate within the context of its gross-out humour, which was then coded as masculine. Feminist potential was also a key concern for many of the female and some of the male bloggers included in my sample, but the debate was here approached in more diverse ways. Some reviews located *Bridesmaids'* feminist discourse in its focus on female friendship, some in the representations of women as complex, and some in the representations of women as funny. Other reviews stressed that the film complies with patriarchal ideology through its representations of conventionally feminine pursuits (Annie's cupcake baking and the wedding preparations), through its preoccupation with women as competitors and through the narrative strand that develops Annie's heterosexual romance. Across these readings, the gross-out elements were constructed variously as disrupting conventions of femininity or as "pandering" to male viewers, which demonstrates the polysemia of such comedic transgressions (King 2006).

For some bloggers, there was a distinct sense of disappointment at *Bridesmaids'* failure to live up to a perceived feminist hype. This comment was posted by a reader in response to a very positive review:

> I think if I just thought of this as a kind of low-brow comedy that copies that Hangover with women I would have enjoyed it more. But thinking of this as something different made me feel sad because I felt very alone. I feel like the only person in this country who didn't like this movie! But as I type this, I am also feeling like I'm a little crazy for wanting so much from a comedy. Maybe the problem is that there are just so few comedies with women as leads that I wanted this one to do everything!

The comment drew attention to the ways in which the *Bridesmaids* as exception discourse often inscribed the film with a range of expectations and responsibilities. Across the blogs, *Bridesmaids* was constructed as responsible for "proving" that women could be funny on film, "carry" a comedy and pull in male and female audiences, *and* responsible for satisfying feminist viewers long deprived of progressive representations in Hollywood productions. The requirement for change *and* critical acclaim *and* commercial success might be seen as an intersection between feminist concerns and the patriarchal expectation that women should please everyone.

The discourse of responsibility has been addressed by female comedians in different ways. Mindy Kaling has been confronted with expectations that she, as an Asian-American woman, is responsible for casting more non-white women in her sitcom, *The Mindy Project* (Fox since 2012). Initially expressing anger and frustration, Kaling subsequently concluded that she had to "accept" that she was held responsible in a way that white comedians were not, and that she had "to do more" (Braxton 2014). Similarly, Lena Dunham has accepted criticism that her comedy drama *Girls* (HBO since 2012) lacked diversity: "I've learned so much in the past few years about intersectionality, the way that feminism has underserved women of colour. I really try to educate myself in those areas" (Nicholson 2014b). However, the responsibility to convince men that women can be funny was firmly rejected by Tina Fey (2011) in her book *Bossypants*. Sharing an anecdote from the *Saturday Night Live* writers room, she praises Amy Poehler for dismissing a complaint from a male comedian that her joke was "not cute" with "I don't fucking care if you like it" and recommends this rebuttal as a general response that is useful for "women in the workplace" ("I don't Care If You Like It").

So, then, the blog reception of *Bridesmaids* was largely very positive, and the reviews were particularly interested in the extent to which the film succeeded as a comedy and in the centring of women as comedians and as characters. The connections between those two concerns were most clearly articulated through the excitement about the film's representation of funny yet complex women and through the *Bridesmaids* as exception discourse. Since its release, Hollywood has certainly not seen a great boost in "women's blockbusters" (York 2010), but *Bridesmaids* became a significant paratext for Feig's subsequent female-driven comedies *The Heat*, *Spy* (2015) and *Ghostbusters* (2016). The latter is the focus of the next part of this chapter.

Pre-Viewing *Ghostbusters* in the Twittersphere

The first two *Ghostbusters* films (1984 and 1989) were written by Harold Ramis and Dan Aykroyd and directed and produced by Ivan Reitman; they starred Bill Murray, Dan Aykroyd, Harold Ramis and Ernie Hudson as four parapsychologists who run a ghost-catching business in New York. Then, 25 years later, on the 8th of October 2014, @paulfeig tweeted:

> It's official. I'm making a new Ghostbusters & writing it with @ katiedippold & yes, it will star hilarious women. That's who I'm gonna call.

On the 27th of January 2015, he followed this up by tweeting an image featuring close-ups of Kristen Wiig, Melissa McCarthy, Leslie Jones and Kate McKinnon. Feig's tweets can be considered "entryway paratexts" that try to "direct our initial interpretations" and expectations (Gray 2010: 79) of *Ghostbusters*. Audiences will of course also interpret the paratexts themselves (Hills 2015), and they may draw on that *interpretation* when they imagine what the film will be like.

In my own reading of this first paratext, the decision to launch the film news through Feig's tweet located *Ghostbusters* within his body of work, which set up *Bridesmaids*, *The Heat* and *Spy* as significant paratexts alongside the two previous franchise instalments. The emphasis on his authorship was reinforced through his identification of Katie Dippold as co-scriptwriter (she wrote *The Heat*) and his announcement that "it will star hilarious women", which connected *Ghostbusters* with his previous female-driven comedy films and distinguished it from the two previous, male-driven *Ghostbusters* films. Finally, Feig's reworking of the catch phrase "Who you gonna call?" worked both to locate the news within *Ghostbusters* fandom and to stress his agency within that structure by reaffirming his decision to shift the gendered focus of the franchise.

The tweet hinted at the complex paratextual dialogue surrounding this news. Feig's announcement disrupted 25 years of "post-object fandom" (Williams 2015) where fans had seen previous attempts at resurrection fail, and so the tweets would interact with existing texts from the *Ghostbusters* transmedia franchise (which comprised TV series, comic books, video games and a novel in addition to the two films) as well as previous and contemporary media coverage and studio news, fan discourse, the stardom of cast members from the previous films and this new film, and so on. As Williams (2015) notes, such disruptions involve an element of risk for fans:

> While a resuscitated fan object can provide a new focus for fan discussion and may prompt changes in fans' self-identities (causing them, for example, to reassert and strengthen their identity when a film is released or a series returns), this identity and the ontological security it can provide can also be threatened if the resurrection is badly handled or disappointing.
>
> (Williams 2015: 171)

Media corporations have the opportunity to create a "paratextual array" of promotional texts to tailor their address to different audiences (Hills 2015), but this is not possible on Twitter, which collapses all user groups into one audience (Marwick and boyd 2011). So, Feig's brief messages broke the news to the film industry, mainstream media, his own fans, *Ghostbusters* fans and anyone else who happened to read them.

As expected, reactions were diverse. Many fans replied to Feig's tweets with great excitement while some expressed anxiety, and a minority voiced disinterest or hostility. The guarded responses constructed Feig as responsible for protecting their investment in *Ghostbusters*, while angry fans suggested that its value as a fan object was already being undermined by his involvement. These responses demonstrate the fans' keen sense that "the text is always being a contingent entity, either in the process of forming and transforming or vulnerable to further formation or transformation" (Gray 2010: 7).

By choosing to publish the news on a social networking site, Feig gave other users the opportunity to respond directly and immediately to his account. It offered his Twitter followers a sense of being in the know and enabled them to share the news with users in their own networks. At the time of writing, the first announcement had been retweeted 6,194 times, while 4,861 users had marked it as a "favourite". The image of the actresses had been retweeted 3,254 times and been marked "favourite" 3,323 times. However, while the responses can be seen as an example of "participatory culture" (Jenkins 2006), we don't know how many of those tweets Feig read, and he did not reply to any of them. We might therefore think of the announcements as broadcast tweets, which are often used in the promotion of film, TV or individual celebrities. They encourage "just-in-time fandom" by enabling fans to share their speculations, ideas and concerns but also "regulate the opportunities for temporally-licenced 'feedback', and the very horizons of the fan experience" (Hills 2002: 140). As Deller (2011) points out, Twitter may be presented as "an open, democratic environment where everyone can speak", but different users clearly have different levels of power and influence (217).

Clicking on Feig's tweets brings up "related content", which includes tweets that responded to the original posts, as well as responses to the responses. This illustrates how each broadcast or "one-to-many" tweet became a "many-to-many" dialogue (Marwick and boyd 2011: 129) as well as several conversations between small groups of users. The "related content" comprised 609 tweets below Feig's first announcement and 590 tweets below the image post. Examining these data sets, my analysis will start by considering the positive reactions, before moving on to discuss the more guarded and decidedly negative tweets. The approach is informed by Chin and Gray's (2002) study of fan "previews" of the *Lord of the Rings* films (2001, 2003 and 2003) as well as Proctor's (2013) research on fan responses to news about the *Star Wars* franchise, while my analysis will examine the responses through the lenses of paratextuality (e.g. Genette 1997, Gray 2010 and Hills 2015) and post-object fandom (Williams 2015). I attempted to seek informed consent from all Twitter users whose tweets are quoted in full here, although they did not all respond to my request. I still reproduce tweets from those users here, but they have all been anonymised. I made the decision not to contact Twitter users who posted very aggressive tweets in order to protect my own safety. I therefore quote only fragments from such tweets, in addition to paraphrasing and summarizing their content.

With individual tweets being limited to 140 characters, Twitter is perhaps not the ideal space to discuss issues in depth, but it certainly facilitates short outbursts of excitement:

> @paulfeig @katiedippold WOOOHOOOOOO! Best news ever!
> @paulfeig @katiedippold you two. YOU TWO!! Oh this is beyond brilliant

Following Feig's first announcement, such excited approval was expressed in 33 tweets by male users, 52 tweets by female users and 7 tweets by users with a gender-neutral Twitter handle. As Hills (2012, cited in Proctor 2013) observes, franchise resurrections offer "new hope" to audiences, which can lead to "a moment of heightened fan feeling". Whether that feeling is glee, disinterest or worry will depend on how fans imagine the resurrected text (206).

Feig and Dippold's involvement appeared to be key to the excitement some Twitter users expressed about their projected *Ghostbusters*, as seen in the second tweet quoted above. This invoked their previous collaboration, *The Heat*, as a significant paratext, and this connection was sometimes made explicit:

> @paulfeig @katiedippold Make it as funny and action packed as The Heat and I'm in!

For many more posters, however, enthusiasm seemed to be linked to the imagined involvement of specific female comedy performers. This was evident in the 103 tweets that made casting suggestions, a creative practice that one poster compared to the game Fantasy Football:

> @paulfeig We want Melissa McCarthy @Lesdoggg @SarahKSilverman
>
> @RebelWilson Kathryn Hahn and @nickkroll as receptionist #GhostbustersCasting

Interestingly, "fan-casting" tweets were more than twice as likely to be from male Twitter users, while 30 female users responded to Feig's promise to call "hilarious women" by making more or less humorous offers to participate in the film. This suggests a tendency to gender the projected *Ghostbusters* as a feminine space where female pre-viewers could participate directly (however playfully) while male pre-viewers could participate *through* the female comedians they fan-cast in their imagined *Ghostbusters*.

The casting tweets challenged the marginalisation of women in comedy in three key ways. First, the wide range of suggestions drew attention to the number and diversity of female performers in contemporary U.S. comedy. Second, frequent references to performers who had starred in Feig's previous female-driven comedies located *Ghostbusters* within a specific history of female-driven comedy, which disrupted the narrative of successful female-driven comedies as isolated instances (Warner and Savigny 2015) Finally, these performances of female comedian fandom were tweeted by both men and women, which undermined the assumption that the appeal of such performers is limited and gendered (Bore 2010).

A small number of tweets used the fan casting game to draw attention to white privilege in U.S. comedy:

.@paulfeig @katiedippold Great news! Congrats! People are asking: any Black or Hispanic women in new Ghostbusters? @[disguised] #movies

As the debates around ethnicity and casting for *The Mindy Project* and *Girls* indicated, it is specifically *white* masculinity that is privileged in U.S. comedy, and so fan-cast comedians like Mindy Kaling, Leslie Jones, Maya Rudolph, Whoopi Goldberg, Margaret Cho and Aubrey Plaza represent intersectionalities of marginalised gender and racial identities. Responses to Feig's tweeted image of one black actress (Leslie Jones) and three white actresses (Kristen Wiig, Melissa McCarthy and Kate McKinnon) rarely discussed his casting in terms of race, which may suggest that, within the context of a U.S. comedy industry dominated by white performers, most posters considered this line-up to fulfil their limited expectations of ethnic diversity. (The film itself was later criticised for reproducing racial stereotypes by representing the white women as scientists and the black woman as a subway worker, but that debate remains outside the scope of this chapter.)

Feig's image tweet received a wide range of affective responses. Confusion was a frequent component in many of the early replies, and some observed that Feig was teasing his followers by not clarifying what this image post meant:

@paulfeig Are you messing with us right now orrrrrrr … ?

Feig's post contributed to the "hype" surrounding his film. He teased fans to encourage speculation about what the tweet meant, and a "correct" interpretation required knowledge about Feig's involvement in *Ghostbusters* and about the women in the photographs.

Other affective responses to Feig's image tweet included excitement, joy that favoured performers had been chosen and disappointment that others had been left out:

@paulfeig @[disguised] I approve wholeheartedly of anything that involves Kate McKinnon.

@paulfeig Erm excuse me??? If this is for Ghostbusters where is our girl Sandy B?!! What is going on?!!!!!

Feig's casting news worked as an "entryway paratext" by attempting to guide audience expectations (Gray 2010), and, for some fans, it eliminated an "ideal" (11) *Ghostbusters* because it removed the possibility that their fan-cast comedians would feature in the film.

Some posters, however, abstained from fan-casting and instead performed *Ghostbusters* fandom by invoking the 1984 film as the master paratext for the imagined resurrection. Their tweets often suggested that they struggled to reconcile Feig's news with their understanding of the *Ghostbusters* "canon", and this tension was linked to four different concerns. The first of these was a disinterested "rejection discourse" (Williams 2015: 103) that constructed *Ghostbusters* as a concluded text that should never be resurrected:

> When there are no fresh ideas, in the neighborhood ... RT @paulfeig @katiedippold It's official. I'm making a new Ghostbusters

While this tweet reworked a line from the *Ghostbusters* theme song (Parker 1984) to position the film within a Hollywood lacking in ideas for new projects, others identified the death of Harold Ramis as the appropriate endpoint of the *Ghostbusters* film franchise. Writing about how films of TV series respond to a show's perceived decline, Williams (2015) suggests that a rejection discourse can let fans "distance themselves from a show, discursively positioning themselves as critical and non-emotionally involved", which can work as a strategy "for some fans to cope with, and re-narrate, potential ruptures to a sense of identity or self-narrative that the cancellation of a series may provoke" (103). Similarly, adopting a disinterested, critical position may work to insulate *Ghostbusters* fans from the negative impact a disappointing resurrection might otherwise have on their fan identity.

A second recurring concern was articulated by fans who suggested that they had certain hopes and desires for a third *Ghostbusters* film, but that these were incompatible with Feig's back catalogue. Some of these Twitter users articulated anger towards Feig, expressed through hyperbole and expletives, and such hostility became more evident in responses to his casting tweet. This development indicated that he had, by then, become an object of anti-fandom for some *Ghostbusters* fans, who asserted that he would "fuck the Ghostbusters universe" and wished that he would "grow assholes on [his] fingertips and get hemorrhoids". The use of aggressive and creative insults can be seen as performances of "hard" masculinity through "the public exposition of power" (Kehily and Nayak 1997: 73). They displayed "transgression, aggressiveness, naturalness and unsophistication" (Pujolar 2000: 45), but also produced "a space of creativity" where *Ghostbusters* fans could collaborate to use aggressive humour for "new effects" (49). This play constructed Feig's project as abject.

Whereas some anti-fans pointed to *The Heat* or *Bridesmaids* as paratextual forecasts of failure, others participated in fan-casting by "anti-casting" Melissa McCarthy. Such tweets varied in their hostility. Some described her as "lame" or articulated mocking laughter, and others

employed misogynistic discourse to construct her as grotesque and dele-
gitimise her as a comedic performer. At the same time, McCarthy was
one of the most frequently suggested comedians in fan-casting tweets,
and many posters expressed enthusiasm about her confirmed involvement. These conflicting responses to projections of her performance
seem to echo the contested meanings of the unruly woman (Rowe 1995)
that I identified in diverging readings of her character in *Bridesmaids*.

The misogynistic discourse evident in much of the McCarthy anti-
fandom was interlinked with a third concern, which was articulated by
male Twitter users. It focused on Feig's promise to "call" female comedians, and on his confirmed casting of four women. As Whalley (2010)
argues, the first *Ghostbusters* film primarily sought "to retain the
young, male audience that had previously made Murray's films successful" (87), and these tweets policed the gendered boundaries of *Ghostbusters*. Some constructed the gendered shift as "unnatural", while
others represented Feig's project as a hostile intrusion into masculine
fan culture and as a disappointing end to a long period of waiting and
speculation in their post-object fandom. Like the articulation of disinterest discussed above, sarcastic tweets worked to distance fans from
the resurrection. However, the aggression in some of these responses
suggested a greater anxiety about what Feig's film might mean for these
fans' gendered identities.

We might consider the gendered shift in the *Ghostbusters* franchise
within the context of a paratext that connects all three films. *Saturday Night Live* was invoked in several responses to Feig's casting news.
McCarthy has hosted the show several times, whereas Wiig, Jones and
McKinnon have all been cast members. Similarly, Aykroyd and Murray
were also *Saturday Night Live* alumni. Discussing the move into Hollywood comedy by *Saturday Night Live* stars in the 1970s and '80s,
Whalley (2010) notes that "instances of white male bias on *SNL* became
total male domination" (191). Tina Fey then became the first female
head writer in 1999, and, sharing an anecdote about a sketch where the
team cast a male comedian to portray Rocky's wife, she writes:

> ... it illustrates how things were the first week I was there. By the
> time I left nine years later, that would never have happened. Nobody
> would have thought for a second that a dude in drag would be fun-
> nier than Amy [Poehler], Maya [Rudolph], or Kristen [Wiig]. The
> women in the cast took over the show in that decade, and I had the
> pleasure of being there to witness it.
> (Fey 2011: "Peeing in Jars with Boys")

So, within the paratextual dialogue surrounding Feig's film, we can see
that a significant gendered shift within *Saturday Night Live* preceded
such a shift in the *Ghostbusters* franchise.

A fourth concern articulated by Twitter users focused on rumours that Feig's *Ghostbusters* would be a "reboot", rather than a sequel. As Tryon (2013) notes, a "reboot" is a "process of restarting an existing media franchise by returning to its origin point" (432). For Hollywood studios, this is a strategy for combating the ageing and "critical or commercial exhaustion" of franchises (433), though this can be problematic for fans:

> in the world of fictional narratives and long-running, serialized stories, the term is used to indicate a removal or nullification of history in order to "begin again" from "year one" without any requirement of canonical knowledge of previous incarnations (which is, of course, an implausible conceit as the audience cannot be rendered amnesiac at the whim of a corporate monolith).
>
> (Proctor 2012)

Unsurprisingly, then, many tweets suggested that fan imaginings of a reboot were laced with anxiety about how it could offer the pleasures that fans associated with their fan object:

> @paulfeig @katiedippold clearly you will read every tweet & craft the movie based on them, but please - not a total reboot. Keep some lore!

Fans might expect a sequel to offer pleasures associated with continuity, such as the chance to see favourite characters again, or opportunities to revisit places of significance, or a more indefinable sense of experiencing a familiar world. A reboot, on the other hand, means that everything is up in the air, and fans have to negotiate the resulting sense of uncertainty. As Williams argues,

> fandom of specific objects may provide individuals with a sense of ontological security that derives from the fan's devotion to his/her fan object and also from the resultant fan community. Ontological security may develop from the constancy of a fan object, for example television programmes that are screened regularly and that return with each new "season" of television. (2015: 25)

Any *Ghostbusters* resurrection would threaten to undermine the ontological security this film franchise offered its fans because it would change the fan object after a long period of post-object fandom. However, the unpredictability of a reboot resurrection could increase this sense of threat. Such anxieties were evident in fan tweets that constructed the reboot approach as disrespectful, both towards the franchise and towards its fans. Some Twitter users asked Feig to reconsider, at times supporting their requests by pointing to previous reboots that they considered failures or to evidence of anger in *Ghostbusters* fan communities. Other fans expressed such anger themselves, sarcastically wishing him "good luck" and declaring that, "we wouldn't call you if our lives depended on it". These tweets constructed a conflict between Feig's plans and the desires of *Ghostbusters* fans. They worked to valorise and homogenise the established *Ghostbusters* fandom centred around the previous franchise instalments and insisted that this audience group would not be supporting his film.

What appeared to underlie these four recurring concerns was an anxiety that the third film may devalue *Ghostbusters* as a fan object. Responses articulated this worry through encouraging advice and begging:

> @paulfeig Welcome! Make sure you 1) emphasize the banter, 2) respect the tech and 3) make it scary AND funny and you'll be fine! Good luck!

> @paulfeig @katiedippold excited but so scared; please don't ruin my childhood like Michael Bay did to TMNT [Teenage Mutant Ninja Turtles].

Negotiating Twitter's 140 character limitation, these fans hinted at complex affective responses ranging from mild optimism to an angry sense of loss, via intense ambivalence. The two tweets quoted above may be seen as attempts to protect the fan object, but other, aggressive tweets claimed that the damage is inevitable. One fan accused Feig of "taking a dump" on the "memory" of Harold Ramis, and the Ramis "legacy" was given great salience by some fans who positioned themselves in opposition to Feig's film. Other posts privileged Dan Aykroyd's previous attempts at resurrecting the film franchise or insisted that a third film had to star Bill Murray. By constructing *Ghostbusters* as a "classic" that was closely linked to specific individuals, these fans challenged the legitimacy of Feig's film, while one conversation even questioned the legality of Feig's project in light of Aykroyd's rights to the franchise. In these ways, fan tweets repeatedly invoked the "long shadow" (Gray 2010: 19) that the *Ghostbusters* "canon" cast over this resurrection, a shadow that was also maintained by Aykroyd's (cited in Child 2015) continued efforts to make "a more conventional third sequel".

Conclusion

Building on the previous chapter's exploration of how *Parks and Recreation* fans constructed that sitcom as successful, this chapter has begun to investigate some of the ways in which cultural identities can structure our engagement with comedy. My analysis contributed to the debate around the marginalisation of women in comedy by examining blog reviews of *Bridesmaids* and Twitter previews of *Ghostbusters*. I found that blog posts tended to celebrate *Bridesmaids* as an isolated achievement for female-driven comedy. This reproduced a common narrative in the critical reception of female-driven comedy and inscribed the film with responsibilities for "proving" that women can be funny and that female comedians can attract audiences and for promoting feminism through its representations. However, this discourse of isolated achievement was challenged by Twitter pre-views of *Ghostbusters* in two key ways. First, male and female Twitter users performed fandoms of a wide range of female comedians by playfully fan-casting the film. Second, Feig's previous female-driven comedies were frequently invoked as promising or off-putting paratexts as *Ghostbusters* fans imagined what the resurrection might be like. These two forms of responses situated *Ghostbusters* within a comedy culture where female performers and female-driven texts are visible and connected through paratextual dialogue.

However, the privileging of (white) masculinity was still reinforced by tweets that constructed female ghostbusters as an unwelcome intrusion into male fan culture. This aggressive online maintenance of white male privilege later escalated, and Leslie Jones received horrific misogynistic and racist abuse on Twitter after the film was released. The hostility demonstrated that comedies, as fan objects, can become sites of cultural struggles over meaning. I will continue to investigate this significance in the next chapter, where I focus on the national and transnational reception of the Norwegian comedy serial *Lilyhammer.*

Notes

1 Glenn Lovell at CinemaDope.com
2 Blog: *Anna, Look!*
3 Molly Galler of *Pop.Bop.Shop.*
4 The Feminist Guide to Hollywood
5 *Anna, Look!*
6 Glenn Lovell at CinemaDope.com
7 Blogger: Peter Piatkowski.

4 National and Transnational Comedy

Lilyhammer on NRK and Netflix

After examining the significance of gender in online audience engagement with comedy, I now want to shift attention onto the significance of nationality. Informed by literature on the relationship between nationality and humour (e.g. Medhurst 2007), I use *Lilyhammer* as a case study to compare responses from its domestic Norwegian audiences and its transnational audiences. The chapter builds on Sundet's (2016) industry study of *Lilyhammer*, which used interviews with key informants involved in the production and commissioning of the programme to explore how these practitioners "make" its audience. This is a set of processes by which "media workers make sense of the audience, attract it, measure it, and try to serve it" (14). My analysis also builds on a previous project (Bore 2011), where I adopted a focus group approach to examine British and Norwegian audience responses to a set of TV comedies from those two countries. At the time, the idea of a Norwegian TV programme achieving distribution beyond Scandinavia seemed far-fetched, and I had to translate and subtitle the shows myself. However, the international successes of Swedish and Danish dramas such as *Wallander* (TV4 2005–13), *Forbrydelsen/The Killing* (DR1 2007–12), *Borgen* (DR1 2010–13) and *Bron/Broen/The Bridge* (SVT1/DR1 since 2011) have demonstrated that Scandinavian programmes can have value as imports.

It is important to note, though, that *Lilyhammer* is distinct from these three serials, both because it is a comedy and because it is structured around the star text of U.S. musician and actor Steven van Zandt, who played Silvio Dante in *The Sopranos* (HBO 1999–2007). Although the project was commissioned by the Norwegian public service broadcaster NRK from the Norwegian production company Rubicon TV, the production context soon became more complicated:

> [D]uring the production of the first season, Van Zandt pitched Lilyhammer to Netflix, which then entered the production as a co-investor, turning Lilyhammer from an NRK-only series to an "original Netflix series" and redirecting it from its national public service audience to a US streaming audience.
>
> (Sundet 2016: 18)

This case study therefore complicates the notion of "national comedy". I am interested in exploring how Norwegian and transnational audiences read its representations of nationality and how they articulated the significance of nationality for their viewing experiences.

Following *Lilyhammer* across Three Online Spaces

Unlike the approach I take in other chapters in this book, I follow this case study across three different online spaces: The forum on the website of a Norwegian tabloid newspaper; an English-language forum for people interested in film and television; and the official, English-language Facebook page for *Lilyhammer*. This multi-sited approach enables me to compare the responses of Norwegian viewers (addressed to other Norwegian viewers) with those of an international audience, including in-depth and sometimes critical discussions on the film and TV forum, as well as fan responses on the Facebook page.

The Norwegian news site included a very broad range of message boards, with topics such as "The Middle East", "Environment and Climate", "Cars", "Ice Hockey", "Sex" and "Hip Hop". On the busy "TV programmes" forum there were three *Lilyhammer* threads. The thread on the first series had 428 posts, the thread on the second series had 193 posts and the thread on the third and final series had only 15 posts. This decline might suggest a decreasing interest in discussing the show, but it is also possible that users shifted their online discussions to other, perhaps international communities as the programme became more popular abroad. Most participants were very active site users, demonstrated by the post counters displayed under their usernames. Most had contributed at least 1,000 posts, and many had contributed far more. The display of these numbers indicated that prolificity was valorised by the site, and highlights that contributors create content for free and then consume advertising while reading other user-generated content on the board.

The English-language film and TV site had a *Lilyhammer* message board that included 111 threads. Most were quite short, with the busiest thread comprising 63 posts. Here, profiles displayed the duration of site membership rather than number of posts, which valorised experience or commitment rather than prolificity. Both here and on the Norwegian forum, users were anonymous, with self-selected pseudonyms as usernames and profile pictures that clearly did not depict the users. Both message boards were public, and the Norwegian site even included a button that enabled visitors to share individual posts on Facebook or Twitter, which signals the publicness of that space. Neither site provided a facility for contacting contributors, however, so I was unable to ask users for permission to quote their posts. I will therefore refrain from identifying these two sites. My translation of the Norwegian posts into

English will further conceal those user identities, and I have tested that it is not possible to trace extracts from the film and TV forum through Google.

Researching Facebook posts necessitated very careful reflection on the ethics of quoting posts, even though I am focusing on a page that is open to the public. The platform requires users to display their real names, which are often accompanied by portrait photographs, while different and changing security settings blur the boundary between private and public material. I have nonetheless decided to include the site because it is understudied, despite its enormous popularity, and because it might give me access to users who don't self-identify as fans or contribute to sites more frequently associated with fandom (such as Tumblr or DeviantArt). As Lehtinen (forthcoming) observes, engaging with Facebook pages such as this one simply requires users to click a "like" button. To address my ethical concerns, I have not quoted sensitive information, I only use short quotations from Facebook, and I have contacted the users who made those posts in order to seek informed consent. However, Facebook can make it difficult to contact users who are outside of our own networks, and I did not get responses from all of the users to whom I sent messages. I have still decided to include those posts, but I have made sure that it is not possible to identify the users by entering the quotes into search engines.

Comedy, Belonging and (Trans)national Television

Academic work on the relationship between comedy and nationality has tended to focus on the importance of cultural belonging. Mills (2005) observes that TV comedy forms "part of the television process in which broadcasting is used in attempts to define the ways in which a culture presents itself to others" (10), and O'Regan (2000) emphasises the importance of exploring how the international circulation of TV programming produces imagined national identities. For Norway, as a small nation, *Lilyhammer* was a rare opportunity to reach international audiences. It is therefore significant that the show repeatedly invokes the 1994 Winter Olympics hosted by Norway in Lillehammer, in order to position itself within, but also against, the image of Norway promoted by the games and the tourism industry. In the first episode, New York gangster Frank Tagliano joins the FBI's Witness Protection Program, and he chooses to relocate to Lillehammer because he remembers the Olympics and associates the area with "clean air, fresh white snow and gorgeous broads". The show then continues to create comic situations from an incongruity between its representations of Norwegian culture and its representation of Frank's (under the alias Giovanni, shortened to Johnny) U.S. mobster attitude and practices.

This incongruity plays with the question of whether Frank/Johnny "belongs" in small-town Norway. As Medhurst argues, "the ascertaining and labelling of those who do not belong" is a "core element in the construction of nation". This strategy tends to concentrate on "the nearer others" and the "internal others" (28–29):

> These processes work similarly in comedy, of course, which is why British (and especially English) comedians have been so devoted to the Irish joke but have no need of Portuguese jokes, and why jokes about West Indians and Pakistanis only took hold in British popular culture once post-war immigration brought large numbers of people from those cultures to make their homes in Britain.
>
> (Medhurst 2007: 28)

In *Lilyhammer*, the "other" is not the U.S. but the fictional Italian-American mobster figure from U.S. films and TV crime dramas. In the fictional Lillehammer, Johnny functions as a disruptive other that facilitates the satirising of "us", including perceived Norwegian naivety, bureaucracy and self-satisfaction. This satire draws on what Anderson (1991) describes as the imagining of the nation as a community, a process that develops "a deep, horizontal comradeship" (7), despite practices of subordination and exploitation. In Anderson's account, this "profound emotional legitimacy" distinguishes the nation from many other imagined communities (4).

Drawing on Anderson's work, Verdery (1996) argues that the individual national identity is formed through "daily interactions and practices that produce an inherent and often unarticulated feeling of belonging" (229). For example, Dhoest (2007) notes that newspapers and television circulate "representations and interpretations of the nation, continue to provide opportunities for shared 'national' experiences, and institutionalise national cultures by storing cultural elements and memories" (61). Billig (1995) conceptualises such practices as "banal nationalism", which works as "a continual 'flagging', or reminding, of nationhood" (8). Examining discursive constructions of nationality in Norway, Gullestad (2002) argues that a dominant discourse of Egalitarianism produces a problematic notion of "imagined sameness". The cultural emphasis on equality produces an emphasis on homogeneity and a discursive implication that differences cause undesirable tension. The valorisation of commonality and "playing down differences" in social interaction has blurred class boundaries and intensified the marginalisation of non-Western immigrants and asylum seekers (47). This marginalisation is evident in *Lilyhammer*, which uses Johnny's arrival to represent immigration, xenophobia and the processes of integration. I will examine audience discussions of those representations later on in this chapter.

Lilyhammer's Production and Distribution Context

Launched in 1933, Norwegian public service broadcaster Norsk Rik-skringkasting (NRK) was modeled on the BBC, funded by the license fee, and "expressly devoted to a programming policy intended to serve popular/public enlightenment purposes" (Gripsrud 1995: 75). However, due to the expense of establishing and maintaining terrestrial broad-casting in a mountainous, sparsely populated country, the broadcaster has had to rely on a substantial amount of imports to fill its schedules (Syvertsen 2004). This has traditionally tended to be Scandinavian and U.K. programming, whereas the import of U.S. content has been tied to debates around commercialisation and cultural erosion (Gripsrud 1995). The introduction of commercial broadcasters in 1988 dramatically in-creased the availability of U.S. entertainment programming targeting younger Norwegian viewers (Ytreberg 1996). NRK first dropped below a 50 per cent audience share in 1994 (Bastiansen and Syvertsen 1996: 148), and, although their main TV channel NRK1 still enjoys "a loyal audience base" of older viewers (Ihlebæk *et al.* 2014: 475), Sundet (2016) argues that, since the loss of its monopoly, NRK has shown greater in-terest in researching and thinking about its audiences. This "reflects its desire to fulfill its societal, democratic and cultural obligations as a pub-lic service broadcaster", but it is also a response "to deregulation, media convergence and increased competition from commercial channels, new streaming services and other providers of 'TV-like content' such as You-Tube" (16). From their perspective, *Lilyhammer* was commissioned for Norwegian audiences, "as a cost-effective and unconventional television drama with star actor Steven Van Zandt in the lead role". In contrast, Rubicon TV targeted their "drama production" at both domestic and international audiences, seeing them as resource-costly projects that rep-resented "opportunities for export and co-investment" (18).

Netflix launched in 1997 as an online DVD rental service (Jenner 2014), but in 2010 it shifted its main business from DVD delivery to of-fering subscribers unlimited film and TV downloads (Cunningham and Silver 2012). And, as Jenner (2014) notes, "Netflix has now moved into the business of being producer of serialized drama", becoming "the first in the chain of media exhibition" (5). Unlike *House of Cards* (Netflix, since 2013), however, Netflix was the not the first to show *Lilyhammer*, which premiered on NRK1 on the 25th of January 2012, while Netflix released all eight episodes 12 days later (Ratvik 2012). The show was also distributed outside of the U.S. by Red Arrow, which sold the first season to 130 countries (Sørenes 2014). As Sundet (2016) observes, then, "*Lilyhammer* had to serve both a national and an international audience that consumed television in either 'flow' or on-demand modes" (13). By releasing all episodes at the same time, Netflix enabled its users to binge-watch the show, which Jenner (2014) suggests is now "an encouraged mode of viewing all Netflix series" (7). Pittman and Sheehan's (2015) survey of binge-watchers demonstrated that Netflix was their preferred platform for this practice, and the researchers note that Netflix has no ad breaks:

> When one program is nearing the nearing the end of its running time, Netflix will automatically cue up the next episode in that series for you. The user has to opt out when he or she wants to stop. It requires very little effort to binge on Netflix; in fact, it takes more effort to stop than to keep going.
>
> (Pittman and Sheehan 2015)

With *Lilyhammer*'s series being limited to 8 episodes, a run can be completed quite quickly, and I will discuss the implications of this viewing pattern for contributions to the Facebook page later on. Having established the theoretical and industrial contexts for my case study, I will now move on to the analysis, which starts by examining Norwegian responses to the show.

Watching *Lilyhammer* in Norway

Norwegian *Lilyhammer* viewers often foregrounded the "Norwegian-ness" of the show, though they did so in two quite distinct ways. The first approach articulated concerns about how the programme would represent "us" abroad. When the first series started, contributors to the Norwegian forum tended to construct it as a Norwegian TV show starring a U.S. celebrity actor, rather than an international co-production. However, they were aware that the show had international distribution deals, and they frequently invoked an imagined transnational audience. This user was evaluating the very first episode:

> Some funny scenes in this, some a little embarrassing, but nothing too bad. The question is if there's too much Norwegian humour in this, keen to see how well it does considering the Netflix push in the U.S.

This response inscribed the episode with both funniness and shame, but simultaneously contained these affects through the markers "some", "a little" and "nothing too bad", which worked to distance the viewer from the show: They cared a bit, but not "too much". The post illustrates the discomfort viewers can feel in response to perceived comic failure, suggesting that the failure is shameful and that, as witnesses, we become implicated in that shame. However, the contributor then set his or her own affective response aside, suggesting that the key issue at stake was instead the show's reception by U.S. audiences. This shift indicated the perceived significance of *Lilyhammer* as a representative for Norwegian television to the U.S. It also emphasised the cultural specificity of "Norwegian humour", which was constructed as a barrier to transnational audience enjoyment of the show. Here, such national humour drew a distinction between "us", who will have a full understanding of the text, and "them", whose engagement will necessarily be limited. As Critchley observes:

> Humour is a form of cultural insider-knowledge, and might, indeed, be said to function like a linguistic defence mechanism. Its ostensive untranslatability endows native speakers with a palpable sense of their cultural distinctiveness or even superiority. In this sense, having a common sense of humour is like sharing a secret code. (2002: 67–68)

While the "Norwegian-ness" of Norwegian comedy programmes would usually remain the invisible norm for domestic audiences, it was made visible and destabilised by Van Zandt's role and by the show's international distribution. As seen in the post quoted above, the transnational audience was primarily imagined as being from the U.S., even though the show was distributed in other countries via Red Arrow and Netflix. This echoes the definition made by NRK and Rubicon informants in Sundet's (2016) study, and it demonstrates the significance of the U.S. for contemporary television, both as producer and as audience, and the relative discursive invisibility of other territories. Here, the U.S. was invoked as a provider of quality TV and good actors and as an imagined audience who would be evaluating *Lilyhammer*.

Within this context, it is perhaps significant that contributors repeatedly used the word "embarrassing" to describe the performances of Norwegian actors, representations of Norwegian culture, and characters' tendency to address Johnny in Norwegian while he replied mostly in English:

> All that mixing of Norwegian and English when they talk to Johnny is embarrassing to listen to. ... The series would actually be good if they had just spoken to him in English 100%, at least until we could get the impression that he has been in Norway for a while. I reckon the series would be better liked abroad.
>
> I'll suffer through the second episode, if it's as irritating I'll drop the whole thing.

The post suggested that Norwegians were embarrassing themselves in front of an American *within the diegesis*, but it might also suggest that, because of this flawed dialogue, *Lilyhammer* was, or could be, an embarrassing representation of Norway to U.S. audiences. The forum contributor was implicated in this imagined shame, and the viewing experience was described as irritating and constructed as painful labour.

Since the viewer claimed to appreciate other aspects of the show, the affective response to the language use seems strong. Ahmed's (2004) notion of "national shame" offers a way to make sense of this reaction. She argues that "declarations of shame can bring 'the nation' into existence as a felt community' (101):

> Individuals become implicated in national shame insofar as they already belong to the nation, insofar as their allegiance has already been given to the nation, and they can be subject to its address. Our shame is "my shame" insofar as I am already "with" them, insofar as the "our" can be uttered by me. (2004: 102)

Here, contributors articulated a sense of shame as a response to imagined negative perceptions of *Lilyhammer* by U.S. audiences. By seeing the programme as a rare and risky opportunity for Norway to represent itself to others, they constructed "us" as a small nation, with a "peripheral position and marginal language" (Syvertsen 1992: 23).

The post quoted above also hinted at a concern that *Lilyhammer* represented Norwegians as stupid and provincial, with little experience of communicating with English speakers. This worry was articulated more clearly in posts that complained about character appearances and behaviours:

> Several things I reacted to in this series.
> First of all, this sheep's head. Hardly anyone in Lillehammer (or anywhere outside of the west country) eats that, certainly not on a regular weekday.
> Secondly, nobody comes out into their yard with a shotgun just because they haven't seen the car before.
> Thirdly, who the fuck leaves their sheep out in winter?
> Fourthly, there are about 40 wolves in Norway. The probability of one of them being in someone's yard I find very small.
> Fifthly … no, I can't be bothered anymore.
> There were a lot of goofs [English] in this series, despite everything I smiled from time to time.
> I dislike us Norwegians being portrayed in this way.

This explicit concern about representations of nationality invokes the ways in which the listed elements can be seen to confirm existing stereotypes of Norway. For example, this is how Norway has been characterised in Danish jokes:

> Norway is considered a backward country, provincial, in the periphery not only from a Scandinavian perspective, but also in relation to Europe. Norway's modern position as an oil exporter seems to

have no impact on the joke-telling. By the same token, Norway's independence from the European Union is interpreted as a sign of its provincialism. One example of Norway's so-called "pre-modern position" is related to the alleged strong national pride in Norway, which is seen in contrast to other more modern nations' international orientation. (Gundelach 2000: 117)

Lilyhammer, then, was repeatedly invested with the potential to implicate Norwegian viewers in national shame by being an inferior TV programme or by representing Norway as an inferior national culture. The second complaint, however, was dismissed by posters who foregrounded the show's comedic modality and absolved it of "the burden of representation" (Tagg 1988). This was a response to the contributor quoted above:

> You have clearly not understood that this is an entertainment series with actors and imaginative elements, not a documentary film from Lillehammer.

A similar debate took place on the English language film and TV forum. Here, it was initiated by a poster who indicated that he or she was a foreign national residing in Norway and saw Johnny's mobster practices as a threat to "the social trust and cohesion that make Scandinavia such a pleasant place". The post suggested that organised crime is not an appropriate topic for comedy and hinted at a concern about media effects, though this was not made explicit. The first replies to this post dismissed the critique by constructing the contributor as "boring" and arguing that he or she had failed to understand that the show was meant to be entertaining and exciting. This reproduces a discourse of comedy as a license to explore transgression. *Lilyhammer* uses cues to indicate a weak, comedic modality, reminding us that what we are watching is not "real" and discouraging us from worrying about Johnny's behaviour. However, concerns expressed by viewers new to the show indicate that they were sometimes unsure of how to read it. This tension can be traced back to the production process, where Van Zandt wanted *Lilyhammer* to be a "dramedy" that built on his performance in *The Sopranos*, while show runners Anne Bjørnstad and Eilif Skodvin wanted to create a comedy (Sundet 2016: 20). The resulting ambiguity was a desirable characteristic for NRK, who associated it with quality TV and praised the "scruffy style, mix of genres, play with stereotypes and hidden societal critique" of the first series (23). My analysis of data across the three online audience spaces suggests that, following some initial uncertainty, committed viewers read the show as a comedy and valorised representations of crime and violence as important sources of humour in the programme. Having explored some of the initial, anxious responses to *Lilyhammer* by Norwegian contributors, I will now move on to discuss the ways in which Norwegian *Lilyhammer* fans later positioned themselves as privileged members of an imagined international fan community.

From the Periphery to the Centre

The *Lilyhammer* Facebook page promoted the show as a Netflix Original, erasing NRK's involvement. Its function as a promotional tool was underscored by a power structure that only allowed page administrators to start threads, while fans were positioned as followers and respondents. This limits the extent to which the page can function as a participatory space. Lehtinen (forthcoming) observes that the mechanism attempts to contain and shape fan discourse on official Facebook pages, and such sites can therefore provide interesting case study analyses of the relationships between fans and producers. On the *Lilyhammer* page, administrators started each of the 265 threads by posting an image with an accompanying message. The images tended to be screen grabs from the show, with added captions displaying quotes from the dialogue, but they were also sometimes mock-promotional images for Johnny's bar or images of Van Zandt on set. The posts sometimes foregrounded the Norwegian-ness of *Lilyhammer*, for example by including snow, knitwear, skiing or the word "skål", which invited fans to participate in a Norwegian toast. This paratextual emphasis on nationality can be seen as a bid for cultural distinction, setting *Lilyhammer* apart from other TV shows on the basis of its setting. It also invited fans to address this distinction.

One of the last posts to the page featured a screen grab of Johnny leaning over a bar, chewing on a pretzel stick and holding a deck of cards. He is staring thoughtfully ahead, and the caption reads: "I'm turning more Norwegian by the moment". The image was accompanied by the text: "You're not the only one, Boss." This post inscribed *Lilyhammer* with a transformative capacity, suggesting that transnational viewers are not only introduced to Norwegian culture, but are internalizing that culture and gradually *becoming Norwegian*. It unified the imagined international *Lilyhammer* fandom, giving individual viewers a shared quality and setting them apart from other audiences. However, only three Facebook users responded by confirming that they shared this experience, while other replies tended to either express love for the show or ask when the next series would become available. Across the Facebook page, attempts by administrators to encourage a nation-based fan discourse achieved only limited success, and so the significance of the show's Norwegian-ness for transnational viewers was rarely articulated in this space. It might indicate user resistance to the site's attempt to direct fan conversations, as Lehtinen (forthcoming) found in her study of the *True Blood* Facebook page, or it might be because the site's user culture instead privileged other topics, which I will discuss further later on in this chapter. On the English-language film and TV forum, several transnational viewers did valorise *Lilyhammer*'s Norwegian-ness. They argued that its nationality set it apart from U.S. and U.K. TV shows, making it "fresh and interesting", rather than "just another show about NY gangsters". Some also performed viewer competency by includ- ing Norwegian words in their posts. These audience responses aligned with the nation-based distinction promoted by the Facebook page and demonstrated that some transnational viewers did inscribe its perceived cultural difference as pleasurable.

Although transnational audiences rarely invoked this cultural differ- ence on the Facebook page, Norwegian users frequently highlighted their proximity to the show. The previous section of my analysis examined the worries that some Norwegian viewers expressed about how *Lilyhammer* would be received abroad, indicating the perceived risk associated with representing Norway to transnational audiences. However, the Face- book page valorised the show through both admin and user posts, and it therefore represented a safe space for Norwegians to claim ownership of the programme. One of the ways in which they did so was by demon- strating that they had early access to new content:

Oh, how the tables have turned. For once we have something on Norwegian television that the Americans are waiting for and not the other way around. Don't know about you, but I'm set for season 2 episode five on Wednesday! ^^

The post illustrates the recurring assumption that transnational viewers were U.S. viewers and addressed the unequal power relation between the U.S. as an exporter of TV shows and Norway's dependence on imports to fill its TV schedules (Syvertsen 1992). Although U.S. imports were often associated with cheesiness and commercialism in the past (Bore 2011), my sample indicated that there had been a marked shift towards associating U.S. TV with *quality* dramas and sitcoms. This perception is evident in the post quoted above, where the user constructed U.S. im- ports as something Norwegians eagerly await as a peripheral audience. U.S. film and TV releases are distributed in Norway sometime after they are made available to domestic audiences, which poses a challenge for Norwegian viewers who wish to participate in international, online fan communities (Bore and Williams 2010). It also brings the risk of expo- sure to unwanted spoilers. It is unsurprising, then, that the Facebook post articulated a sense of pleasure in finally inhabiting the nation-based centre of an international fandom. The contributor teased U.S. fans about their delayed access to *Lilyhammer*, reminding them that the sec- ond series was well underway in Norway, and that *they* were, for once, on the periphery.

A second way in which Norwegian viewers constructed themselves as privileged *Lilyhammer* fans was by suggesting that their nation-based experiences enabled them to make richer readings of the show. Their knowledge of *Lilyhammer*'s national context informed their readings of the text's representations of social customs, for example, and enabled them to recognise comedic cultural references. As a form of cultural competence, it was seen to give Norwegian viewers access to a more complete understanding of the show and to a greater range of textual pleasures. This audience discourse of privilege was articulated through Norwegian-language posts that identified specific references that transnational viewers were unlikely to understand, as well as through English-language "interventions" into discussions about the show. Here, Norwegian contributors would adopt a position of authority by answering questions about representations, correcting perceived misinterpretations and explaining the wider cultural context of narrative events. The post quoted below was a forum contribution to one of many discussions about why Johnny tends to speak in English while the Norwegian characters tend to address him in their own language:

> I actually know on an American living in Norway who is like that. He will understand everything you throw at him in Norwegian, but will only reply in English, as Norwegians find it easier to understand him in his native English than trying to decipher Norwegian words hidden behind a thick American accent.

Whereas some contributors tried to explain the language shifts by drawing on their understanding of multi-national TV production (Van Zandt didn't have to learn Norwegian) or transnational TV (domestic audiences wanted to hear some Norwegian, while U.S. audiences didn't want to read subtitles), this viewer presented his or her own, embodied experience of communicating with a Norway-based U.S. citizen as evidence of the show's verisimilitude. The valorisation of such embodied experiences of Norway was reproduced by transnational fans who foregrounded their familiarity with the country, for example by identifying their Norwegian cultural heritage or their travels in Norway.

"Americanised" *Lilyhammer*

However, for some Norwegian fans, a perceived Americanisation of series 2 and 3 undermined their claim to the centre of an international *Lilyhammer* fandom. On the Norwegian forum, this development was imagined during the broadcast run of the first series:

> The exciting thing is of course whether you get a "Norwegian" series 2, or whether foreign interests meddle in series 2 and so on.

The post suggested that *Lilyhammer* was inherently Norwegian and that this Norwegian-ness might be seen as an obstacle for international distribution. Once series 2 started on NRK1, another poster also expressed disappointment:

> I had looked forward to Lilyhammer. But after ten minutes: I don't like this, violence is not pleasant. This has gone through NRK's mediocrity machine. The first series had a self-ironic, naive concept. Now it is Americanised and uninteresting to watch.

Here, "Americanisation" was associated with representations of violence, and a second contributor agreed that the shift made him or her "uncomfortable". In response to the same episode, a third contributor complained about changes to the show's visual style:

> Now they've also started with advanced camerawork. NRK doesn't understand what has brought them success. The whole new concept is completely misunderstood.

In both cases, the undesirable development was blamed on the Norwegian public service broadcaster, who was seen to offer a poor, undesirable imitation of U.S. quality TV. However, Sundet's (2016) production study of *Lilyhammer* suggests that NRK actually shared some of these concerns. As Netflix increased its funding contribution, the show's budget doubled for series 2 and again for series 3, when Netflix became the main investor. So, although NRK retained "creative control" in theory, the production context became more complicated (19). For example, Sundet identifies "an ongoing debate regarding the appropriate amount of explicit violence, sex and bad language", which is associated with edgy quality TV in the U.S. but not in the "Western Europe public service context" (20). The concern about Americanisation was a minority view on the Norwegian forum, however. Most contributors expressed excitement about the second series, describing it as "entertaining", "exciting" and "fantastic". Some praised it for being "more professional" or "more adult", while one user infused the term "Americanisation" with value:

> I think it's good that it's a bit Americanised, too Norwegian or the same level as series 1 would quickly become boring in series 2, I think.

Earlier on in this chapter I noted that "Americanisation" has traditionally been associated with cultural imperialism in Norwegian debates around television. Norway was one of the last European countries to establish a TV service, and its cultural elites expressed concerns that television would erode national culture. This anxiety was specifically tied to the influence of *U.S.* popular culture, whereas British imports have traditionally been considered both prestigious and popular (Gripsrud 1995). The distinction between U.S. and Norwegian cultural values was reproduced by the contributor who disapproved of *Lilyhammer*'s representations of violence. The dismissal of its more "advanced" visual style could also be read as resistance to the perceived aesthetic influence of U.S. quality TV, and it is notable that Sundet's (2016) interviewees from NRK preferred the "scruffy style" of the first series (23). In contrast, the contributor quoted above constructed national culture as a constraint that could be disrupted by the influence of U.S. TV. This notion of Norwegian TV fiction as "boring" echoes findings from my previous research (Bore 2011), where young, female participants suggested that NRK was for "older" viewers, while commercial channels TV2 and TVNorge (which both schedule a lot of U.S. imports) were for "younger" viewers (224). These intersections of age-based and nation-based discourses illustrate the significance of *Lilyhammer*'s success with younger Norwegian viewers, with whom NRK have often found it difficult to connect (Sundet 2016).[1] Having explored the significance of *Lilyhammer*'s Norwegian-ness for its domestic audiences, I am now going to look at key ways in which nationality was invoked in English-language discussions about the programme.

Reading Representations of Nationality

On the English-language film and TV forum, *Lilyhammer* was repeatedly constructed as a "fish out of water" or "culture shock" story that represented a clash between two value systems. However, this did not replicate the Norwegian debate around Americanisation. Johnny's value system was consistently associated with *fictional* gangsters from U.S. film and TV, rather than with U.S. national culture. This pattern suggests the circulation of a shared interpretive repertoire, developed through audience engagement with gangster screen fiction. In contrast, readings of other characters and the local community were more varied. Most readings saw *Lilyhammer* as satirizing, critiquing or making fun of certain aspects of Norwegian culture, but they identified different targets for this critique and different messages. This diversity indicates the slipperiness that is often associated with a satirical mode (Griffin 1994). Although satirical texts might use a variety of techniques to anchor meaning and clarify their arguments, their ambiguity may be amplified in transnational viewing contexts. As Gray observes in his study of audience responses to *The Simpsons*, representations can have different sets of meanings in national and transnational contexts:

> American viewers may well detect the cultural signs in programs such as *The Simpsons*, *King of the Hill*, or *The Jerry Springer Show* that these characters and the lives being toyed with represent small town, "middle America"; but, outside of the nation, such a

distinction might be lost on or irrelevant to international viewers without the cultural codes to distinguish between types of Americans, who will look at a cheap joke on *Springer* directed at "redneck trailer trash" as a joke on Americans in general. (2007: 144)

So, transnational *Lilyhammer* viewers might miss some of the show's cultural nuances, and some contributors expressed their uncertainty about how they should interpret the naivety of local characters:

> I can't see these people being this dim witted and so slow on the uptake.

Some transnational viewers also inscribed the show with a range of values that they had developed within their own affective-discursive environments. For example, this contributor argued that *Lilyhammer* uses Johnny to promote a libertarian ideology:

> The show presents an interesting contrast. On the one hand there is a nation of well-behaved drones living under the yoke of an administrative state. Sure it appears to be pleasant aesthetically speaking but is this the natural state of the human race? Along comes a flawed individual who comes from a place that is relatively freer. The locals are drawn to him because he lives his life on his own terms.

This reading invested *Lilyhammer* with an anti-government message that is at odds with the public service broadcasting ideology of the NRK but echoes discourses circulating in U.S. political debates. Problematically, it privileges violent crime as an example of agency, which rather ignores the ways in which Johnny's actions often limit the agency of other characters.

Most notably, however, nationality was invested with salience in discussions around *Lilyhammer*'s representations of immigration, which are initially structured around Johnny's encounters with official "integration" initiatives. Several contributors offered racist and xenophobic readings that saw the show as a critique of Norway's perceived efforts to "integrate" immigrants and refugees. The interpretations othered characters who were represented as immigrants, inscribing ethnic minority groups as rude, indecent, exploitative, threatening, and so on. The posts often conflated othered characters with real immigrants and refugees, so that contributors presented their own racist readings of *Lilyhammer* as evidence that Norway, as a nation, was being exploited. This argument employed a discourse of "host and guest relations":

> [D]iscrimination and racism is naturalized and reduced to something that happens to the host as he or she is provoked or abused by guests who refuse to act according to the etiquette set for guests.

The annoying, visible cultural difference of the guests take a heavy toll on the host's tolerance, and eventually leads to outbursts against the guests as a culturally and, in some cases, racially distinct group.
(Hervik 2004: 263)

As Ahmed (2004) argues, such narratives create "a subject that is endangered by imagined others whose proximity threatens not only to take something away from the subject (jobs, security, wealth), but to take the place of the subject". Here, the white "host" is also the "victim", and the "nation" is "under threat" (43). Forum contributors created such narratives of hate by drawing on racist and xenophobic discourses circulating within and across national contexts. They sometimes referred to immigration debates from Britain or the U.S. to position themselves alongside white Norwegians within an imagined community of "Western nations" that needed to protect their "soft underbelly of tolerance" from others "who would rip our guts out to take what we have spent generations to build". Drawing on Ahmed (2004), I see this use of imagery as turning "whiteness into a familial tie" and shaping "Western nations" as a singular body, with skin that is "soft, weak, porous" and "vulnerable to abuse" (2).

In contrast, other forum contributors challenged such racist readings, maintaining that *Lilyhammer* actually intended "to highlight the ignorance of the Norwegians" and offered "caricatures of norwegian stereotype predjudice". These diverging readings illustrate the risk associated with satire. As Kuipers (2006) argues, our enjoyment of satire will often depend on whether we agree with its perceived intent, and my findings demonstrate that *Lilyhammer* viewers were able to invest the show with quite distinct intentions. This indicates a textual openness that may have been partly facilitated by shifts between its different comedic, dramatic and action modalities. The resulting ambiguity is addressed in Sundet's (2016) production study, which explores an underlying debate over whether the show should be "a television 'dramedy' about the welfare state and its stereotypes, aimed at a Norwegian public service audience, or an American action drama about a mafia boss in hiding, aimed at Netflix's pay-TV audience" (20). However, the international distribution of the programme may also have opened the text up for a wider set of readings. First, textual cues that anchor meaning in a Norwegian viewing context may not be recognised by transnational audiences, and, second, their readings will draw on experiences and interpretive repertoires developed in a range of different cultural contexts. I am now turning my attention to the ways in which national contexts became important for *how* audiences watched the show. This was a key theme on the official *Lilyhammer* Facebook page.

The Imagined, International *Lilyhammer* Fan Community

Fan contributions to the *Lilyhammer* Facebook page were dominated by cycles of excitement, desire and frustration. On the 12th of December 2013, the administrators posted a timeline image that featured a neon pink flamingo (the logo for Johnny's bar) and the text "1 DAY TO GO." against the dark background of a starry night. The bottom of the image was dominated by Netflix branding against white snow, labelling *Lilyhammer* "A NETFLIX ORIGINAL SERIES" that was "ONLY ON Netflix" and promising "ALL NEW EPISODES DECEMBER 13". The caption read: "Your name's on the list. See you there tomorrow for #Lilyhammer Season 2". Page followers responded with excitement:

Is it tomorrow yet?

Yipeeeeeee! ;-}} ^^~

Perfect! We're going to be snowed in this weekend, so we can have a Lilyhammer binge party!

As the third response indicates, however, the simultaneous publishing of all eight episodes facilitated binge-watching. Mittell (2015) notes that watching several episodes in a row can provide "a more immersive and attentive viewing experience" (39), whereas "simultaneous viewership" (40) enables fans to use the time between episodes to get together to discuss, critique and share their audience pleasures. This distinction was evident in my study. Discussions on the Norwegian-language forum were largely structured by the weekly broadcast of each episode on NRK1, and contributors would evaluate the latest instalment and share their affective responses. In contrast, there were few exchanges about specific episodes on the Facebook page, where users were not watching the show at the same time or at the same pace. Some contributors offered brief evaluations after completing a series, but such comments rarely received replies from other users, and there was little evidence of sustained site engagement. This can be seen to illustrate Bury's (2016) argument that Facebook facilitates "a number of fannish pleasures" but does not "enable community formation" (2). Although the *Lilyhammer* page enables fans to connect "with people with specific fannish interests" (18), its hierarchical structure positions fans as consumers rather than as members of a participatory community. With 155,322 registered users, the site is so big that it is difficult for users to develop relationships, while the structure prevents them from developing and congregating in their own corners of the space. It might be more useful, then, to think of the Facebook page as a space for the performance of *Lilyhammer* fandom, rather than as the home of a fan community.

The periods of audience excitement were short-lived on Facebook. Outside of the brief time periods surrounding the publishing of new series on Netflix, the page was dominated by desire and frustration:

> watched 8 episodes is that the whole season? Want more!

> Well that's that! What I've waited for about a year is over in the matter of days. There had better be a Season 4 since Sigrid did leave a little sumpin' for Johnny (Frankie) to clean up!

These posts illustrate that the 8-episode *Lilyhammer* seasons were unusually short, by U.S. standards, and this compounded the experience of an imbalance between waiting time and viewing time. Some users articulated a resulting tension between a desire for the immersive viewing experienced that can be achieved by watching "an excessive amount of episodes" (Jenner 2015: 11), and a desire to extend the viewing pleasure by delaying the completion of the series:

> Pace yourself, resist temptation to watch 8 straight hours. RIGHT!

For many contributors, then, the period characterised by excitement was soon replaced by feelings of desire and frustration as they, once again, waited for new episodes.

However, the dominant cycles of excitement, desire and frustration were specifically structured by the publication of new episodes on Netflix *in the U.S.* Viewers in other territories often accessed the show at different points in time. I have already noted the sometimes smug posts from Norwegians who watched *Lilyhammer* on NRK1 before it was published on Netflix. In contrast, other users sometimes expressed a sense of being left behind:

> I love Frankie the fixer to!, but can't see it in New Zealand. Please please, get Netflix to make it available here.

> We haven't even seen season 2 in France

> Why isn't there a streaming on Netflix in Sweden?? #WTF

These discrepancies point to a key tension in the site's promotion of *Lilyhammer* as a Netflix show. By focusing their promotional strategy on U.S. audiences, the administrators glossed over national differences in the Netflix publishing pattern. And the strict hierarchy that positioned administrators over users prevented viewers in other territories from starting their own discussion threads on the page. Instead, their requests, protests and other affective-discursive responses remained dispersed across the comment threads for official posts. This marginalised their viewing experiences, reinforcing a centre/margin structure despite the international expansion of the Netflix brand.

The nation-based diversity of the page user group was nonetheless often valorised in posts. On the 21ˢᵗ of November 2014, the administrators wrote:

> Skål to Season 3, now on Netflix! #DrinkWithJohnny http://nflx.it/
> LilyhammerUS

The text was accompanied by an image instructing users how they could participate in the fan game. They were encouraged to "POUR YOURSELF A BEVERAGE", "SNAP A PHOTO OF YOURSELF WATCHING SEASON 3 WITH THE BEVERAGE" and "SHARE IT IN THE COMMENTS BELOW #DRINKWITHJOHNNY". The post received 1.2k "likes", 129 shares and 132 comments. Some of these comments followed the instructions, and administrators replied to such posts with "Skål!" and promises of fan rewards, which indicate the value of such fan labour for shows and for brands like Netflix.

> Attagirl! Nice work on your #DrinkWithJohnny photo. Send a direct message to the Lilyhammer Facebook page for a special Lilyhammer surprise.

Some participants positioned themselves within an imagined, international *Lilyhammer* fan community by identifying their location:

> Enjoying the new season in the UK !
>
> Just a little Fireball with Johnny! Cheers from North Dakota!

This anchoring of fan identities in specific national, regional and local spaces drew attention to television viewing and fandom as situated, lived experience. At the same time, it valorised the mosaic of such experiences within the imagined fan community. The narrative of togetherness was disrupted, however, by users who highlighted that their marginality once again prevented them from joining in:

> I would skål if season 3 were available in Finland.

Conclusion

This chapter continued my investigation of the relationship between comedy and cultural identities by shifting attention from gender to nationality. I chose *Lilyhammer* as my case study because the increasing involvement of Netflix problematises the programme's definition as a Norwegian comedy and, by extension, the homogenising discourse of "national comedy". It enabled me to examine some of the complexities and shifts in how the show's domestic and transnational audiences invoked nationality and inscribed it with affects. I traced this engagement across a Norwegian-language discussion forum, an English-language forum focused on film and television and the official *Lilyhammer* Facebook page. This multi-sited approach facilitated a comparison of national and transnational responses to the serial, but it also let me examine how the specific characteristics of each space facilitated different kinds of audience responses and interaction.

I found that some Norwegian viewers were initially concerned about how the show, as a rare TV export, would represent Norwegian comedy and Norwegian television to U.S. audiences. This affective response articulated a sense of cultural belonging by invoking the possibility that the show's transnational comic failure would implicate Norwegians in "national shame" (Ahmed 2004: 101). In contrast, the *Lilyhammer* Facebook page later offered Norwegian users a "safe" space to claim ownership of the show. Some here expressed a sense of inherent privilege within international *Lilyhammer* fandom, produced by their nation-based cultural capital.

Across the responses from transnational viewers, nationality was invoked in two key ways. On the forum, participants evaluated and discussed different aspects of *Lilyhammer*, and this included its representations of nationality. My analysis identified conflicting readings, which I connected to the slipperiness of satire and the shifting comedic/action/gangster modalities of this particular text. The resulting textual openness enabled transnational viewers to inscribe the show with a range of national affects and values. For example, some contributors used *Lilyhammer* to claim a sense of cultural belonging within an imagined *white* community that crossed national borders. The Facebook page did not encourage discussion of the text, but invited users to identify as *Lilyhammer* fans. Here, transnational viewers positioned themselves within an imagined, international *Lilyhammer* fan community while simultaneously constructing their fandom as lived experience situated in specific national, regional and local contexts. Importantly, they highlighted that these geographical contexts determined their access to the show, demonstrating that the U.S.-centric focus of the Facebook page worked to marginalise users based in many other locations.

The next chapter continues my exploration of cultural identities in audience engagement with comedy by shifting attention onto "race". Through my analysis of YouTube responses to the British web comedy *Brothers with No Game*, I want to examine the significance of blackness for its audiences, but its genre will also be an important part of that discussion.

Note

1 More recently, however, NRK has had success with online teen drama *Skam* (since 2015), which has also received attention from transnational fans and media.

5 Black Web Comedy

Brothers with No Game on YouTube

This chapter bridges my explorations of the significance of cultural identities (chapters 3 and 4) and genre (chapters 6 and 7) in comedy. Focusing on the British web comedy *Brothers with No Game*,[1] I use this case study to examine some of the opportunities and challenges this form poses for producers and audiences. In particular, I here want to situate *Brothers with No Game* within academic debates around the marginalisation of blackness on British television and consider some of the affective-discursive ways in which YouTube users positioned this text as a black show through their comments. My analysis explores audience discussions around *Brothers with No Game*'s representations of black masculinities and femininities, as well as their articulations of a pleasurable sense of cultural belonging within an international, black diasporic audience. It reflects on the extent to which web comedy and its online communities *can* provide spaces for marginalised voices to challenge cultural hierarchies and processes of othering. It also considers what role humour might play in such practice.

I am, as Ross (1996) advises, "cautious" about examining audience responses to a text that "can only ever have second-hand resonances" for me as a white, Norwegian-born immigrant living in Britain. However, I also note her warning against "dismissing the critical gaze simply because the object and the subject do not share the same ethnicity" (163), as well as the call for greater attention to people of colour in fan studies (e.g. Wanzo 2015 and Warner 2015). I therefore want to acknowledge that my interpretations of the YouTube responses to *Brothers with No Game* are necessarily grounded in my own lived experience, though I have attempted to confront and destabilise my white perspective by engaging with extant literature on black British cultures (e.g. Carby 1982/2005, Gilroy 1993, Hall 1990, Malik 2002, Mercer 1994) and black audiences (e.g. hooks 1992, Coleman 1998).

Introducing *Brothers with No Game*

Brothers with No Game started out in 2010 as a comedic blog created by Masibu Manima, Leon Mayne, Henry Oladele and Paul Samuel. The blog was developed into a comedic web series, and the first episode was released on YouTube in 2012. To distinguish web series from TV series, I understand the former as being produced specifically for web distribution, rather than TV series that are simultaneously or subsequently also made available online. Kuhn (2014) notes that web series episodes tend to be between 3 and 10 minutes long and that the shows tend to emphasise seriality by extending storylines across multiple short episodes. At the time of writing, *Brothers with No Game* consisted of two series, while their website promises that "Season 3 is coming soon". Set in London, it focuses on the work, friendships and romantic relationships of the four friends Dorian, Junior, Marcus and Theo. The *Brothers with No Game* YouTube channel has received 1,371,011 views and has 20,431 subscribers. The show was also broadcast (in a somewhat different form) by local TV station London Live in 2014 and made available with French subtitles by video on demand platform Afrostream in 2015.

YouTube was launched in 2005 as a video sharing website that "provided a very simple, integrated interface within which users could upload, publish, and view streaming videos without high levels of technical knowledge, and within the technological constraints of standard browser software and relatively modest bandwith" (Burgess and Green 2009: 1). However, Kim (2012) notes that, after YouTube was bought by Google in 2006, the site added tools that facilitated the identification of materials that infringed copyright, enabling copyright holders to block or monetise such video sharing. Second, it introduced advertisements, sharing "the revenue with the copyright holders of the videos" (56), and, third, media companies started using YouTube to promote their own content. So, although amateur YouTube users continue to view and upload videos, Kim argues that the site has shifted its prime emphasis away from UGC content onto "professionally generated content". As a space, then, YouTube is characterised by a tension between DIY culture and a drive towards monetisation. Exploring this environment through a case study of U.S., YouTubers Higa and Wu, Guo and Lee (2013) found that these amateur producers were able to challenge dominant discourses of Asian/ Asian Americans and build a community based around the platform. However, the researchers also maintain that the counter-hegemonic potential of this practice was constrained by "YouTube's institutional agency and its entertainment principle of 'LOL or Leave'", which privileged the provision of entertainment, rather than education by connecting revenue to view counts (404).

This conclusion can be contrasted with Bradley's (2015) analysis of Issa Rae's web series *The Mis-adventures of Awkward Black Girl* (2011–2013), which was also distributed on YouTube. Bradley focuses on critical comedy, exploring how Rae uses humour to construct "a sense of black agency by introducing the possibility of black women as human beings". She argues that the series challenges discursive othering "by displaying 'normal' everyday experiences" and "teasing out the complexities of contemporary black women" (149). This concern about representations is also echoed in interviews with the writers and cast of *Brothers with No Game*. In *The Guardian* (Adewunmi 2012), Mayne argued that "There's a narrow representation of what it means to be black; there need to be different stories told", while actor David Avery told *The Voice* that his work on *Brothers with No Game* differed to his other roles:

> In the mainstream work that I do, 80 per cent of it tends to be that I'm wanted by police or I'm up to no good, but this was the complete opposite, but it was still representing urban males from London … We're actually a bit silly, we're a bit vulnerable and that kind of role is rare and refreshing.
>
> (Avery quoted in Grant 2013)

This chapter aims to engage with the debate around the significance of web series as a space for marginalised voices by shifting attention onto its audience. How do the viewers position it in relation to other screen texts? How do they inscribe it with meanings and pleasures? And how do they articulate identities as viewers? My sample includes the comment threads for all 15 *Brothers with No Game* episodes. YouTube does not include a facility for contacting users, and so I have not been able to secure consent for quoting individual contributors. I will therefore only quote users who were operating with a pseudonym that concealed their offline identity, although I will also refrain from sharing such pseudonyms here.

Positioning *Brothers with No Game* as Amateur Media

The YouTube comments posted in response to individual *Brothers with No Game* episodes repeatedly constructed the show as amateur media. They addressed its creators and cast directly, offering praise, critique and advice:

> Good stuff, improve the sound though, every time i have to turn volume up high to hear.

> Well shot and thought about show people. I like how use converted your blog into a show. Fresh idea! I would say though, the one thing it's missing is soundtrack during the dialogue. Very important. Just some constructive criticism. Keep it coming though. Nice one

These evaluations indicated that *Brothers with No Game* failed to meet the standard viewers associated with professionally produced screen fiction. However, the contributors also suggested that the producers should *aspire* to that standard, and they constructed themselves as participants in this development by identifying shortcomings that should be resolved and praising perceived improvements. Occasional "official" responses worked to legitimate the comment threads as a space for user/producer interaction, but these responses did not invite viewers to participate in the creation of *Brothers with No Game* other than as financial donors:

> BrothersWithNoGame:
>
> Thank you for the support and donations so far.
>
> Every little really does help. £2 from each subscriber would allow us to bring you season 2. It was a tremendous effort from the team to bring you a quality product on a limited budget. A bigger budget is required to ensure that we do not have further hiccups experienced in Season 1, such as: delayed launches, sound and technical difficulties etc.
>
> Hope you can appreciate the entire teams efforts with a small donation.
>
> Thanks in advance.
>
> Brothers With No Game

This message responded to audience concerns about the production values of the first series by acknowledging specific "hiccups" that YouTube contributors had identified and by drawing attention to a challenging production process that was labour intensive and had a "limited" budget. The message then invested "subscribers" with the power to reduce these obstacles by donating to the *Brothers with No Game* crowdfunding campaign. Importantly, subscribers were here addressed as consumers of a commodity, rather than as fans of a cultural text. This discursive strategy maintained a conventional producer/consumer hierarchy and contained audience "contributions to offerings of capital" (Scott 2015: 174).

The *Brothers with No Game* campaign profile on crowdfunding platform Indigogo made more use of fan discourse. For example, the reward or "perk" promised to backers who made a £50 contribution depended on whether they identified as "Team Vanessa" or "Team Remy", which referred to Junior's two love interests in the show. These options acknowledged that fans will have different affective investments in the show and legitimated the fan practice of "shipping". The opportunity to move from fan-consumer to fan-participant was nonetheless only available to those who made £500 donations, who could: "Contribute to the scripting process for the second half of season 2. Credited as Associate Producer" (Indiegogo). Nobody claimed this prize, and the average donor contribution was under £17. So, although *Brothers with No Game* can be considered an example of "amateur and independent media" (Christian 2011: 1.5) that has taken advantage of online spaces to grow an audience and fund the project, its model for user participation remains close to that associated with television. This practice may reflect a wider trend for web shows:

> What the history of web entertainments shows is that it has never deviated from legacy media, including television, even at its most anarchic and open. Instead television has been an object of desire and abjection for those seeking an edge in online markets.
>
> (Christian 2012: 352)

The relationship between web comedy and television comedy is key to my explorations in this chapter. The next part of my analysis will approach this distinction by looking at how YouTube contributors engaged with ideas of marginalised voices, absences and representation.

Positioning *Brothers with No Game* as a Black Show

Writing about the Channel 4 sitcom *Desmond's* (1989–1994), Osborne (2016) introduces it as "the first situation comedy series in Britain to be created and scripted by a black writer of African Caribbean descent" (167). Reflecting on the show's legacy, her study then concludes: "The achievements of programming *Desmond's* did not accomplish any lasting impact in reconfiguring the broader field of television" (179). Black voices remain marginalised on British TV and on U.S. network television, but Acham (2012) argues that they are "flourishing" in online spaces (65). This TV/web distinction was echoed in the YouTube user responses to *Brothers with No Game*.

A number of users suggested they were underserved as TV audiences, some expressed dismay that *Brothers with No Game* was not shown on TV, and some suggested that their consumption of screen fiction was shifting from TV programming to web shows:

> These web series have come so far these days, that i go to youtube before reaching for my cable remote. Other than suits, scandal and white collar nothing else is worth watching on TV.

Fan comments often situated *Brothers with No Game* within a valorised body of web series centred around black characters, including *The Mis-adventures of Awkward Black Girl*, *The Unwritten Rules* (since 2012) and *Venus vs Mars* (2012), and one contributor explicitly argued that web series enabled black producers to create work on their own terms.

I read this debate as revolving around two key issues. The first was the perceived absence of "quality" British and U.S. TV shows that were made by black producers and had black characters in lead roles.

The second issue was the notion that black voices are constrained within the white structures of television. Web series here emerged as a space where black producers could operate with a sense of agency and create new narratives grounded in their own lived experience. This perceived potential was often highlighted through comparisons between *Brothers with No Game* and TV representations of blackness:

> Cause tv will only give people like tyler perry offers that set blacks back another 100 years smh.......[2]

This comment illustrated the assumption that black cultural producers speak for "a supposedly homogeneous and monolithic community", a notion that inscribes them with social responsibilities that bind them "ever more closely to the burden of being 'representative'" (Mercer 1994: 248). Here, black U.S. actor and TV producer Tyler Perry was constructed simultaneously as a black producer that has been favoured by mainstream (white) U.S. television and as capable of, and responsible for, "setting back" black Americans. Stressing the significance of Perry, Smith-Shomade (2012) argues that he "has transformed a theatrical cottage industry for Black audiences into a multimedia empire" (8). The contributor's rejection of Tyler expressed frustration with the ways in which blackness has been represented on U.S. television, and it echoed concerns voiced by viewers who took part in Coleman's (1998) study on black U.S. audiences. Her research participants identified recurring representations of black Americans "as abnormal and dysfunctional", with "negative stereotypes" that mock "Black culture and communities" and require "African American performers to, so frequently and irresponsibly, play the buffoon" (164).

Across the YouTube threads, *Brothers with No Game* was often constructed as a welcome relief from stereotypical representations of blackness. In particular, the show was positioned in opposition to film and television texts that situate young black people within crime cultures:

> A black drama that doesn't have anything to do with guns or gangs or any of that stereotypical stuff, that's why I love this show! Showing young, attractive and professional black people, keep it up. :)

These comments engaged with the discourse of social responsibility by valorising what they constructed as "positive" representations. This particular user focused on *Brothers with No Game*'s representations of young black people who are "attractive and professional", which can be seen to praise representations of conformity to neoliberal cultural norms. However, within the dual context of marginalisation and screen stereotypes that mark blackness as abject, narratives of cultural conformity or "normalcy" offer disruption and critique:

Web series provide a space for Black people to see everyday stories about life's complications or joys or culturally specific vignettes. Due to their wide range of characters, these narratives show us the diversity of Black life in terms of class, gender, and sexuality— opportunities that white audiences get every day on television. While Black people are certainly not absent on network television, consistent Black narratives are.

(Acham 2012: 72–3)

Moreover, as Pelle (2010) observes in her analysis of work by Asian American comedian Margaret Cho, "there is always pleasure to be had in intelligibility, in not having to fight and struggle against those who hate us for who we are" (32). We might therefore situate the reception of *Brothers with No Game* within an affective economy that circulates affects of frustration and anger at marginalisation, absences and stereotyping, as well as desire for visibility, recognition and cultural belonging. These affects were articulated further in debates around *Brothers with No Game*'s representations of black men and women.

Black Masculinities and Femininities

On YouTube, *Brothers with No Game* is presented as a "web series in which four guys come to terms with quarter-life crisis in the form of dating, relationships, work and self-improvement", which positions the show as an entertaining exploration of contemporary black masculinity. The hyperbole of the term "quarter-life crisis" suggests both comedy and drama, and YouTube responses indicated that the show's modality shifts worked to offer a range of viewing pleasures. Crucially, for a web comedy, commenters found *Brothers with No Game* funny, often expressing amusement through affective Internet jargon such as "lol" and "lmao". In particular, they singled out moments of observational comedy that provided a sense of recognition. These are comments from two different contributors:

OMG, these guys are classic British-Nigerian lads. Had me dying laughing all the way through.

"I expect water to be free. £7 for water? That's like three happy meals and a lotto ticket."

Brothers with No Game offered black viewers a feeling of cultural belonging in a range of different ways. For example, viewers could engage with representations of black characters in familiar, everyday situations. They could laugh "at inside jokes or vernacular that is particular to various Black audiences" (Acham 2012: 67), and they could read and contribute to discussions between black audience members.

Brothers with No Game most frequently invited viewers to laugh at and with the four central male characters, known collectively as "the brothers". Viewers inscribed them with comedic pleasures that were connected to performances, witty lines and their comic failures in heterosexual romance. These failures are foregrounded by the title *Brothers with No Game*, and they work both to undermine the stereotype of hyper-sexualised black masculinity and to set up the project of self-improvement promised in the YouTube show description. For example, these are two comments in response to episode 4 of the first series, where the unemployed Junior has a failed first date with Remy in an expensive restaurant (rather than the more affordable chain restaurant Nando's, which he had suggested), is unable to fulfil her expectation that he should pay for the meal and ends the episode by making a phone call to apply for unemployment benefit support:

> Wow! That was a funny episode but serious too. Almost too real. It was cool to see his boys had his back while encouraging him to file for unemployment. Can't wait to see the next episode!

> This episode just made me love this show even more. There is comedy, romance, professionalism, and then real issues are addressed. All of the guys have emotions and feelings based on real issues. I am so glad to be watching stories of men that are not cardboard cut-outs.

These responses valorised the modality shifts that allowed the restaurant scene to create comic incongruities between Remy's and Junior's perspectives, while also inviting viewers to sympathise with Junior's plight. However, other contributors adopted a position of comic superiority, reading his failures as laughable:

> Nandos! ive been taken to Nandos on a 1st date ...needless to say it was the last date lol

These conflicting readings were part of a wider debate around audience perceptions of what constituted "successful" black masculinities. As Worsley (2010) observes, this "is not a static concept, but reflects the ever-shifting needs and political goals of black communities" (107). Here, a particularly contested issue was the significance of wealth or the financial ability to "treat" women, which forms part of "a masculine identity rooted in the patriarchal ideal" (hooks 1992: 88). Some contributors saw representations of black unemployment or poverty as reinforcing stereotypes, some dismissed the relevance of wealth to masculinity, and some called attention to racist social structures:

> Well more us brothers would have our stuff together if not for systemic racism and oppression. We have the highest rates of unemployment for a reason.

Brothers with No Game, within its YouTube context, functioned as a site for affective-discursive struggles over the meanings of black masculinity. It demonstrated that the show can "work dually at creating Black community while providing a space for Black expression" (Acham 2012: 67), including debates around social problems:

> Why is everyone cussing Jr.? He's down on his luck and trying to get back on his feet. A very true representation of many young adults today: recession, loss of job, unemployment etc.

Like a number of the other comments I have quoted here, this contribution constructed representations in *Brothers with No Game* as "true" or close to reality. Despite the show's use of observational comedy, then, it was nonetheless often seen to adopt a strong modality through its use of complex characters who faced recognisable challenges. For some viewers, this perception of verisimilitude may have ruptured the "comic insulation" (Palmer 1987: 45) provided by the show's comedic modality and reinforced the inscription of the *Brothers with No Game* team as socially responsible for representing black communities in specific ways (Mercer 1994). The heterogeneity of the audience community meant that such preferences remained contested.

Although *Brothers with No Game* narratives are primarily centred on its male characters, YouTube contributors also drew attention to its representations of black women. These discussions echoed concerns about the importance of representing diversity in black communities, with some viewers praising its inclusion of diverse black femininities and others expressing dismay at reproductions of stereotypes. These are comments from two different users:

> One thing I like about these web series is the fact that the women aren't so cookie cutter. Some are natural some are relaxed. Some are light, some are dark or in between. Some are bohemians, some are glamazons. There's so much more variety when it comes to female beauty.

> I love the fact you have beautiful dark black women on your show...

Both of these posts rejected white supremacist notions of ideal femininity by inscribing "natural" black hair and "dark" skin with beauty. The first comment identified the prevalence of monolithic representations of black women and situated *Brothers with No Game* within a wider body of "black-themed" web series (Acham 2012: 63) that provide greater diversity. Such nuance offers black female audiences more opportunities for affective experiences of recognition and cultural belonging.

The posts both focused on the appearances of female characters, and I found that this emphasis was reproduced in other comments that praised the show's representations of women. The pattern might reflect the privileging of male character development in *Brothers with No Game*, where we are offered far less insight into the motivations and experiences of female characters. However, it might also indicate the salience viewers attached to discourses of black feminine beauty and style. Warner (2015) notes that "hair culture is a major part of the Black community and conversations about natural versus relaxed hair textures, hairstyles, weaves and wigs are commonplace" (44), while Mercer (1994) argues that "patterns of style" can be seen "as creative responses to the experience of oppression and dispossession" (100):

> With its organizing principles of biological determinism, racism first politicized our hair by burdening it with a range of negative social and psychological meanings. Devalorized as a "problem", each of the many stylizing practices brought to bear on this element of ethnic differentiation articulate ever so many "solutions". Through aesthetic stylization each black hairstyle seeks to revalorize the ethnic signifier, and the political significance of each rearticulation of value and meaning depends on the historical conditions under which each style emerges.
>
> (Mercer 1994: 121)

However, although *Brothers with No Game* was praised for diverse representations of black feminine beauty and style, it was also sometimes criticised for stereotyping black women in other ways. In particular, such critique targeted the episode portraying Junior and Remy's date. These are comments from two different contributors:

> This is a really good series. [...] Can we see a friendly, laid back, kind and gentle black woman who is willing to pay half or all of the bill? Let's not reinforce tired stereotypes.

> LOL Funny stuff. Dude could sing. Why the sista gotta always be portrayed as the gold digger and the Caucasian women is sweet and understanding?

These critiques could be seen to reference the "Sapphire" stereotype, which Biswas and Choudhury (2016) describe as "a depiction of black women as evil, bitchy, stubborn, hateful, demonic and treacherous" (674). They position this figure within a set of "stereotypical and derogatory images of black women which tend to their commodification and degeneration" (673), and the YouTube commenters often articulated a sense of exasperation through their critiques. In her account of black female cinemagoers, hook (1992) describes a feeling of pain for audiences who "looked too deep" at the screen (121), and argues for the importance of developing "an oppositional gaze" that constructs "a critical space" (122) for deconstruction and disruption. I read the comments above as suggesting compound affective responses that simultaneously pulled the viewers closer to the text and pushed them away from it. However, although affective responses to stereotyping might sometimes have disrupted the potential for *Brothers with No Game* to offer these black female viewers a sense of cultural belonging, the YouTube comment threads still facilitated their *critical participation* in the audience community that developed over the course of the two series.

Although Thelwall *et al.* (2012) suggest that YouTube comments are likely to be read only infrequently, *Brothers with No Game* comments often engaged with previous posts. This produced "a discourse that voice matters" (Carpentier 2014: 1014) and worked to valorise YouTube as a space to connect with other black audience members. The series creators have further reinforced the notion of community by adding other web series to their YouTube channel (and to their own website) and rebranding themselves as "BWNG TV, a platform for independent creatives to to [sic] produce creative and unique narratives. Join the movement!" This can be seen as a bid for cultural distinction, positioning the platform as an alternative cultural space that enables "creatives" to work outside the structures of the TV industries and offers audiences narratives that are not available elsewhere. This space continued to centre black voices and narratives, for example through Monique Needham's comedy series *HouseMates* (2014–15), which focuses on a group of female friends, and the BWNG team's own *A Day in the Life of Daddy* (2014–15), which is described as a "Drama series about a father reconnecting with his daughter after the emergence of another man in her mum's life".

Romance and Desire

Alongside expressions of amusement and discussions of representation, participants also used the comment threads to articulate lust for the men and women on their screens. What Collie (2017) terms "the lens of desire" (223) emerged as a key part of audience engagement with *Brothers with No Game* performers and characters, who were "physically close" while remaining "tantalisingly absent" (Wheatley 2016: 206):

And Theo, honey, dont let me see you on the streets; I will attack! yum yum yum!! *he so fione* lol

How the FUUUCK!!!! did you get all that beautiful chicks in the same room!!! OOOOMMMMGGG!!!....I still haven't finished watching this because i just paused it on the one of the chicks... the BUFFEST DARK SKIN alive!!!...I want to to do that girl!!!...(A bit offensive) BUT SERIOUSLY!...I WANT TO DO THAT GIRL!!!!!

These comments foregrounded heterosexual desire and arousal, employing discursive devices such as multiple exclamation marks, block capitals and phonetic transcription to emphasise the intensity of affective responses (see chapter 7 for a further discussion of such rhetorical choices). However, this was a desire for unavailable bodies, which echoes Theo, Marcus, Junior and Dorian's lack of "game" and the show's portrayal of frustrated attraction and desire. Negotiating this absence, the first contributor conjured up a fantasy of meeting Theo "on the streets", while the second viewer paused the episode to concentrate fully on what appears to be a minor character or extra, investing her with erotic spectacle.

Both contributors articulated their wishes quite explicitly, making the male and female bodies "occupy the place of erotic object" (Collie 2017: 233) and positioning themselves in the active role of the subject who would "attack", consume or "do". These comments can be seen to transgress a private/public boundary, but they negotiated this transgression in different ways. The first comment addressed the fictional character of "Theo", rather than the performer, containing the statement within the realm of fantasy. It also ended with "lol", which worked as a discursive mechanism that framed the promise to "attack" as humorous hyperbole. The second contributor briefly but explicitly inscribed his own expression of desire with transgression by inserting "(A bit offensive)". It remains unclear which cultural norms he saw himself transgressing; it could perhaps be the public and explicit expression of desire or the objectifying of a female performer. In any case, he swiftly disregarded the imagined offence by reasserting and emphasising his sexual desire, privileging its expression over the maintenance of cultural norms. The YouTube comment threads, then, seem to offer a safe public space for participants to share articulations of sexual desire, although they sometimes still invoked and negotiated conventions that attempt to regulate such feelings. This sense of relative safety may be facilitated in part by the anonymity provided by usernames and, for female contributors, "shifts in the discourses of female sexual and social identities away from expectations of passivity and submissiveness and towards a wider social acceptance of expressions of women's sexuality and sexual desire" (Toffoletti and Mewett 2012: 103).

The frequent foregrounding of attraction and desire in audience responses to *Brothers with No Game* may also reflect a sense of intimacy facilitated by the small screen viewing experience (Wheatley 2016) and the aesthetic required for such screens. Creeber (2011) suggests that the web series style is characterised by "an emphasis on the close-up, direct address and intimate revelation" (602), which promotes familiarity. Within *Brothers with No Game*, these devices are primarily used to enable Theo, Dorian, Junior and Marcus to share their perspectives and feelings with the audience, both for comedic effect and to invite viewers to invest emotionally in characters and storylines. My analysis of the

YouTube comments suggested that this investment was concentrated in portrayals of heterosexual romance.

Fans articulated their affective responses to representations of romance through speculations about future developments, shipping of specific pairings and longer posts offering in-depth analysis and discussion. These are two examples:

> i hope junior doesn't back track with vanessa! seems like him and remy could have something great :)

> It's not like I thought it was between Junior & Vanessa @ alll! He should go with her. His mom is in Ghana, he has no job/prospects & things were just starting w/Remy. He should've kept his word & went w/her in the 1st place!! I hope Dorian still has a chance w/Lisa, Theo falls deeper in love & Marcus leaves that girl alone & gets w/a woman! Great finale y'all.

As these posts suggested, Remy's character was often read as more complex and sympathetic after her initial introduction, and the subsequent return of Junior's ex-girlfriend Vanessa produced two different shipping factions on the comment threads. The second contributor quoted above engaged with a dramatic modality that employed romantic conflict and revelations about characters' pasts. The comedic elements of *Brothers with No Game* here became invisible, which reflected a wider pattern in responses to the series one final:

> How can Vanessa give Jay [Junior] an ultimatum like that fucking hell, this series is actually quality

This contributor articulated a sense of surprise, both at Vanessa's perceived behaviour and at her own investment in the show. The evaluation indicated that "quality" was facilitated by a perceived shift from a comedic modality to a dramatic modality. This discourse of quality reproduced a cultural hierarchy of screen genres and privileged emotional investment over laughter. (I discuss this hierarchy further in chapter 7, where I focus on responses to romantic comedy.)

The pattern provides an interesting contrast to Williams's (2011a) study of shipping in *The West Wing* fandom (NBC 2000–2006). She found that some fans employed a "masculinised" discourse to devalue "feminised" shipping practices, which were seen to contaminate "the 'purity' of the drama genre" by focusing on narrative elements associated with soap opera (271). Although comedy culture privileges masculinised discourse, there were no objections to shipping or to discussions of romance on the comment threads. Perhaps this reflected the low cultural status of comedy and an association between emotional investment and the more culturally valued drama genre. Or perhaps the salience of romance was reinforced because these audience discussions overlapped with debates around gendered protocols for dating, romance and sexual relationships. Drawing on their readings of available information, participants evaluated characters' behaviour across different situations and made normative judgements about what they should do next. This worked to ground discussions of romance within wider debates around heterosexual black femininities and masculinities.

The *Brothers with No Game* creators facilitated fan investment in romantic relationships by combining "contained episodes" with "ongoing seriality" (Mittell 2015: 34) and then exploited such investment by using cliff hangers to maintain interest until they were ready to release the next episode. Some fans responded to these delayed resolutions with great frustration:

> You guys do this every single time.
> I cant take this anymore.
> The cliffhangers popping out of everywhere…. Its too mcuh.
> I dont think i wanna donate anymore,
> My hearts might not be able to handle a season 2.

In contrast, fans who primarily read *Brothers with No Game* as a comedy maintained a distance that enabled them to see romantic conflict as a source of humorous pleasure:

> I was just saying to my homegirl it'll be dope if they bring Vanessa back and she try to get back with my BOY!!! LMAO!!! This series is on repeat!

The cliff hangers represent one way in which the *Brothers with No Game* scriptwriting model negotiated the challenges of the production context, audience expectations of distribution patterns and narrative conventions of narrative comedy and serialised drama. More broadly, the show's modality shifts and unconventional narrative structure can be seen as examples of "new practices of script development" associated with web series (Taylor 2015). Writing about television, Mittell notes that the "structure of serial form is a temporal system with story installments parceled out over time with gaps between entries through a strictly regimented use of screen time" (27). However, in the case of *Brothers with No Game*, like many other web series, screen time varies markedly because episodes and the gaps between them were of varying length. For example, the final episode of series one ran to 27 minutes, which made it much longer than previous instalments. The increase was applauded on YouTube, where two fans suggested they were going to prepare for viewing by making, respectively, popcorn and a cup of tea. This constructed the viewing experience as a significant event to be savoured, rather than a fleeting moment of consumption.

Taylor (2015) argues that the flexible approach to webisode length liberates scriptwriters from the need to maintain set episodic and serial arcs that determine "the turning points and story peaks that drive the structure and tone of the scripts". She also maintains that the "hits, shares [and] fans" of successful web series work to legitimise these new scriptwriting practices, as do their transfer to "those same mainstream, corporate institutions that would arguably be unlikely to risk such a free range approach to script development within their own commissions". In the case of *Brothers with No Game*'s transfer to London Live, commissioner Derren Lawford (interviewed by the BBC) explains that the channel worked with the web series creators to make certain changes:

> For a start, none of the episodes were the same length so we had to devise a format and narrative structure that would sustain 22 minutes per episode and we had 13 of those to curate. ... We agreed on a house style for graphics, opening titles, in-character pieces to camera and discussed new elements.

This process indicates a negotiation between the practices of web series production on the one hand and sitcom conventions on the other, resulting in a shift towards greater stylistic coherence and traditional episode length.

Cultural Belonging and Diaspora

The notion of cultural belonging has already emerged a few times in this chapter, connected to the marginalisation of black voices on British television, representations of black masculinities and femininities and participation in an audience community based around the *Brothers with No Game* YouTube channel. For the remainder of the chapter, I want to develop a more in-depth exploration of how cultural belonging was evoked in the comment threads, what locations and groups it was connected to, and what its affective-discursive significance seemed to be. First, some London-based audience members articulated pleasure in seeing "their" city represented. One contributor even attempted to identify the specific part of London, adding "It's nice to see black British lads from my area". Of course, London features often in British film and television, but *Brothers with No Game* represents a young, "black London" (Gates 1997/2000: 183) that is rarely included. Alongside this sense of belonging in the city of London, fans connected this affective response to their British national identity:

> This shows makes me proud to be British!! These episodes are not long enough lol, they just seem to fly by as i'm watching, at the end i was thinking 'huh, 27 minutes have passed already damn!'

Brothers with No Game was here inscribed as a source of nation-based pride, and I would like to draw a connection to my discussion of *Lilyhammer* in the previous chapter. There, I explored the ways in which Norwegian viewers inscribed the NRK/Netflix production with pride or shame as they imagined how this rare export would be perceived abroad. Unlike Norway, Britain exports numerous TV programmes, including comedies, and so individual productions pose less risk to its imagined reputation. However, *Brothers with No Game* might offer black British viewers a sense of belonging within a Britain where young blackness is centred and heterogeneous. This may facilitate feelings of national pride, particularly within a space where notions of Britain and Britishness were made significant in positive responses from transnational viewers.

Transnational viewers drew on their own lived experiences to invest London and Britain with cultural similarities as well as cultural differences. For example, one U.S.-based commenter expressed a sense of pleasurable surprise in recognising "how similar Brits are to us", illustrating her viewing competence by interpreting a fleeting moment in the episode. Several other contributors highlighted the significance of the characters' London accents for their enjoyment of the show:

> ....sigh...need to go to london...those accents are killing me...smh lol sexi...

Here, the London accents were made significant as a desirable cultural difference that anchored the absent characters within a foreign city. However, contributors also negotiated the transnational viewing context by foregrounding textual elements that they connected to their own cultural heritage. This is an extract from a longer exchange among several participants:

> The girl that couldn't cook was pretty and Im loving the accents. I was born in Jamaica and it was cracking me up how they kiss their teeth when annoyed. Very common w. Jamaicans lol
>
> yea, it's mostly Black people who do it. Iv'e never seen a white person do it b4...lol..yea not its called kiss my teeth or "kmt" Nigerians even write it like this : "mcheeew" lmao
>
> Haitians call it tchupe. I laughed out loud when he did it ahahah

The exchange worked to highlight "the transatlantic connections of the African diaspora" (Mercer 1994: 252), and participants expressed amusement at recognising the representation of this shared cultural practice in the show. Such pleasurable recognition was a recurring theme across the threads, with participants foregrounding moments where the show referenced their own cultural heritage:

LOL DO YOU HAVE SOME SAUCE OR STEW, AI IS HE AFRICAN!

yes, Ghana has the BEST fanta!!!

love how u guys keep repping my island Jamaica!

As seen in the third post here, such references were sometimes labelled "shout outs" or "repping" (representing), which indicated the salience attached to such moments. As Wright (2004) emphasises, "Blacks in the diaspora possess an intimidating array of different historical, cultural, national, ethnic, religious, and ancestral origins and influences" (2). By making visible the cultural heritage of its characters, *Brothers with No Game* valorised the heterogeneity of black Britishness and located it within a wider African diaspora. This discursive strategy also worked to offer black transnational viewers a sense of cultural belonging within an imagined international community:

As an African-American woman, I've never seen depictions of other young Africans from the diaspora. I am very much excited about this series & keep up the great work!!

Mercer (1994) observes that diaspora, as a concept, "disrupts the centrality of the categories of 'nation' and nationhood that are so often taken for granted" (246). The African diaspora in the U.S. has had a high international profile because of the widespread availability and popularity of some black U.S. popular culture. However, the U.S. viewer quoted above suggested that the structure of her own engagement with black culture had remained nation-based, and she constructed *Brothers with No Game* as a welcome disruption that made visible another group within the diaspora as imagined community (Tsagarousianou 2004).

The imagining of *Brothers with No Game*'s audience as diasporic rather than national is demonstrated by its transfer to the French SVOD service Afrostream. This platform is available internationally and claims to offer "The best black films and TV series". Content promoted on the front page includes *Brothers with No Game* alongside productions from Nigeria, France and the U.S. The site and its offerings can be situated within a shift towards diasporic television that has provided ethnic minorities with an alternative to national TV through cable and satellite providers (Malik 2013). Stressing the significance of connectivity for diasporic communities, Tsagarousianou (2004) argues that transnational diasporic media "can provide a sense of contemporaneity and synchronicity to the dispersed populations that make up a diaspora and to their everyday lives" (62). Its position outside British broadcasting helped *Brothers with No Game* to facilitate such connectivity across complex diaspora groups in different locations.

Conclusions

This chapter has continued my examination of the significance of cultural identities in comedy cultures, building on my study of women in Hollywood comedy (chapter 3) and my analysis of the national and transnational audiences of *Lilyhammer* (chapter 4). Here, I have explored the ways in which articulations of blackness intersected with gender and nationality in audience engagement with the web series *Brothers with No Game*. My analysis was particularly concerned with exploring the extent to which this show, within its YouTube context, might provide a space for marginalised black voices. I found that the show offered domestic and transnational audiences pleasurable opportunities to recognise and laugh at specific aspects of their own heritage and lived experience. But it also provided opportunities for individual viewers to feel a sense of belonging to a wider, imagined diasporic audience who were laughing together and had shared concerns. This heterogeneous community became visible on the comment threads, which were used to voice pleasure, critique and frustration.

As part of this discussion, I have considered some of the generic specificities of web comedy, including the ways in which participants positioned *Brothers with No Game* as amateur media and the intimacy facilitated by small screen viewing and its articulation of the web series style. I stressed that participants situated the show within a wider culture of black web series, which drew attention to the absence of black narratives on television and valorised this cultural form as a significant alternative to TV comedy. The next two chapters will continue this exploration of genre in screen comedy, focusing on the television sitcom in chapter 6 and the romcom film in chapter 7.

Notes

1 Thank you to Mark Boosey at The British Comedy Guide, who recommended that I look at this web series.
2 "smh" is an abbreviation of "shaking my head".

6 Sitcom Audiences and Genre Developments

Everybody Hates Chris,
Miranda and *Gavin & Stacey*

Following on from my discussion of web comedy, this chapter continues my exploration of the significance of genre for audience engagement with comedy by shifting attention onto the sitcom. This genre has had an enduring popularity in the U.S. and the U.K., but its popular appeal has often co-existed with critical disdain for its formulaic narrative structure, use of stereotypes and a lack of innovation (Becker 2008). So although traditional sitcoms certainly continue to draw audiences, it is perhaps unsurprising that many productions have departed from generic conventions in various ways. Mills (2009) identifies two additional strands of sitcoms that "define themselves in terms of their look and aesthetics": One "has the realist/naturalist look of drama and/or documentary" (such as the different versions of *The Office*), while the other "makes an explicit display of its use of the image" (such as *Arrested Development*, Fox, 2003–2006) (128–29). This chapter examines how audiences respond to such negotiations of generic conventions through a multi-sited reception analysis of three sitcoms that have all had mainstream success: *Everybody Hates Chris, Gavin & Stacey* and *Miranda*. Reflecting on the extent to which humour theory and cue theory can help us make sense of audience responses to a contemporary sitcom, I consider how viewers in different online contexts articulated criteria for "good" sitcom and how the programmes were evaluated against these criteria. As part of that analysis, I draw attention to the ways in which such responses might be facilitated and constrained by the characteristics of the online spaces in which they are expressed. What discourses of sitcom circulate within and across these three reception contexts? And what can this tell us about the cultural meanings and positions of British and U.S. sitcom today?

None of the sites I focus on here included a facility for contacting contributors, and so I was unable to seek informed consent to reproduce posts. Although the sites are all public, I therefore refrain from identifying two of the sites (the profile of the third site, Amazon.com, means that it cannot be effectively disguised), and I only quote posts from contributors who were clearly using pseudonyms.

Everybody Hates Chris and Viewers as Consumers

Single-camera sitcom *Everybody Hates Chris* was co-created by U.S. stand-up comedian Chris Rock (with Ali LeRoi) and purports to be "inspired" by his own experiences as a black teenager in Bedford-Stuyvesant, Brooklyn, and as a student at "a predominantly white junior high school" (Associated Press 2005). I here examine how this sitcom was reviewed on the U.S. site Amazon.com, where viewers are positioned as consumer-reviewers and evaluations often refer to screen texts as "products" and comment on delivery time, picture quality, packaging, price and so on. At one point, reviews had to be at least 20 words long, though that rule has since been revoked:

> Everybody hates Chris is appropriate for all ages and still hilarious for all ages, it's a winner, five stars all day everyday for sure without a doubt. Is this twenty words yet?

This contributor drew attention to the (unpaid) labour that reviewers undertake for the world's largest online retailer, even though they have already paid for their purchased products. Other customers can "reward" the labour by indicating that the review is "helpful", which impacts on the reviewer's rank. In a 2011 study of the top-rated 1,000 Amazon.com reviewers, Pinch and Kesler note that such reviewers often get free products in return for reviews. They found that their respondents tended to be male (70%), aged between 30 and 70 and university educated. The median age was 51–60. So, although the demographic makeup of reviewers will necessarily vary widely depending on the product, the site's broader user culture is dominated by middle-aged, middle-class men.

My analysis examined all available reviews of three "products": The season 1 DVD (32 reviews), Season 2 as DVD or streamed from the site (103 reviews), and the full series box set (67 reviews).

All three products had an average rating that was close to the full score of 5 stars. Since the contributors had already chosen to spend money on *Everybody Hates Chris*, I did not expect to see a wide range of positive and negative reviews. Instead, I wanted to explore how the user culture of Amazon.com facilitates and constrains the ways in which comedy is talked about there through its privileging of a consumer discourse that constructs comedy as a commodity and evaluates its success in fulfilling desired functions. Across these reviews, I identified three recurring criteria that focused on *Everybody Hates Chris* as offering comedic pleasures, social commentary and viewing experiences that could be shared by the whole family. I will discuss these in turn.

The Amazon reviews of *Everybody Hates Chris* foregrounded the show's comedic modality. Contributors valorised laughter as a viewer response by describing the show as a "belly buster" that will "make your cheeks ache" but also by devoting review space to link this affective response to specific textual elements. For example, contributors frequently constructed Chris Rock's narration as a source of comic pleasure. The device was discussed both in terms of Rock's authorship of funny stories and in terms of his funny delivery of those stories:

> Chris Rocks' hilarious narration delivers bursts of precisely executed humor into each exceptional episode.

As Neale and Krutnik (1990: 47–48) observe, "jokes, wisecracks, and funny lines ... require formal closure, often in the form of a punchline", and this means that they are less suited to providing "a springboard for narrative development" and "much more suited to constructing or marking a pause or digression in the ongoing flow of a story". However, Rock's extra-diegetic voice-over in *Everybody Hates Chris* provides a flexible comic device that can incorporate such verbal humour while also contributing to narrative development.

The review cited above emphasises Rock's skill and craft as a comedian, which draws attention to the affective labour that is required to offer audiences "good times" (Thomas 2015: 7). This work is often concealed because, as Graefer (2016) notes, "Humour needs to seem effortless in order to fulfil its aim of being funny" (148). References to such efforts were rare across the reviews, but Rock was repeatedly inscribed with significance in other ways. Some contributors focused on the connection between *Everybody Hates Chris* and Rock's own life experiences, which was often constructed as a source of authenticity, while others situated the show within the wider comedic output of a star comedian (Whalley 2010: 193). This illustrated the movements of practitioners and audiences among different forms within comedy culture, with Rock's star text spilling across stand-up, TV sketch comedy, sitcom, film and so on. As a disembodied authorial voice in *Everybody Hates Chris* he reproduces and reworks his stand-up material, blurring the boundary between his own life and the events that happen to Chris as character.

The praise for Rock's narration also formed part of a wider celebration of cast performances, which were identified as a key source of comic pleasure. A small minority of reviews praised the actors for seeming "natural", with one reviewer adding: "It's not like your watching a show". This evaluation concentrated on acting as characterisation (Jenkins and Karnick 1995: 150) and reproduced a discourse of the sitcom genre that values a move away from its theatrical roots and towards the "realist/naturalist" style of TV drama (Mills 2009: 127–28). However, most discussions of the cast focused on their performances as including both characterisation and comic "showmanship" (Jenkins and

Karnick 1995: 150). Reviews stressed the importance of "comic timing", for example, and several contributors identified the portrayal of Chris's mother as particularly enjoyable:

> Tichina Arnold as Rochelle is one of the best physical comedians ever, male or female—what she can do with her face, body, and voice is amazing.

This review challenged cultural hierarchies of comedy that privilege verbal humour by positioning Arnold within a history of valued physical comedians and inscribing her with an impressive "repertoire of performance skills" (Jenkins and Karnick 1995: 150).

Across the Amazon reviews, the valorising of *Everybody Hates Chris*'s comedic modality was situated within a consumer discourse where customers advised other customers that "if you enjoyed the 1st season, you'll enjoy the 2nd season as well" or "Cant go wrong , this show is classic". Here, the generation of laughter became a desirable product function, which was often complemented by "thinking" or "learning":

> I love this series. It's especially fun to watch it with my son and teach him about Black social issues and history through it. He's laughing and enjoying the storyline and not realizing how much he's learning!

This reviewer foregrounded and valorised the programme's representations of blackness, assigning the show an educational function that was masked by entertainment. Other contributors also highlighted its representations of "race" and class, suggesting that it offered "life lessons" or "social commentary" about "inner-city life" or about "blue-collar" African American families. Some reviewers signalled their own blackness through such readings, which illustrates Medhurst's argument that "comedy is an invitation to belong":

> Comedy's consoling fantasy is that however difficult life might be, however much forces way beyond your control try to rip you to pieces, there can still be moments where – right here, right now – you can join those who are like you in a celebratory rite of communal recognition. Comedy says to us: you're among friends, relax, join in.
> (Medhurst 2007: 19)

Other reviewers seemed to feel less certain about their own position in relation to the programme. For example, one contributor suggested that he had questioned whether *Everybody Hates Chris* would appeal to him as a "white male". He described enjoying it, but constructed the premise of the show as "a black guy's perspective of LIFE in a mostly white school". This discursive strategy provided a marked contrast to the centring of black audiences in the YouTube responses to *Brothers with No Game*. Here, the Amazon reviewer framed *Everybody Hates Chris* as a narrative world where whiteness is the norm, and reaffirmed the privileged position of white viewers as "us".

Constructions of *Everybody Hates Chris* as social commentary frequently described the show as "serious but funny", making a recurring distinction between humour and seriousness. However, reviews tended to inscribe both categories with value, and some compared the show favourably to sitcoms that were constructed as "sentimental" or "lecturing". The show's successful negotiation of this balancing act was often linked to notions of authenticity, with reviewers constructing its representations as "real", "realistic" or "honest". Some located this authenticity in similarities between the show and their own experiences, writing that it reminded them of their own childhood or that specific characters reminded them of people they knew:

> This show takes you back to your childhood in a hilarious way. It is like traveling back in time and reliving all the things that were huge problems then but now seem trivial.

Other reviewers constructed the show as a window on a specific place at a specific time, with one contributor describing it as "a small glimpse of life of growing up black in the 70's in the inner city". Some located this "realness" in Rock's authorship and the show's autobiographical elements:

> I love how he talks about his life and Chris Rock paints a picture of his life right before your very eyes.

The idea of Rock representing his life by "talking" and "painting" connects his identities as stand-up comedian and sitcom (co-)creator, while the blurring of comedian and character can be situated within a history of star-focused TV comedies such as *I Love Lucy* (e.g. Mellencamp 2003), *Roseanne* (e.g. Rowe 2003) and *Miranda* (which I discuss later on in this chapter) and of stand-up comedians incorporating "autobiographical performance" (Gilbert 1997: 317) into their stage routines. This blurring complicates the use of superiority theory to understand what and whom the audience might be laughing at (Mills 2011). Although Chris is sometimes constructed as the butt of the joke, Rock is the comedian-creator who invites us to laugh at him, other characters and ourselves. As Gilbert notes:

> Because of the "us against them" nature of marginal humor (humor performed by any marginal group, e.g., African-American, gay/lesbian, Jewish comics etc.), marginal comics often construct

themselves as victims. In doing so, however, they may subvert their own status by embodying the potential power of powerlessness. Their social critique is potent and, because it is offered in a comedic context, safe from retribution as well. (1997: 317)

Thinking of *Everybody Hates Chris* in terms of marginal humour offers one explanation for why some reviewers inscribed the sitcom with social significance. However, although reviews often drew attention to the show's representation of a black, working-class family and (sometimes) their financial difficulties, this tended not to be constructed as social critique of class divisions. Instead, some reviews identified the "penny-pinching" father (Terry Crews) as a source of comic pleasure, while others signalled their own "blue-collar" or black identities by suggesting that they could relate more to *Everybody Hates Chris* than to sitcoms like *The Cosby Show* or *Fresh Prince of Bel-Air* (NBC 1990–1996), which feature black upper-middle-class characters. Within this discourse, the representations of black, working-class characters became an indicator of "authenticity", rather than of critique.

Some reviewers did identify representations of racism, however, referring to "racial stereotyping", "racial slurs" and racist characters like Chris's teacher Ms. Morello (Jacqueline Mazarella) and school bully Caruso (Travis T. Flory). Whereas a small minority of contributors constructed these representations as "offensive", most tended instead to situate them within the programme's social commentary. For these viewers, then, *Everybody Hates Chris* functioned as a safe space to explore racism:

> In comedy, we expect the unexpected. If gags and jokes often function as neuralgic points, as points at which the conventionally censored or repressed find expression, they are performing a permissible, indeed institutionalized, function. Thus comedy in general, and the comic in particular, become, somewhat paradoxically perhaps, the appropriate site for the inappropriate, the proper place for indecorum, the field in which the unlikely is likely to occur.
> (Neale and Krutnik 1990: 91)

So, the show's comedic modality offers a form of "insulation" (Palmer 1987: 45) that can make it easier for audiences to laugh at difficult subject matter and to experience a sense of relief that racism has been acknowledged and positioned as an object of laughter. The 1980s setting also sometimes seemed to provide additional distance, with one reviewer writing that the series "Reminds us of how times have changed and how to laugh at ourselves".

This sense of safety was frequently indicated by contributors who described the show as family friendly:

This is a great show for the WHOLE FAMILY! My 3 kids (esp my 12yr old son) absolutely LOVE it. (...) While I don't condone a lot that's on TV, this show seemed to be pretty nice for the middle school crowd and we are sorry to see it go.

Like this reviewer, many contributors identified themselves as parents or grandparents. Some reported buying the series for their children or grandchildren, suggesting that it is suitable for younger viewers because it is "clean" or "wholesome", and positioning it against the "trash" TV that would otherwise be available to them. Many others inscribed the programme with a cross-generational appeal that was often linked to a sense of recognition, for example of 1980s culture, of family life or of childhood experiences. This valorisation of family viewing complicated the narrative of the stratifying TV audience, in which viewers "gather according to social formations of taste", often along the lines of age, gender and "sexual preference" (Brunsdon and Spiegel 2008: 2). It also problematised the distinction between mainstream, multi-camera sitcoms and single-camera sitcoms developed for niche audiences (Mills 2009: 55). These viewers indicated that they had bought the DVD or paid for the streaming of episodes in order to access the show when they could sit down as a family and to continue doing so after the series had concluded. So, these responses located the communal experience of comedy within the (nuclear) family and the home, rather than within an imagined, wider audience that shared tastes and values. This suggests that the sitcom still has the potential to provide a temporary "family hearth" (Tueth 2005: 12), with the aid of time-shifting.

Miranda and Viewers as TV Forum Participants

The second part of my sitcom case study focuses on responses to *Miranda* (BBC2/1, 2009–2015), which is written by and stars Miranda Hart. Like Chris Rock, Hart illustrates the transmediality of many comedians as celebrity texts. She has done stand-up comedy, her TV sitcom *Miranda* was based on the radio sitcom *Miranda Hart's Joke Shop* (BBC Radio 2, 2007–2008) and she has performed in film comedies (e.g. Paul Feig's *Spy*, 2015). *Miranda* the sitcom focuses on the title character's life as a single and uncommonly tall and clumsy woman in her thirties. It challenges the cultural hierarchies of this genre by focusing on a female performer, by adopting a multi-camera shooting style and by incorporating a laugh track from the live studio audience. The show was nonetheless successful with both critics and audiences, moving from BBC2 to the flagship channel BBC1 for its third series.

I am here examining the ways in which *Miranda* was talked about on a popular British website that hosts message boards dedicated to a range of media and entertainment topics. In 2014 I collected all posts from two forum threads that explicitly invited users to articulate what they found funny or not funny about *Miranda* (67 posts), as well as the first 100 posts each on the main thread for series 1 and the main thread for series 2.

My intention was to capture a broad range of responses to the start of the sitcom as well as the responses of viewers who continued to follow the show. Compared to the Amazon.com reviews of *Everybody Hates Chris*, these posts engaged more explicitly in a *dialogue* around *Miranda*. The exchanges offered little sense that contributors were familiar with each other (although this changed somewhat for the thread on series 2), but tended to focus on sharing and discussing personal responses to the programme. The contributor post tallies tended to be in the thousands or tens of thousands, so the responses can be situated within a very large and loose-knit but also busy and interactive online community based around a shared interest in TV entertainment. Across the threads, I found that evaluations of *Miranda* tended to focus on innovation, humour style and character engagement.

The value of sitcom innovation was debated extensively across the treads. Some posters evaluated *Miranda* against a requirement for originality, describing it as a "step backwards", arguing that it is not "clever or funny enough to pull of the old-fashioned style", suggesting that contemporary audiences "expect better than the old-fashioned sitcoms", and criticising it for using "70s jokes". In contrast, other posters identified this criterion only to resist it. They praised *Miranda* for being "traditional" and argued that it is "refreshing" precisely because it differs from what Mills terms "comedies of distinction":

> [T]hese are sitcoms which offer audiences the pleasures of *not* being traditional, and engage in industrial and textual work in order to distinguish themselves from traditional sitcom as much as possible.
>
> (Mills 2009: 134)

So, if we situate these audience responses within the context of current genre developments, it seems that *Miranda* became a site of struggle over definitions of sitcom and expectations of sitcom pleasures. As one poster wrote:

> "Old fashioned" it may be - but I find it entertainingly FUNNY compared to some of the "modern sit-coms" (which aren't sit-coms at all!)

Like the IMDb reviewers of *(500) Days of Summer* I discuss in the next chapter, this poster can be seen to address a reception discourse produced by professional critics. We can think of professional reviewers as "taste makers and gatekeepers" (Shrum 1996: 40) whose work has the potential to influence both the kinds of comedy that get made and the ways in which audiences engage with comedy. TV critics, columnists and comedy critics employed by newspapers "pass aesthetic judgment on comedy" through a critical discourse that is "mass-mediated and widely visible" (Friedman 2014: 125). Becker (2008) notes that the sitcom genre has frequently been dismissed as "artificial" and "stale", while Friedman's (2014) analysis of comedy reviews argues that "experiments with comic form were so highly regarded by critics that they often seemed to transcend any assessment of quality" (134). In the case of sitcoms, this discourse devalues established conventions that focus on generating laughs from a fairly static situation. These include the circular narrative, the multi-camera shooting style, the laugh track and comedic devices such as punch line jokes and slapstick.

Returning to the forum post quoted above, then, it is interesting to note that this poster rejected the critical demand for innovation in sitcom. Instead, he or she argued that the more traditional *Miranda* offers viewing pleasures that are not available in sitcoms that have moved away from generic conventions and finally attempted to re-draw the boundaries of the sitcom genre by expelling such "modern" versions. This counter-discourse was also articulated by Sioned Wiliam (Controller of Comedy at ITV) in an interview with Mills (2009), where she expressed frustration that critics only like comedy that "is perceived to be pushing the envelope" (63). It seems, then, that the affective economy of the sitcom remains unstable, with producers, audiences and critics continuing to debate what this genre should offer.

Across the threads, this struggle often focused on what is sometimes referred to as "humor styles". For example, Kuipers (2015) examines humour styles as specific understandings of what "good" and "bad" humour is. Her analysis of interviews with Dutch audience members identifies clear distinctions between "highbrow" and "lowbrow" humour styles, which map onto social class distinctions. Audiences preferring a highbrow humour style "like more ambiguous, ironical humor, that is sharp and sometimes unpleasant", while the lowbrow humour style "favors comedians and television programs that are exuberantly and emphatically funny". Importantly, she maintains: "These styles are generally mutually exclusive, in an asymmetric way: people who like popular humor are generally puzzled by highbrow humor, whereas people who favour intellectual humor look down upon popular humor" (113).

Across the threads, *Miranda* was constructed as lowbrow comedy. Several posters praised the series for being "entertaining", "light hearted", an "easy watch", "unsophisticated", "silly" and for "not taking itself seriously". Many contributors were very enthusiastic about this perceived dedication to the pleasures of traditional entertainment, which might suggest that these audience members felt that the sitcom genre was starting to privilege more highbrow humour. One poster claimed that "there is nothing like it on television", while others described it as "amazing", "brilliant" and "excellent". In contrast, those disliking *Miranda* dismissed it as "simple", "clichéd", "crude", "brash" and "juvenile", while its use of penis jokes was repeatedly singled out as objectionable:

> I like Miranda Hart, and Pat Hodge (haven't seen her for years), and Sally Phillips, but the programme last night was just awful. Putting in willy jokes right at the start is a sure sign of poor material. Rubbish, rubbish, rubbish.
>
> Having said that, it is part of a tradition of screechy, brash, simple BBC sitcoms stretching back for decades (for example, Are you Being Served), so there must be a significant section of the public which likes it.

In her study of Dutch comedy audiences, Kuipers (2006) suggests that her research participants received "status gratification" from their dismissal of lowbrow comedy (373). Similarly, this post invoked a discourse of working-class culture as abject while positioning the contributor firmly outside the "significant section of the public" that keep tuning in to watch the despised sitcoms. The evaluation polices "the symbolic boundary between 'us' and 'them'" (Friedman 2015: 116) by constructing *Miranda*'s viewers as part of a wider audience of which the poster had no knowledge.

However, in between *Miranda*'s fans and anti-fans there were non-fans (Gray 2003) who articulated only mild affective responses, describing the show as "ok" or "quite amusing", and a group of what we might call reluctant fans, who seemed to struggle to reconcile their enjoyment of *Miranda* with their perception of their own humour styles and comedy viewer identities:

> It's funny, I really shouldn't like Miranda. I like more considered, clever comedy and usually think shows like this are just really cheap, easy shows to make.
>
> But I find it incredibly entertaining and I'm not sure why!

Similarly, another poster found that "despite my best efforts to hate it, it makes me laugh", while some explained that they liked *Miranda* more than they thought they would, or more than they "should". As Bourdieu (1984) argues, "each taste feels itself to be natural" and so "tastes are perhaps first and foremost distastes, disgust provoked by horror or visceral intolerance" (56). These viewers seem to indicate that *Miranda* failed the evaluation criteria associated with their "natural" comedy tastes, but that their laughter nonetheless inscribed the show with funniness. This response differed from distanced "ironic consumption" (McCoy and Scarborough 2014: 42) and from "critical, subversive fandom" (Haig 2014: 12). Their acceptance of *Miranda*'s invitation to laugh was experienced as surprising and inappropriate. The sitcom somehow resonated with them, but when sharing that pleasurable experience on the message board, they constructed it as an *exception*. This tension simultaneously demonstrates the potential for fissures in the boundaries between audience humour styles and the significance of those boundaries for comedy viewer identities.

As in the Amazon.com reviews of *Everybody Hates Chris*, performance was a recurring theme across the forum threads. However, Hart's performance style was evaluated in quite different ways. One contributor wrote:

> I really like Miranda's "non-acting" style, though I can see how it might grate on other people, and it was good to see some good old-fashioned slapstick falling over too.

Hart's performance style departs both from conventional sitcom acting and from the more naturalistic performance styles associated with recent sitcom trends. As Walters (2013) notes in his discussion of *The Trip*, shooting "on location breaks from comedy performance as a rehearsed and choreographed theatrical event" (114). In contrast, Hart's performance style draws attention to its theatricality and can be seen as part of *Miranda*'s self-reflexive style. She often looks to the camera and addresses the audience, for example to share an insight, to invite sympathy or to highlight her awareness that she is making a very conventional joke. At the end of each episode, the performers also wave goodbye to the viewers at home. However, whereas some posters clearly enjoyed Hart's performances and praised her comic timing and her pratfalls, other contributors described it as "fake", complained that "she cracks up all the time" and dismissed her as a "bad actor". As those responses indicated, *Miranda*'s self-reflexivity repeatedly draws our attention to the constructedness of the sitcom and to Hart as a comedian.

Writing about *The Office*, Mills (2004) argues that the series uses David Brent's embarrassing attempts at being a workplace comedian to set up "a laughable disparity between such conventional comedic performance and the 'realistic' office environment" in order to reposition "traditional comedy … as merely ridiculous, to be laughed *at* and not *with*" (73). In *Miranda*, however, I think the self-reflexivity invites audiences to respond simultaneously to Hart-as-comedian and to Miranda-as-character. While it draws attention to the constructed nature of the sitcom events, the blurring of comedian and character can be seen as a bid for authenticity and as an invitation to viewers to invest affectively in Hart/Miranda.

Many posters who found *Miranda* funny focused their evaluations of Hart's performance of her comedian persona, which includes this character as well as her stand-up comedy, celebrity interviews and so on. They talked about liking or even "loving" her, and of "relating" to her clumsiness or her dating disasters, for example:

> I LOVE Miranda. Miranda is me☺

I think this is the kind of affective response that the show tries to invite. The opening monologues addressed to the audience and the subsequent asides to the camera not only "align" the viewer with the character (Smith 1995: 82–83), but also are attempts to position the viewer as a friend and co-conspirator, someone who understands and can share anything with Hart/Miranda. So, while the sitcom foregrounds Miranda's failures and shortcomings, I think it often resists the application of superiority theory. While viewers might laugh *at* Miranda and feel superior to her, many posts demonstrated that contributors found her funny even when they recognised their own failures or misfortune in the character. Such responses might indicate what Freud describes as the pleasures of the "comic" (Freud 1905/1991: 239). For example, if viewers think Miranda spends too much physical energy and not enough mental energy in a situation, that difference might appear comic to them, and they might "experience a pleasurable empathy with the person who is pitted against this harsh world" (Mellencamp 2003: 52–53).

However, if a viewer doesn't like the Hart/Miranda persona, he or she is unlikely to accept her invitation to enter into an "allegiance" (Smith 1995: 82–83). Some posters described her as "hyperactive", complained that she was "too boarding school" or summed up both offenses through the label "jolly hockey sticks" (according to various online dictionaries this means an annoyingly enthusiastic upper- or middle-class girl or woman). These negative evaluations, then, were often classed. However, there was an interesting tension between the disdain for "posh" Hart/Miranda and the disdain for lowbrow humour I discussed earlier, and some posters inscribed *Miranda* with unacceptable transgressions of class and gender distinctions:

> Apparently a tall overwieght women pulling funny faces and talking directly to the camera in a 'jolly hockey sticks' accent constitutes hilarious comedy in the year 2011.
>
> God help us all !!!!!!!

As Kotthoff (2006) notes, clowning and deliberate foolishness have traditionally been considered inappropriate behaviours for women, because patriarchal norms of femininity emphasise prettiness and modesty (5–7). These expectations are particularly associated with middle-class femininity. However, Miranda is too tall, tells dirty jokes, falls over, gets caught lying, gets mistaken for a man, and so on. These comic incongruities can be thought of as carnivalesque inversions of high and low, with an emphasis on "excess" and the "topsy-turvy" (Stallybrass and White 1986: 8). However, while the viewer quoted above responded to such transgressions by rejecting Hart/Miranda as abject, others suggested that they had experienced comic relief:

> I suppose I find it funny cos I identify with many of the situations… and sometimes the only difference between many of us and Miranda is that she says out loud what many of us keep in our heads LOL

Here, the contributor identified Miranda's breaches of social conventions within recognisable situations as a key source of viewing pleasure. And whereas the previous post positioned Hart/Miranda as an "other" and refused her the power to "be" funny, this viewer included her among "us". As Medhurst (2007) observes, comedy can work both to reinforce bonds through shared laughter and to exclude, working as "a fence keeping you out as much as a gate letting you in" (20). In the case of these threads, such affective-discursive gatekeeping seemed to be performed by audience members who perceived *Miranda* and its fans as incompatible with their own viewing identities and humour styles.

Gavin & Stacey and Viewers as Experts

The third and final site for my sitcom case study is a thread about *Gavin & Stacey* (BBC3/1, 2007–2010) on a forum dedicated to British comedy. Like *Everybody Hates Chris* and *Miranda*, this sitcom stars its own writers, with James Corden as Smithy and Ruth Jones as Nessa. The main characters, however, are Gavin (Matthew Horne) from Billericay in South East England and Stacey (Joanna Page) from Barry in South Wales. The sitcom focuses on their developing romance across national and class boundaries and the relationships among their friends and families. It adopts a single camera shooting style, emphasises the development of narrative strands across episodes and fits quite neatly into Mills's (2009) category of sitcoms with "the realist/naturalist look of drama" (128–29). *Gavin & Stacey* was a hit with British viewers and critics, while the attempted U.S. remake *Us & Them* (FOX) failed to get broadcast (Thielman 2014).

In 2009 I collected all 665 posts on the *Gavin & Stacey* thread. This sample included responses to series 1, series 2 and the 2008 Christmas special episode, but not responses to the third and final series, which aired later. The website incorporates several message boards dedicated to the discussion of comedy, but also boards for new comedy writers, where they can discuss comedy production and critique each other's work. The discussion of *Gavin & Stacey* can therefore be situated within an online culture that included participants with a strong interest in watching and discussing comedy, as well as participants who were also writing their own comedy, with varying levels of success. I was interested in how this culture facilitated particular ways of talking about sitcom and found that contributors tended to value subcultural capital (Thornton 1995) specific to comedy, including knowledge about the British TV comedy industry and an understanding of script writing, as well as close analysis and vigorous debate. My discussion will focus on the three key themes that emerged through my analysis: *Gavin & Stacey*'s combination of comedy and drama elements, its dialogue, and the originality of the show.

Within an affective economy that values drama over comedy, *Gavin & Stacey*'s rejection of key sitcom conventions and its adoption of a "naturalist/realist mode" (Mills 2009: 135) can be seen as a bid for "quality". However, for some viewers, this style positioned the programme outside of the sitcom genre. Posters repeatedly debated whether it could really be defined as a sitcom, rather than a comedy drama, and the thread was moved back and forth between the sitcom forum and a forum dedicated to other forms of comedy. A key issue of debate was the importance of jokes in sitcoms, with some contributors insisting that *Gavin & Stacey* did not have enough jokes to fit within this genre.

According to Palmer's (1987) incongruity theory, a successful joke structure has a preparation stage and a culmination stage that surprises the audience. What makes this surprise a *comic* surprise is, in his view, a tension between plausibility and implausibility at this culmination stage (40). The argument that *Gavin & Stacey* was not a sitcom because it lacked jokes was met with various counter-arguments. Although nobody challenged the centrality of humour to sitcom, many responses constructed the humour in *Gavin & Stacey* as "subtle", and some positioned the programme within a trend of sitcoms that have moved away from "punch line jokes". This is an extract from a lengthy post defending the show against accusations of "lazy writing":

> The show gets funnier the more you watch it, because the jokes are all in the characters and the situation they are in. I agree that Gavin and Stacey isn't a "sit-com" as we know it, this for me is a plus. It's so much more. It's funnier than most stuff on television, in my opinion, and yet so moving and touching.

Like this post, many others constructed *Gavin & Stacey* as superior to traditional sitcoms, praising its "charm", its "warmth", and its success in making viewers care about its characters:

> I went from loving Smiffy and his stupid Gavlar and Pamalarr stuff and his general interaction with Steadman to quickly thinking by the end of the first series "christ this show is making me feel wierd! It's a comedy and I actually "care" about the characters and what happens to them.

These viewers valued the programme's combination of comedic, dramatic and romantic modalities and the wide affective register that provided. However, while the next chapter will argue that reviews of *(500) Days of Summer* focused on romance rather than comedy, the established user culture on this site placed humour at the centre of the dialogue. Critical posts maintained that the "drama" in *Gavin & Stacey* is actually just poor writing, with some blaming the writers' lack of experience or a rushed writing process. This is one example:

> I once attended a speech where a producer said, 'If your comedy isn't very funny, you refer to it as a comedy/drama.'
>
> This would be comedy/drama then.

Other contributors rejected the notion of drama as failed comedy, instead locating the distinction between comedy and drama in formal elements, such as episode duration and narrative structure, or in extra-textual cues, such as genre labels in listings and promotional materials.

However, this debate demonstrates that the move away from circular narratives and the multi-camera shooting style means that some sitcoms challenge audience expectations of what sitcoms are like. For many viewers, the "sitcom" or "comedy drama" label may not matter much, but for some of these budding comedy writers, genre definitions were important because they themselves struggled with the balance of sameness and difference required by TV commissioners. This is an extract from a much longer post:

> ...what I mean is, people get perfectly decent stuff rejected because it's 'old fashioned'. What most BBC readers and producers would call old fashioned is what people on these forums call classic sitcoms.
>
> Sitcom doesn't really exist any more as you or I know it. It is 'narrative comedy'.

While I, as an academic and as an audience member, find the development of the sitcom genre quite fascinating, this post constructed the shift in narrative mode from series to serial as a constraint imposed on sitcom writers by the industry. This concern drew attention to the precariousness of sitcom writing as a form of affective labour, not only because it is very competitive and contracts tend to be short (Mills 2016), but also because writers have to second guess the development of the genre and the changing tastes of commissioners and audiences. As U.S. comedy writer and performer Tina Fey writes in her book *Bossypants*:

> We shoot *30 Rock* on film, like a little movie each week. This means that we film every line of dialogue about five times from about five different angles. Every time we switch angles it takes about twenty

minutes to move the cameras around. Every five minutes the cameras run out of film and we have to reload ... We only shoot in this "single camera" style because it is currently the fashion.

(Fey 2011: "Doing, Learning, Dying")

The debate around the generic definition of *Gavin & Stacey* intersected with a discussion of its dialogue. Some anti-fans provided detailed analysis of exchanges that they constructed as comic failures, with one poster even re-writing a conversation so that it complied with the conventional structure of jokes. In contrast, *Gavin & Stacey* fans highlighted comic situations and "hidden" or "throwaway" humorous lines, with one contributor noting an example of smutty word play:

> One line I assume must have been worded that way on purpose, that made me laugh...
>
> Gavin: Come on mate.
> Smithy: Don't come on me mate.

While the anti-fans set up an adherence to the preparation/surprising culmination convention of jokes as a marker of good sitcom, the fans tended instead to value the experience of "discovering" humour in the text. One post commented on this distinction and drew on the idea of textual openness to set up a hierarchy of comedy forms and comedy audiences:

> It's like reader-response criticism: the viewer is judged intelligent enough to interpret and find various situations funny without a crafted punchline delivering a specific payload. They're different sub-genres I suppose, and I imagine would appeal to different personality types (e.g. presumably those further along the autistic spectrum would prefer fixed, classic in-your-face "gags").

This post devalued sitcoms that are clearly cued as humorous because they were seen to require less "work" from the audience. Rather than emphasising laughter as a desired affective response to comedy, the contributor privileged the process of interpreting textual elements as comical and pathologised audiences who enjoy conventional jokes. The post echoed what Friedman (2015) terms a style of comic appreciation that values "difficulty" and is based on "the idea that good comedy should involve some effort and knowledge on the part of the audience" (69). In his sociological study, this style was associated with audiences who had high levels of cultural capital, and the contributor quoted above also performed such capital through the reference to "reader-response criticism".

The third recurring theme in this discussion of *Gavin & Stacey* focused on originality. The anti-fans dismissed the show as "derivative" and "clichéd", singling out specific scenes for critique and likening them to other comedies they disliked, such as *The Catherine Tate Show* (BBC2/BBC1 2004–2015) or *Little Britain* (BBC3/BBC1 2003–2007). The fans, on the other hand, rejected innovation as a necessary marker of good sitcom. Instead, some posters focused on the importance of "truthfulness":

> This is meant to be true-to-life, are you telling me that there is a way to write a true-to-life sitcom without approaching subjects that have already been performed before?

These contributors tended to read *Gavin & Stacey* as observational comedy, pointing to recognisable characters and situations in the show. However, anti-fans argued that such recognition was not enough:

> I recognise that situation as being true to life – i just dont see why its funny.

It seems to me that this perceived lack of originality or innovation may be a key issue in this particular discussion of *Gavin and Stacey*. The programme was seen to break with some important sitcom conventions in terms of its use of dramatic and romantic modalities and in terms of its lack of conventionally structured jokes. However, unlike *The Office*, for example, it wasn't different *enough* to impress viewers as an example of generic innovation. This position appeared to be particularly problematic for some of the budding sitcom writers posting to this thread, as they often expressed dismay with the show's success. And while many posters emphasised the role of subjective interpretation in audience engagement with comedy, one prolific poster insisted that judging the quality of a comedy script was "not about personal taste":

> What i can't understand, and you haven't addressed this - is why I don't think it's well written and they do. We're both using the same critical standards and tools. One of us is wrong. You would say it was me – I of course would say it's them.

While my analysis throughout this chapter (and throughout the book) demonstrates that different viewers evaluate comedy in different ways, this post focused on aesthetics and critical discourse, rather than taste. The contributor argued that, within the industry ("they"), there is a shared system for evaluating comedy, but that it can be applied correctly or incorrectly. This desire for universally accepted rules of comedy indicated the frustration that comedy writers can experience as their affective labour does not just entail writing something they deem to be funny, but also negotiating a complex industry to get their work onto the screen. As Mills (2015) observed in his study of the British TV comedy industry, even established comedy writers spend most of their affective labour on projects that never actually get produced.

Conclusion

This chapter explores the circulation of discourses of sitcom within and across three online sites that each has a set of characteristics and a set of cultural conventions that encourage particular kinds of audience responses. The retail site Amazon.com positions viewers as individual consumer-reviewers and encourages them to assess the values of their purchase. The media and entertainment site has a large and very busy forum that invites users to discuss relevant topics, and the dialogue around *Miranda* focused on discussing users' personal responses to the show. The comedy site, on the other hand, favours critical analysis and discussion that demonstrates knowledge about comedy and the production of comedy. Across these different sites, I identified a focus on traditional sitcom. *Everybody Hates Chris* reviewers wanted a sitcom that they could enjoy together as a family. *Miranda* fans expressed delight at a multi-camera sitcom that foregrounds jokes and slapstick. And *Gavin & Stacey* anti-fans were frustrated that "classic" sitcoms were being reframed as "old-fashioned" and replaced by "narrative comedy". I don't wish to gloss over the many voices that articulated other preferences, but I think this resistance to current genre developments is noteworthy because it demonstrates a continued audience appetite for the pleasures offered by conventional sitcom. The next chapter continues this exploration of audience engagement with generic developments, and I will there expand on my discussion of the relationship between amateur and professional reviewers.

7 Reviewing Romcom
(500) Days of Summer on IMDb

Film and TV reviews have traditionally been the preserve of the cultural elite, represented by professional critics in print and broadcast media. When it comes to comedies, we expect reviewers to tell us what kind of comedy we're looking at, who's in it, and whether or not they found it funny. More recently, however, these critics have been joined by regular audience members who contribute reviews to websites like IMDb and Rotten Tomatoes, post comments underneath professional review articles, discuss films and programmes on message boards, and so on. This means that amateur critics now have the opportunity to contribute to public debates around comedy – about what they want from different comedic genres, about what kinds of performances they appreciate, about what it's okay to make fun of, and so on. I began to reflect on such amateur criticism in the previous chapter, and I will here develop that discussion further through a case study that examines IMDb user reviews of the 2009 romantic comedy *(500) Days of Summer*. At the time of writing, the film had been rated by 75,716 IMDb users and had an average score of 8.0 out of 10. This clearly suggests a favourable reception, but the 348 IMDb reviews also provide qualitative data that can offer insight into *how* the film has been evaluated.

The romantic comedy genre is very popular but critically rather maligned. Professional critics have often dismissed it either as formulaic, girly fluff or as reactionary fantasies peddling sexist ideologies (Abbot and Jermyn 2009: 3–4), but looking at amateur reviews can tell us something about why such films continue to draw crowds and what audiences get out of them. This chapter will draw on existing studies on the romantic comedy genre, including essays from collections edited by Evans and Deleyto (1998) and Abbot and Jermyn (2009), as well as analyses by Babington and Evans (1989), Jeffers McDonald (2007) and Rowe (1995). However, this area of literature is overwhelmingly dominated by analyses of romcom as text, and the chapter therefore also aims to contribute to the field by shifting attention onto audience responses. In particular, I examine what kinds of evaluation criteria the reviews applied, what elements of the film were singled out as important for the moviegoer's experience, and how the film was seen to fail for some reviewers.

I also consider the role of the amateur reviewer and the ways in which their outputs resemble or differ from those of professional critics. Importantly, I want to argue that although sites like IMDb may offer audience members the opportunity to voice an alternative discourse on film, the reviews tend to negotiate ideas that have already been established by professional critics. For example, enjoyment of *(500) Days of Summer* was often seen as an exception to the rule that romcoms have little value, rather than as evidence of the genre's ability to offer viewing pleasures.

(500) Days of Summer

Directed by Marc Webb for Fox Searchlight Pictures, *(500) Days of Summer* was promoted with the tagline "Boy meets girl. Boy falls in love. Girl doesn't". This presents the film as an unconventional romantic comedy in at least three ways: First, it suggests that these two characters will not actually end up together, which challenges the idea of the romcom couple as "meant to be". Second, it presents the possibility that audiences might not get the happy ending we usually expect from comedy. And finally, the tagline casts the boy, rather than the girl, in the role of yearning romantic, thereby challenging the traditional gender roles of heterosexual relationships. Within the film itself, a narrator proclaims: "This is not a love story", and we are then presented with protagonist Tom's (Joseph Gordon-Levitt) memories of his 500 days of being in love with Summer (Zooey Deschanel), a woman who claims that she does not believe in romantic relationships. The non-linear narrative starts with day 488 and then shifts forwards and backwards in time, showing both happy and miserable moments from this period in Tom's life. I chose *(500) Days of Summer* as a case study for this chapter because I thought that the way the film positions itself simultaneously within and against the romcom genre might encourage IMDb reviewers to articulate their perceptions of romcom conventions and of how these are negotiated in the film.

Researching Online Romcom Audiences

I chose to collect reviews from IMDb because it is one of the most well-known online resources for information on specific films, cast members and production personnel and because it had a high number of reviews of *(500) Days of Summer*. Of the 348 IMDb reviews posted at the time of data collection, I collected the first 50 reviews, which were posted between January 19, 2009 and August 5, 2009, and the last 50 reviews, which were posted between July 17, 2010 and May 17, 2011. My goal was not to compare findings across the two periods, but to capture a broad range of responses both from initial cinema audiences and subsequent DVD viewers. The reviews were then coded to identify different kinds of responses to the film, including emotional responses, pleasures and displeasures, evaluations of specific filmic devices, interpretations of the film's themes, and perceptions of its target audience. I contacted all reviewers quoted here in an attempt to seek informed consent to quote their posts. However, although I only received positive responses, many reviewers did not get back to me.

It is important to stress that this chapter clearly focuses on very specific film audiences. Most reviewers included in this particular sample were registered with a U.S. location, though it also includes contributions from IMDb users appearing to be from other countries, including Australia, Brazil, China, Egypt, Estonia and the U.K. Aside from demographic limitations, we also know that most viewers don't bother publishing reviews when they watch a film. Few users will even think of doing so, while others may be put off by the effort it requires: "First, users must register with IMDB. Second, IMDB requires at least 10 lines of comments to publish a review. Third, the user must read all the disclaimers regarding spoilers and spoiler warnings" (Jurca and Faltings 2007: 3). In addition to that, some reviewers may be more inclined to share their responses when they have really liked or really disliked something.

Romcom Viewers as Reviewers

I want to begin by looking at how the IMDb review process works. This site can be seen as part of a wider phenomenon of "online feedback forums", which have "become an important channel for *Word-of-mouth* regarding products, services or other types of commercial interactions" (Jurca and Faltings 2007: 1). However, in order to help users navigate through large numbers of reviews that may be of varying quality, sites tend to rank them in some way (Kim et al. 2006: 423). On IMDb, users are asked to "review the review". At the end of each review, the site asks readers: "Was the review useful to you?" We can tick "yes" or "no", and the results are then displayed alongside the reviews themselves: "271 of 371 people found this review helpful". Their default review display is in this order of perceived utility (labelled "Best"), although other options include "Chronological", "Prolific Authors", "Loved It" or "Hated It". Otterbacher (2011: 425) underlines that we don't know much about how participants choose which reviews they want to read, among the large numbers on offer. She suggests three potential reader strategies: Using utility rankings like the one on IMDb; choosing reviews that express views similar to those we already hold; and checking the reviewer's profile to see if our tastes are compatible.

At the time of writing, the highest ranking review of *(500) Days of Summer* was deemed "useful" by 317 out of 388 people. This score could indicate that the reviewer had a particularly high status in the IMDb review community, but he or she had actually only contributed three other IMDb reviews, none of which was highly ranked. So, while this particular review was clearly well received by other users, the high ranking probably had a lot to do with the fact that it was one of the very first reviews posted for this film. If it was deemed "useful" by a few users early on, and subsequent users displayed reviews in order of perceived utility, this particular review would have had the opportunity to keep being read and voted for by a large number of people.

Based on her investigation of how different kinds of user-generated reviews are displayed on Amazon, IMDb and Yelp, Otterbach (2011: 440) argues that "the prominently displayed reviews" in these communities "are written in a manner that one would expect of professionally produced content, while the least prominent reviews are those of a more amateur nature". Based on this, it seems that the adoption of a "professional" writing style is a useful strategy for writers who want to maximise the readership for their reviews. Within my sample, some IMDb reviews conformed quite closely to the conventions of traditional film reviews that are written by professional critics and published in newspapers and magazines. They included expected elements such as an eye-catching opening line, information about cast and crew, a brief synopsis that doesn't give too much away, and evaluations of script, performances and direction. This is an extract from one such review:

> Here is a rom-com with a number of differences, starting with the title. This Summer is not a season (even Los Angeles does not have that much sun) but a girl (the cute Zooey Deschanel) amorously pursued by Tom (talented Joseph Gordon-Levitt), both of whom work for a greeting cards company trading on triteness. The structure of the narrative is terribly post-modern in being non-chronological and the genre is subverted in not following the conventional formula. The final major novelty is a series of intersected cinematic flourishes such as - my favourites - an open-air dance sequence of triumph and a split screen depicting expectation and reality.

Using the established discourse of professional film critics could be seen as a strategy to invest reviews with a sense of expertise and authority. For example, this reviewer demonstrated an awareness of romcom conventions and postmodern narrative structures. This display of expertise was reinforced by a rather formal and detached writing style that presented the writer's value judgements as objective.

Some IMDb users will simply post the odd review, but others demonstrate greater investment in their film reviewer identities by producing large numbers of reviews and developing their own signature review styles. For example, some users adopted their own scoring systems, in addition to scoring each film on IMDb's own ten-point scale. In my sample, one user had produced 3769 reviews and developed his own tagline.

This was the conclusion to his *(500) Days of Summer* review: "Bob's[1] Evaluation—2 of 3: Has some interesting elements". "Bob's" user profile linked to an external website that described him as a "writer and consultant", while other *(500) Days of Summer* reviews also included links to external sites focusing on film or entertainment media more broadly. Beyond assessing individual films, then, such reviews clearly functioned to promote the status of the reviewer as a film commentator.

However, not all IMDb reviews follow the conventions and writing style of professional film critics. Crucially, many in this sample provide very detailed information about the plot. Whereas reviews found in newspapers and magazines will always avoid giving away a film's ending, IMDb reviews often reveal endings as well as major plot twists:

> PS: I don't like Summer. I like the story, but I do agree that Summer is cold and didn't care much for Tom's feelings. And I do agree that she got married very soon after she broke up with Tom.

Revelations like this one were often flagged up by the heading "*** This review may contain spoilers ***", which gives readers the option of avoiding that kind of information. However, although some audience members actively seek out spoilers (e.g. Gray and Mittell 2007, Caldwell 1999), these clearly labelled spoiler reviews would necessarily exclude any reader who preferred the opportunity to be surprised by the film. Therefore, rather than offering readers a basis for deciding whether they want to see the film, spoiler reviews might function more as a way for the reviewer to contribute to critical debates around the film.

The IMDb review section also includes spoiler reviews that have *not* been labelled as such. The following extract is from a review that did not give readers any warning that they are about to find out whether Tom and Summer will end up together:

> I always wasn't too keen on the solution of the movie and the way Tom passed on to Autumn. The whole sequence felt a bit stale - as if the scriptwriter got hit by a deadline and quickly pasted on the first ending that came to mind.

While the promotion of *(500) Days of Summer* certainly suggests that the film challenges the romcom formula, new viewers may well still want to experience "the details of the journey" (Stilwell 2009: 27) and wonder if the couple will overcome the challenges "thrown in their way", so that "romance triumphs in the end" (Harbidge 2009: 179). Such moviegoers may therefore avoid reading IMDb reviews before seeing a film, which could clearly limit the overall readership for the site's review section.

However, the user reviews can also be seen as a facility where audiences can continue to engage with films *after* the viewing experience has ended. For example, some reviews commented on opinions expressed in other reviews, as seen in the following extracts from three different users:

> Some reviewers claim this movie is refreshing for a romantic comedy and I have to agree and will help notice the little things in relationships as well.

> A lot of people have commented that this movie is fresh, charming, delightful… well I don't see much of those characteristics.

> Man, who's rating these movies?

So, beyond storing an extensive supply of user-generated recommendations and warnings, the IMDb review section offers a way for audience members to extend their engagement with a film they have already seen. By posting or reading reviews, they can share their pleasurable experiences, frustrations and disappointments with fellow viewers.

The second key way in which some IMDb reviews diverged from established film review conventions is in terms of writing style. In particular, some reviews abandoned any pretence of detachment and objectivity, as seen in the following extract from a review that gave *(500) Days of Summer* 3/10:

> If you want a romantic movie, to watch with your partner and have fun, and feel warm and happy at the end (and then proceed with your OWN romance.. is not that the goal of romantic movies?..).. SKIP THIS ONE!..

Reviews like this adopted a personal tone and focused on articulating subjective, emotional responses to the film. As seen here, emotive language, block capitals and exclamation marks are also sometimes used for emphasis in such responses. Only 1 out of 2 IMDb users rated this review as "useful". Discussing the potential impact of spelling and grammatical errors on the perceived credibility of reviews, Otterbacher (2011: 430) argues that poor writing can "devalue" a user review. However, she also underlines the tendency of many online users to adopt a writing style that is closer to speech, and to use "unconventional symbolic representations to substitute for richer clues such as body language" in order to "enhance communication". As such, more prominent reviews may not necessarily use more conventional language, and my sample demonstrated that different approaches to writing and editing were evident among both the "best" and "worst" reviews.

The disappointment expressed in the review cited above could, in some ways, also been seen as specific to reviews of romantic films. The viewer wanted to experience the affects of romance, and the film clearly failed to fulfil that expectation. In contrast, other contributors enthused about their emotional investment in the relationship between Tom and Summer. This review gave the film a score of 9/10:

> We really fall in love with Tom and feel so much sympathy for him during all of the tragic bouts of his relationship with Summer. The film opens with Summer breaking up with him, then the rest jumps around in their relationship. It is all told ingeniously and with the perfect amount of organization to the development of the story that it is able to elicit the maximum amount of sympathy and passion out of the audience.

As Sutton (2009: 45) notes, the romantic film text "provides the spectator with a *mise-en-scène* that 'ravishes' him or her, which provokes his or her loving desire, provokes an active, performative engagement with the film". The reviewer here celebrated the film's success in eliciting a sense of passion and a sense of being in love. Abbot and Jermyn (2009: 2) identify this affective response as a key factor in "[t]he low critical esteem that typically meets the rom-com in contemporary cinema", arguing that "romantic fiction generally is thought to be essentially calculating in its execution, cynically manipulating an emotional and sentimental response from the viewer".

I think what is interesting here, then, is that the IMDb reviews I have looked at demonstrated the circulation of an amateur review discourse that drew heavily on that associated with professional film critics, *alongside* a different critical discourse that celebrated the affective responses that are encouraged by romcoms and derided by critics. The rest of this chapter explores such responses in more detail by outlining how reviews could be seen to assess *(500) Days of Summer* against four key criteria: Authenticity, emotional impact, funniness and originality.

Authenticity

Much academic work on the romcom genre has examined the extent to which such films offer ideologically progressive or conservative representations of gender and sexuality (e.g. Kendall 1990, Lent 1995, del Rio 1998). As McCabe (2009: 163–64) argues: "Nothing quite troubles post-feminist scholarship more than our continued cultural investment in the scripted fantasy of heterosexual romance conditioning our desires, our fantasies, our expectations of finding *the* one, our need to be undone by love". The idea of romantic love is of course central to the "rom" part of the romcom genre, and while the narrator in *(500) Days of Summer* proclaims that "this is not a love story", perceptions of how the film portrays romantic love tended to frame IMDb discussions of its themes, characters, performances and overall cultural value.

Reviewers interpreted the key theme in *(500) Days of Summer* in different ways, as seen in the following extracts from two different reviews:

> This movie is about A relationship, A great love of your life but not THE ONE TRUE love of your life that you end up being with. In real life, we will all meet and fall in love most likely with more than one person in our lifetime ... The beauty of love isn't that it MIGHT last forever because sadly it doesn't always happen. The beauty of love is that it happens AT ALL.

> Tom holds movies, songs, and even greeting cards responsible for preventing people from saying what they really feel and for the corruption of emotions, causing them (especially love) to be completely indefinable. It's a fantasy that can only be recognized by or compared to peers who believe they've attained it. During his evolving perception of love, we see a spectrum as diverse as the special effects and soundtrack that compliment the imagery.[2]

However, although reviews offered diverging views on *why* Tom and Summer's romance fails, they still tended to valorise the film's portrayal of the "highs and lows" of relationships, heartbreak and the process of learning from relationships. These representations were inscribed as important, whether the reviewers suggested that Summer "learns what true love is" or, more frequently, that Tom learns to accept "that the one woman in his life may not be the right one". Such readings clearly differed from those associated with more traditional romcoms, such as *You've Got Mail* (1998) or *While You Were Sleeping* (1995):

> Like any genre, the rom-com relies on a basic formula and reiterates expected narrative and ideological elements. Thus, most commonly, two people meet, various obstacles are thrown in their way, yet romance triumphs in the end and the genre is seen finally to celebrate the sanctity of the couple.
>
> (Harbidge 2009: 179)

However, rather than seeing *(500) Days of Summer* as a complete departure from this premise, I would argue that it negotiates ongoing developments in romcom conventions. For example, it can be seen to draw on discourses around gender relations, romance and sexuality that have been articulated in a number of previous romcoms. In particular, the focus on heartbreak, rather than a successful relationship, can be traced back to the so-called "radical" romcoms of the 1970s (e.g. *Annie Hall*, 1977, *Starting Over*, 1979), which explored the "transience" of love (Jeffers McDonald 2009: 150). Some IMDb reviewers described this portrayal of heartbreak as "insightful", suggesting that audiences could learn from the characters' experiences:

What undoubtedly ends up making this picture so brilliant is how relatable it is to its victims and victimizers a like. When all is said and done, there is most definitely a lesson to be learned by Tom's experiences ... In the end nothing lasts forever, relationships begin, relationships end. Try to be thankful for all the people that broke your heart, they more than likely helped you find yourself in the process...especially you, Summer... bitch.

This idea of the film as "intelligent" and "insightful" was often linked to notions of verisimilitude, with a large number of reviews describing the film as "realistic", "authentic", "genuine" and "true". These are examples from two different reviews:

I'm 60, so I've had some experiences and seen some movies, and I think that this is the first film (that my old brain still remembers) to truly depict what it feels like to be in love, particularly when the feelings are unequal! Despite the humor of many scenes, the emotions expressed were very realistic. The scene with the dancing, etc., in the park? Yes, that IS what it feels like!

But this romantic comedy actually has a realistic beat to it. Not that fairy tale happily ever Hollywood crap. Like this movie was about a REAL relationship. It's about heartbreak and coping with it, with kind of a dark sort of comedy feel to it.

However, the film's mediation of "reality" was a topic of some debate. First, the emphasis on the "everyday" was precisely the reason the film was seen to fail for one reviewer:

The movie was really disappointing, what depicts reflects real life, every day stuff, but let's be honest ... if you go with your girlfriend to the cinema with the promise of a romantic movie, you'll feel robbed with this movie!

Romcoms are often associated with an "air of fantasy and detachment" (Babington and Evans 1989: 6), as seen in films like *Pretty Woman* (1990), *Maid in Manhattan* (2002) and *While You Were Sleeping* (1995). For this reviewer, this modality of romantic fantasy was clearly more desirable than representations of mundane "reality", and *(500) Days of Summer* failed to provide the expected viewing experience.

In contrast, a small number of reviews complained that the film *lacked* verisimilitude, describing it as "overwritten", "contrived" and "calculated":

Hmmm ... Hard to imagine so many people were taken in by this over-calculated, over-worked and relatively minor film ... I like chick-flicks immensely, but there really seemed little meaningful content with a lot of stilted dialog and characters.

Such reviews also dismissed the idea that the film offers any valuable insight, describing it as "cod philosophy", as having "no substance", and as being "a fluffy romantic comedy". These dismissive reviews all located the film's failure in that it is trying "too hard" to be "original" or "cool and kooky". This response can perhaps be seen as a rejection of increased self-awareness in the romcom genre (e.g. Stilwell 2009: 28, Harbidge 2009: 178), which I will return to later on in this chapter. For now, I would like to emphasise the centrality of debates around verisimilitude and authenticity in these reviews: While many reviewers valued the perceived "sincerity" of the film's portrayal of romance and heartbreak, some identified pretence as the film's main shortcoming. In any case, a sense of authenticity appeared to be a key criterion in audience evaluations of this particular romcom.

Being "Swept Away"

In addition to discussions of the film's verisimilitude and its potential for teaching viewers about romantic relationships, a recurring focus across the reviews was the emotional impact of following this "roller coaster romance". Some described the experience of "rooting for" Tom, of wanting Summer "to *see* love in Tom", of falling in love with the characters, and of finding the film "brutally heartbreaking". This is what Babington and Evans (1989: 5) call "the pain of romantic comedy". As Sutton (2009: 45) argues in his discussion of love in romcoms, such films actively seek "a direct, affective relation with the spectator", and this sense of experiencing romance was identified as a key source of pleasure in many reviews. *(500) Days of Summer* was seen to facilitate this experience in various ways, but reviews tended to connect it to the film's "likeable" and "interesting" characters, its convincing performances, and the "chemistry" between Joseph Gordon-Levitt as Tom and Zooey Deschanel as Summer. The following examples are extracts from two different reviews:

> Zooey Deschnael and Joseph Gordon-Levitt were both incredible, the latter particularly. He was sweet and charming, and it was easy to be swept up into his world.

> Joseph truly deserves an Academy Award for literally placing us, the viewer right into his shoes......every height of ecstasy he feels when he interprets a kiss from Summer or a sweet and touching hand holding session as a declaration of love (sadly reading more into it than is actually there) to every agonizing low he feels when Summer leaves/breaks up with him.

However, a far smaller number of reviews saw *(500) Days of Summer* as failing to offer this desired emotional response:

The two leads do maintain some kind of chemistry, but it's told to us from the very beginning that this is not a love story, so there's no reason to get caught up in their romance ... Basically, it relies on melodrama (music set to action) to elicit some kind of emotional response, and a lot of it is repetitive. As far as charming or delightful go, this is a break up movie. It's depressing more than anything.

These diverging views demonstrate that, while the wider critical reception of romcoms has derided the genre's perceived manipulation of emotional responses from its audience members (Abbot and Jermyn 2009: 2), such responses tended to be valorised by the IMDb reviewers. They disagreed over whether the film's focus on a failing relationship actually *succeeded* in offering them a pleasurable viewing experience, but the feeling of being invested in the romance was a second key criterion in their evaluation of this romcom.

Comedy

A third recurring criterion was the film's perceived comedic value. The majority of the sampled reviews described the film as "funny" or "witty", although few provided much further detail about what the reviewer had found funny about it. This might suggest that the film was seen to lack clearly signalled comedic moments, such as jokes, instead relying more on humour as "a general tone, pervading all parts of a text, and existing even when nothing specifically funny is taking place" (Mills 2005: 16). For example, some reviews explicitly constructed the humour as "subtle" or contrasted it with "laugh out loud" comedy:

Now this is a very original romantic comedy, sure it isn't a laugh out loud movie but the story and everything else is so well done I couldn't careless.

It's not a full-on laugh out loud affair, but it doesn't need to be. We already have the characters, and their non-linear track of things as they come, and the filmmakers go for an approach to heighten whatever moods are on display.

Others constructed the film as "charming", "endearing" or "cute", rather than funny. This lack of emphasis on humour might indicate that many reviewers privileged the "rom" over the "com" in this film and perhaps also suggests that *(500) Days of Summer* retains the "emphasis on the importance of tears" associated with "post-classical" romcom (Jeffers McDonald 2007: 85). In contrast, romcoms like *Bridget Jones's Diary* (2001), *Juno* (2007) or *Knocked Up* (2007) place far more emphasis on comedic elements.

However, the marginalisation of comedic modalities can also be seen in much academic literature on this hybrid genre. Important exceptions include Babington and Evans (1989), Deleyto (1998), Jeffers McDonald (2009), Redmond (2009) and Rowe (1995), but analyses of romcom tend to pay little attention to how comedic elements contribute to the films' meanings and pleasures. As Abbot and Jermyn (2009: 2) note, there is a cultural assumption that "eliciting laughs from the audience is antithetical to 'serious' reflection". Both romantic and comedic texts are often culturally devalued, and romcoms therefore face critical dismissal both as lightweight chick flicks and as frivolous and anti-intellectual comedies. However, romance has been brought onto the academic agenda through a feminist concern with exploring texts targeting female audiences, and this has perhaps led to a privileging of discussions of more "serious" issues around gender and sexuality in romcom.

Nevertheless, across the sampled IMDb reviews, there were reviews that described *(500) Days of Summer* as "hilarious", rather than as having "subtle" humour, while some foregrounded its comedic modality by identifying specific elements that they found funny:

> There are funny moments here too, even in the frequent brooding. On a date with a new girl there is ex-embellishing followed by drunken karaoke that is so horribly real you have to laugh.

> At one point, we break into an extremely lively and hilarious musical number full of marching bands and a little animated bluebird tweeting precociously. At another point, we are thrust out of the story and directly into the offices of a record company where business executives try to figure out why there was a huge spike in sales of the Belle And Sebastian CD The Boy With The Arab Strap in northern Michigan. Trust me, in context, it is quite funny.

Reviews often described the humorous tone of this film as "quirky", "offbeat", "whimsical" or "dark". In many cases, these elements were constructed as enjoyable, and reviewers used these labels to position the film in opposition to "mainstream" romcom. In his discussion of audience responses to films that are characterised as "off-beat", Barker (2008) argues that this is "a vernacular label: temporary, unstable, seeking to include films providing the right kind of challenge and sense of belonging to a wished-for interpretive community". Drawing on this idea, I would argue that IMDb reviews used terms like "quirky" and "off-beat" to position themselves against viewers of conventional or "mainstream" romcom. The next section will explore this idea in more detail.

Originality

The low cultural status of the romcom genre was highlighted by the large number of reviews emphasising that *(500) Days of Summer* is not a typical romcom, and by statements such as these:

I am not into the typical romance film genre but this film delivers a
common theme in such a intelligent and cleaver way that leaves you
wanting to see it over and over again.

I was pretty reluctant to see this movie, but I had a free pass (for an
advanced screening of it) so I went. I expected a cheesy chick-flick
love story. It was a sort of love story, but I'm thrilled I saw it.

So, although this film was often seen to offer pleasures associated with the
romcom genre, including laughs and a powerful emotional investment in
the depicted romance, many reviews seemed intent on "rescuing" *(500)
Days of Summer* from this devalued genre. The second extract highlighted that romcom films are commonly dismissed as "chick flicks",
which "are frequently critically constructed as inherently trite or lightweight" (Abbot and Jermyn 2009: 2). Earlier in this chapter I examined
review discussions around the ability of *(500) Days of Summer* to offer
valuable insights into romantic relationships, and this debate could now
be seen to map onto the question of whether this film belongs to the
category of lightweight chick flick. Importantly, however, only two reviewers explicitly dismissed the film as such, while five maintained that
it would appeal to both men and women, and two argued that it was
primarily a film for *male* audiences.

Considering that the romcom audience is generally assumed "to be predominantly female" (Abbot and Jermyn 2009: 2), the question of the film's
gendered appeal received surprisingly little attention in the sampled reviews. This may well be because *(500) Days of Summer* focuses primarily
on the male protagonist, rather than on the couple. This narrative strategy
can also be seen in romcoms like *Four Weddings and a Funeral* (1994),
Swingers (1996) and *Forgetting Sarah Marshall* (2008). Jeffers McDonald
(2007: 109) terms such films "hommecom" and argues that they frequently
focus on gender role reversals and "set out to prove the male hero can be
as sensitive, as heartsick and desperate for love as the female". The IMDb
reviews also identified those themes in *(500) Days of Summer*:

> We have the great and charismatic Joseph Gordon-Levitt who plays
> 'Tom' (3rd Rock from the Sun, Brick, INCEPTION) who wholly
> represents the hopefully romantic and perhaps foolish romantic who
> wants that one great person in his life … His yin to his coherent
> yang is Zoe Deschanel's character 'Summer' who has an aura of
> melancholy and nostalgia of previous non-standing relationship sur-
> rounding her, whilst JGL's character tries affectionately to break her
> hard-shell prejudices of there being "no such thing as love".

> Summer is the 'dude,' looking for casual, no-pressure romance,
> taking the role of the stereotypical, uncaring guy and not the
> relationship-demanding, over-affectionate girl.[3]

This gender role reversal can be seen as one way in which this film challenges the romcom's reputation for being "slavishly formulaic, adhering to well-worn and obvious conventions (boy meets girl; boy and girl face obstacles to their romantic union; boy and girl conquer obstacles to find true love)" (Abbot and Jermyn 2009: 2). The extent to which *(500) Days of Summer* challenges or adheres to established romcom conventions was a hot topic in the IMDb review section, which demonstrated that "originality" was a fourth key criterion in evaluations of this film.

A large number of reviews constructed it as "fresh", "innovative", "creative" or "surprising", focusing particularly on its depiction of an unsuccessful relationship and its use of various stylistic devices. Reviews most frequently highlighted the film's non-linear narrative, but some mentioned a scene that looks like a musical or a scene that uses a split screen to contrast Tom's expectations with the realities of his meeting with Summer after their breakup. These examples are from two different reviews:

> The plot was interesting, original and unpredictable (Completely opposed to the bland and formulaic romantic comedies that appear every year)

> The originality and creativity present in this movie is, honestly, the best thing about it. It's just so damn easy to fall in love with it. The setup of time passing, the cinematography, the inventive narration, hell, even the after-sex dance party in the streets were simply phenomenal.

In contrast, a much smaller number of reviews dismissed the idea of this film as innovative, instead describing it as "formulaic", "predictable" and "dull". When elaborating on these descriptions, however, reviews tended *not* to construct *(500) Days of Summer* as a "mainstream" romcom, but instead argued that it was following the conventions of indie movies:

> Remember when independent films were really independent? 500 Days Of Summer is so dull and Sundance friendly that I felt angry leaving the theater. What really made me nuts was reading after that the creators of the film actually thought they were making some kind of radical romantic comedy.

As a Fox Searchlight Pictures production, *(500) Days of Summer* is clearly the product of an international media corporation, rather than a financially independent production. However, as Stilwell (2009: 26–27) points out: "Indie music, like indie film, began as a financial definition but became a genre determined more by style and attitude", and "many major film companies now have their indie arm" designed to target audiences that oppose "mainstream" Hollywood movies. Earlier in this chapter, I mentioned that some reviews accused the film of trying "too hard" to be "cool". These criticisms can be seen as part of a wider discourse that addressed a perceived tension between subcultural opposition and "artistic authenticity" (Thornton 1995: 30) on the one hand and corporate marketing strategies on the other.

Conclusion

Analysing 100 IMDb reviews of *(500) Days of Summer*, this chapter has examined how these audience members adopted the role of film reviewer, highlighting ways in which different reviews could be seen to follow or break with the established discourse of critical film reception. Arguing that the use of such a "professional" tone could be seen as a strategy to invest the review with a sense of "authority", the analysis also contrasted this approach with reviews that foregrounded subjective audience experiences of the emotional responses encouraged by the romcom genre. I have begun to reflect on how these different review styles might be received by other IMDb users, but I don't think we know enough about how audience members make use of such review sites to plan future viewings or extend their engagement with films that they have already seen. There is a lot of scope for further research here.

My analysis of the IMDb reviews also aimed to shed some light on how audience members evaluate romcom in terms of form and content. The discussion identified four key evaluation criteria. The first was the perceived "authenticity" of the romantic relationship portrayed in the film, and the interpretation of the characters' experiences as "real". The second criterion was the experience of a powerful emotional investment in Tom and Summer's romance, which challenged the cultural devaluing of such affective responses. Moreover, the evidence that such enjoyment can be gained from a film about a breakup also shows the potential for narrative pleasures outside of those associated with the conventional romcom plot:

> Part of the joy for the audience is knowing that no matter the contrivances of the plot, the couple will end up together at the end. Occasional plots that cast at least some doubt on which characters will end up together, like those of *Sabrina* (1954) or *While You Were Sleeping* (1995), are rare. The pleasure is in the details of the journey, just as it is in the details of a conventionally structured 32-bar pop song or its verse–chorus descendants.
>
> (Stilwell 2009: 27)

The third evaluation criterion I identified was the film's ability to offer comedic pleasures, and my analysis highlighted that readings variously described the film as "hilarious" and "subtly" humorous. However, the comedic modality tended to be marginalised by an emphasis on romance. Noting that this pattern can also be seen in much academic analysis of romcom, I stressed the need for further studies focusing on the role of *comedy* in this hybrid genre. The fourth evaluation criterion was the requirement for originality, and although the majority of reviews constructed *(500) Days of Summer* as "fresh" or "innovative" in terms of its non-linear narrative and its ending, some dismissed the film as a "calculated" attempt at targeting indie audiences.

As my discussion has suggested, then, the reviews could frequently be seen to "rescue" this film from the devalued romcom genre through their articulation and negotiation of evaluation criteria and through the repeated claim that "this is not a typical romcom". In that sense, while sites like IMDb offer audience members the opportunity to act as film reviewers, their evaluations can be seen to continue to orient themselves in relation to ideas established by pre-existing critical discourse. This chapter has concluded my three-part investigation into the significance of genre for online audience responses to screen comedy. I will now move on to an analysis of how viewers engage with transgressive comedy.

Notes

1 The username has been changed.
2 The Massie Twins (GoneWithTheTwins.com).
3 The Massie Twins (GoneWithTheTwins.com).

8 Comedy and Transgression
Pinning Amy Schumer

Public debates around film and TV comedy often focus on content that is identified as transgressive, with opposing sides defending the right to free speech or calling for regulation. Such concerns tend to focus on two key issues. The first is the argument that a comedic representation is offensive because it is "kicking down" within social hierarchies. It might stereotype minority groups, for example, or humiliate those who are considered vulnerable, reinforcing their marginalisation in society. Complaints about such content usually draw on discourses around identity politics, prejudice, oppression and "political correctness". The second issue focuses on language or imagery that is deemed offensive because it is in "bad taste". This includes blasphemy, obscene language, and "gross" images, often featuring bodily functions. In both of these cases, debates revolve around who or what audiences are invited to laugh at, what it is acceptable to joke about, and to what extent humour provides a license to go beyond established cultural norms. Within academic humour and comedy studies, a key way that scholarship has engaged with such debates is by exploring the progressive or conservative potential of comedic transgression, particularly in relation to race (e.g. Malik 2010) and gender (e.g. Rowe 1995).

In this chapter, I want to contribute to this body of work by exploring the reception of transgressive comedy through a case study of Amy Schumer paratexts on the social bookmarking site Pinterest. Schumer's comedy has frequently been identified as transgressive in popular media, where she has been criticised for telling jokes that "provide a safe vehicle to share stereotypes, release inhibitions and spread racism" (e.g. Patton and Leonard 2015), but also lauded for presenting an "eviscerating takedown of patriarchal self-importance and beauty standards" (Gennis 2015). We can also see women's stand-up comedy as transgressive in itself, since this cultural form "is interpreted as an assertive, if not aggressive, mode of performance" (Pelle 2010: 28) that requires women "to make a spectacle out of" (Russo 1994: 53) themselves. My analysis approaches this case study by examining how the "pinning" of material by and about Schumer privileges particular readings of her as a (white, female) comedian-celebrity and how this practice forms part of

Pinterest's "training ground for self-representation" (Andò 2015: 227). The case study builds on my previous discussion of women in Hollywood comedy (chapter 3) and draws on Mizejewski's (2014) argument that "women's comedy has become a space where feminist topics emerge" (11) across stand-up, sitcoms, film and the debates around those texts.

Contextualising my analysis within literature on Pinterest and the "unruly woman" (Rowe 1995), I will argue that this online space facilitated an affective repertoire that inscribed Schumer as desirable, inspirational and funny. She was frequently positioned within a feminine project of self-development, where her celebrity-comedian text offered a set of symbolic resources for female Pinterest users. This project focused on two contrasting goals: The first goal was to improve one's female body by appropriating beauty and style products worn by Schumer in celebrity imagery. The second, more prominent, goal was to valorise one's embodied self and claim agency within a patriarchal society, inspired by Schumer's utterances. Reflecting on the ambiguity of Schumer's comedian-celebrity text, my analysis will also problematise the gendered discourse of self-improvement, drawing attention to its "regulative dimensions", which draw "new lines and demarcations ... between those subjects who are judged responsive to the regime of personal responsibility, and those who fail miserably" (McRobbie 2004: 261). Finally, I will discuss this Pinterest use as a practice of "ordinary fandom" (Sandvoss and Kearns 2016), reflecting on how it differs from the creative and textually productive fandoms that have been the key focus of fan studies. The lack of attention given to comedy fandom within this field might be a result of a desire to valorise fans as unique audiences by focusing on the intensities of cult fandom and the creative activities of some fans, and I will argue that Sandvoss and Kearns' emphasis on everydayness and emotional attachment offers a useful way into thinking about both celebrity fandom and comedy fandom.

Transgressive Femininities in Comedy

Rowe's (1995) work on "the unruly woman" remains a key text in the vibrant body of academic work on transgressive femininities in comedy. Her study draws on Bakthin's (1968) idea of the carnivalesque (which I outlined in chapter 1) and the studies of feminist critics who have identified gendered gaps in his account of the carnival. Importantly, Rowe's (1995) investigation is informed by Russo's (1988) essay "Female Grotesques: Carnival and Theory", which notes the significance of laughing, "senile, pregnant hags" in Bakhtin's account of the grotesque, and goes on to explore "the meaning of their laughter" (Rowe 1995: 2). Continuing this investigation into "female spectacle making" (2), Rowe explores "the power of female grotesques and female laughter to challenge the social and symbolic systems that would keep women in their place" (3).

These connections among laughter, power, gender conventions and the female body remain a focal point in recent scholarship, most notably in Mizejewski's (2014) book *Pretty/Funny: Women Comedians and Body Politics.* Presenting case studies of female comedians Kathy Griffin, Tina Fey, Sara Silverman, Margaret Cho, Wanda Sykes and Ellen DeGeneres, she argues:

> [I]n the historic binary of "pretty" versus "funny", women comics, no matter what they look like, have been located in opposition to "pretty", enabling them to engage in a transgressive comedy grounded in the female body – its looks, its race and sexuality, and its relationships to ideal versions of femininity. In this strand of comedy, "pretty" is the topic and target, the ideal that is exposed as funny."
>
> (Mizejewski 2014: 5)

The comedic exploitation of ideal femininities is also a central concern in existing work on Amy Schumer. Foy (2015) analyses how Schumer's stand-up comedy incorporates "sexually transgressive" (707) material while "maintaining an alliance with the audience" by "dismantling or appropriating the male gaze" (712). This, Foy argues, enables the comedian "to harness the power of sexually subversive humor and to negotiate the discomfort it can produce" (703). Goltz (2015) offers a reading of Schumer's "ironic performativity" of multiple white femininities at the *Comedy Central Roast of Charlie Sheen* in 2011, focusing on her "disruption of sexism" and her "doing" of racisms (277). He emphasises the ambiguity of ironic performativity and the requirement "that we, as audience, accept and examine our roles, our commitments, and our complicities" (283) through our engagement with her comedy. I share Foy and Goltz's interest in examining the active role that Schumer's audiences play in the production of meaning, and I here want to shift attention to the paratextual dialogue that extends our engagement with Schumer beyond the moments of her performances. Drawing on this body of work on female grotesques, the unruly woman and women in contemporary comedy, I want to explore how Schumer's transgressive and ambiguous comedian-celebrity text is positioned on Pinterest and how that positioning might be seen to negotiate patriarchal conventions of gender.

Pinterest

Pinterest was launched in 2010. According to a study by Duggan (2015), it is used by about 31% of online U.S. adults. U.S. Pinterest users are far more likely to be women than men (44% of female Internet users versus 16% of male Internet users), they tend to be under 50 years old, and they are relatively evenly spread across the categories "white, non-Hispanic", "black, non-Hispanic" and "Hispanic" (11). The site is based on the concept of a pin board or a scrapbook. Users "pin" images they find online and organise them into labelled collections called "boards". The website invites us to "save creative ideas from around the web" and to "find and save recipes, parenting hacks, style inspiration and other ideas to try" (Pinterest). Gilbert *et al.* (2013) have noted that this "focus on 'things' has made Pinterest of great interest to online retailers and marketers" (2427), and their quantitative study revealed that the most frequently used verbs on the platform were "'use', 'look', 'want', and 'need'" (2435). A qualitative study of Pinterest users by Linder *et al.* (2014) found that their participants "use[d] boards to express interests and motivate personal change", while their repeated engagement with the pins of other users worked as "tacit social proof, making new goals and personally untested ideas appear achievable" (6). We might usefully think of this as an example of "digital DIY identity work" (Kanai 2015: 2) that is public, yet solitary. Although Pinterest now allows users to have secret boards, most remain public. And although it enables users to comment on pins and (since 2014) message each other, the study by Linder *et al.* (2014) indicated that users perceived "other social media, such as Facebook, as spaces for conversation", while Pinterest was seen "as a solitary space for collecting ideas" (5).

As an online culture, then, Pinterest privileges connections among femininity, creativity, self-improvement and consumption. Within this context, how do its users inscribe Amy Schumer with meanings through their pins? Using the site tools, I collected my data by re-pinning the 100 most popular pins tagged "Amy Schumer" on my own "Schumer" board (where, predictably, it sat alongside boards called "winter garden", "bikes" and "kids party") and coding content by adding comments into my pins. As in my discussion of *Parks and Recreation* fandom on Tumblr (chapter 2), I am here interested in thinking about these paratexts as part of a wider comedy quotation culture and in exploring how such quotations contribute to the formation of the "popular memory" of comedy and comedians. In his study of the online quotation culture around *Pulp Fiction* (1994), Newman (2014) argues that some elements are quoted frequently "in part because of the ways they express particular sensibilities that mesh with ideological constructions of identity", while other elements might remain "unquoted" because they are "too troubling to remember" (16). In my sample, critiques that accuse Schumer of racism remained invisible, for example, while a less troubling accusation of plagiarism was included. I will now explore some of the key ways in which Amy Schumer's comedian-celebrity text was inscribed within the affective economy of Pinterest.

Inspirational Amy Schumer

The majority of pins in my sample circulated celebrity news and interviews, which privileged Schumer's celebrity identity over her comedian identity. On a platform that foregrounds images, Schumer's celebrity-comedian text became a mosaic dominated by photographs from magazine shoots, talk show appearances, red carpets and paparazzi shots. This highlights that Schumer conforms to ideals for postfeminist celebrities in important ways: She is white, blond and pretty, and she wears make up and fashionable, sexy outfits. Moreover, even when these images were attached to longer articles focusing on Schumer's work, they tended to be pinned to boards focusing on fashion and beauty. This practice ignores Schumer's transgressive comedy, which challenges "the cultural identification of women with their bodies" (Mizejewski 2014: 92), and repositions her as a symbolic resource in a feminine project of self-improvement through culturally sanctioned consumption. This can be seen as part of a wider pattern in the media coverage of women in comedy, as illustrated by Tina Fey's frustration with answering interview questions about "her diet and skin-care regime" (Lauzen 2014: 108) and the hiring of Ellen DeGeneres as the face of Cover Girl Cosmetics (Mizejewski 2014).

However, these celebrity images were not the most popular pins in my sample, as indicated by re-pinning frequency. Those were instead found among the 46 pins that foregrounded verbal quotations from Schumer's comedy, speeches or interviews. The quotes were often valorised as inspirational, either through their presentation or through user comments on pins. For example, some were presented as motivational posters, with words superimposed over images of nature or combined with photographs of Schumer. One image featured a close-up of Schumer against a grey background, with these words in white letters, superimposed on the bottom part of the photograph:

I say if I'm beautiful. I say if
I'm strong. You will not
determine my story – I will.
—Amy Schumer

The image is not taken from the moment when Schumer made this utterance, which works to sever the statement from its original context, including what she said before and afterwards, to whom she said it, and how she said it. Instead, the poster works to isolate the quotation from the rest of Schumer's output and celebrity persona and suggests an intimate connection between the utterance and her "authentic" self, as represented by the close-up photograph. Schumer is softly lit, and she is looking thoughtfully into the camera with a very slight smile, her head supported by her right hand and her wrist turned towards us. The image is cropped to focus on her face, with its white skin, made-up, blue eyes and pink lips, and on her long, wavy blond hair. The image inscribes Schumer with calm, white, feminine authority and her words with significance. By re-pinning the quote, Pinterest users are able to appropriate Schumer's direct address to those who police patriarchal gender norms.

Unlike the ironic performativity associated with Schumer's stand-up (Goltz 2015), the "I say …" quote adopts seriousness as a discursive strategy and presents an unambiguous argument. The image presents Schumer as pretty and serious, rather than amusing, which function as markers of a stronger modality. This is not a representation of the unruly woman as grotesque, with her excessive body and her "voracious and shrewish female mouth" (Rowe 1995: 37). Yet neither does it comply with Bakhtin's (1968) notion of the classic body that is "entirely finished, completed, strictly limited" with no "signs of its inner life" (320). Schumer's body is in development, and it has a "story". The quote evokes the contested meanings of that body and the multiplicity of its possible stories while simultaneously claiming Schumer's ultimate right to choose those meanings. In particular, it is concerned with her right to inscribe herself with beauty, which is crucial to ideal femininity, and with strength, which is associated with ideal masculinity. In doing so, the quote confronts patriarchal ideology, claiming that, from a space of white celebrity privilege, Schumer can reject its authority.

This image had been pinned by Notey.com, a platform that curates blogs and publications on specific topics, encouraging users to "Search. Discover. Share." Clicking on "Read it" in my pin takes me to Notey, which shares the article "10 Amy Schumer quotes that prove how awesome she really is" (Hansen 2015) from HelloGiggles. This second site, co-founded by comedian Zooey Deschanel in 2011, describes itself as "a positive online community for women (although men are always welcome!) covering the latest in culture, female empowerment, style, relationships, friendship, careers, and issues that matter most to young women's lives" (hellogiggles.com). Starting with an introductory overview of Schumer's career development as a comedian, the article then shares the list of quotes. The image from Pinterest is not included here (instead, the article uses another softly lit close-up of Schumer looking thoughtfully into the camera with a very slight smile), but when I click on the "I say …" quote, I am taken to vulture.com, where I can read the full transcript of Schumer's "intense, inspirational speech" to the Gloria Awards and Gala, which was hosted by the Ms. Foundation for Women (Vineyard 2014). This speech, along with Deschanel's website (and Poehler's Smart Girls initiative, which I discuss in chapter 2), illustrates the labour that female comedians undertake outside of stand-up, films and TV shows. For example, many have written books, like Mindy Kaling's (2011) *Is Everybody Hanging out without Me?* and Schumer's (2016) *The Girl with the Lower Back Tattoo*, while Fey and Poehler have hosted the Golden Globe Awards three times, and Lena Dunham runs her feminist newsletter *Lenny* with Jenni Konner. This diversity of outlets enables female comedians to shift between humorous and serious discourse, engaging with their audiences and with cultural debates in complex ways.

The links I followed demonstrate how Pinterest drives traffic to other sites, facilitating the consumption of online content. They also locate Schumer within a paratextual dialogue that reconstructs ideal femininity as "inspirational" and "positive". Across the pinned material in my sample, there was a marked tendency to label Schumer as "inspirational", "motivational" or as a "role model". Writers frequently connected this status to her perceived insightfulness, which enabled her to provide valuable "life advice", "relationship advice" and "life lessons", and to her perceived authenticity, which enabled her to voice her insights in an "honest" and "real" way. These two qualities can be linked to Schumer's celebrity-*comedian* persona. Stand-up comedy is commonly associated with autobiographical content, and Schumer's material has foregrounded intimacy and confession. However, this discourse glosses over the ironic performativity of her comedy and the contradictions and messiness in her celebrity text. The complex gendered negotiations of everyday life comprise a crucial topic in Schumer's output, but, appropriated and recontextualised through the practices of quotation culture and inspiration discourse, her utterances construct female agency as seductively attainable. This reading strategy can also be contextualised within wider discourses around the subjectivity of young women, who are expected to achieve independence through "self-monitoring, the setting up of personal plans and the search for individual solutions" (McRobbie 2007: 723).

The reading of Schumer as inspirational was also evident in Pinterest user practices. The "I say …" quote had been repinned to 1.3k Pinterest boards, many of which were labelled "Feminist", "motivational", "Inspiration and beauty", "Inspiring women", "quotes", "words to live by", "WISDOM", "Truth", "healthy for me", and so on. The image, and similar "poster" images of Schumer quotes on Pinterest, can be seen as part of the wider pattern of the platform being used to "motivate personal change" (Linder *et al.* 2014: 6). Examining this trend further, Wilson and Yochim (2015) argue that "what so often circulates across the affective networks of Pinterest is happiness, or rather the promise of happiness", held in curated material such as "inspiration or funny quotes, books one loved or hopes to love, recipes one plans to try, and so on" (242). The authors draw on Ahmed's (2010) argument that "happiness is an orientation towards the objects we come into contact with" (24), suggesting that:

> Pinterest can be thought of as an affective network for curating and sharing the good life, for displaying that one desires the right kind of things and takes pleasures in the right kind of ways. Thus, it is also a

site of social and cultural privilege: Its happiness is primarily reserved
for those who are already invested in, and have access to, a particular raced, gendered, and classed conception of the good life for those
who already have a taste for it.

(Wilson and Yochim 2015: 244)

Schumer becomes such a promise of happiness, demonstrating the possibility of a female agency that rejects "sexist expectations of politeness,
cuteness, and white feminine modes of accommodation" (Goltz 2015:
273). This possibility is validated both by Schumer's successful career
and by the endorsement of the quote provided by other pinners. However, Wilson and Yochim's (2015) argument hints at a tension in this audience practice. Her feminist/subversive power is claimed from a position
of privilege. As Goltz (2015) notes, Schumer "is a normatively attractive
and feminine white blond woman who strategically uses her bright smile
and rosy cheeks to pander to and then upset gendered norms" (273). Her
specific promise of happiness, then, might primarily be available to other
white, middle-class women who are already invested in (popular) feminisms. Different promises are circulated among different user groups.
For example, Nicholson (2014) has examined how black female celebrities in the U.S. were constructed through comments on their Instagram
and Pinterest pages. He considers the extent to which this engagement
challenges existing scripts of black femininity and argues that it has the
potential to give black female Internet users a voice "in the conversation
about representation and portrayal" of black women (287).

The "I say ..." image and user pinning practices indicate Schumer's
participation in celebrity feminism, which Keller and Ringrose (2015)
describe as "a form of popular feminism made visible recently by young
celebrity women eager to publicly claim a feminist identity" (132). Frequently cited examples include Beyoncé and Emma Watson, as well as
comedians Lena Dunham, Tina Fey and Amy Poehler, with Hamad and
Taylor (2015) suggesting that "the figure of the self professed feminist
celebrity" has turned into "a sustained and ongoing flashpoint of the
cross-media celebrity landscape" (124). However, "[f]eminism's implication in the circuits of celebrity has routinely been figured as problematic"
because it is "seen as antithetical to feminist modes of activism and a
refusal of hierarchies" (Taylor 2014: 75). Similarly, Mizejewski (2012: 8)
highlights feminist debates about "what 'counts' as 'feminist comedy' -
what topics can be satirised, what standard tropes such as self-deprecation
can be deployed, what ideals need to be met or represented". Exploring
such tensions, Brady (2016) foregrounds "feminism as (a) *movement*, as
something as perpetually incomplete as the subjectivities and collectiv-
ities of those whom it seeks to represent", suggesting that "the value of
celebrity feminism might be precisely in the inability of feminists to agree
on which celebrity feminists are hurting or hindering 'feminism'" (438).

The tensions in Schumer's comedian-celebrity text, produced by her sexy outfits, her ironic performance of white femininities, her serious critiques of gender roles and her claiming of a feminist identity (e.g. Leal 2015), illustrate such struggles over meaning. Despite the emphasis on inspiration and empowerment in my sample, only three of the pinned paratexts explicitly identified Schumer as a feminist. This included an article from *Time* called "How Amy Schumer Gets Guys to Think Feminists Are Funny" (Dockterman 2014), which cites *Inside Amy Schumer* as evidence that "feminism and comedy can go together" and "a feminist comic [can] draw a wide crowd", because it has succeeded on *Comedy Central*, "even though the network's audience is 60% male". The article has been pinned to 1.2k boards, but the pinning practices demonstrate that Pinterest's separation of the image and the article text facilitates very diverse readings. Despite the explicit focus on feminism in the headline, the pin was included on boards such as "Girl Power", "Legs – oh they make us ...", "Amy Schumer", "Everyday Outfit", "famous", "Hot Chicks" and "Funny Gals". This illustrates that one of the challenges of promoting feminism through celebrity texts is the process of appropriation and recontextualisation of materials in the digital public sphere. Although "Schumer's entire persona can be seen as breaking down the male gaze because it asks the audience to 'look again' at the image they think they see, and to evaluate the comedian through language rather than her image" (Foy 2015: 711), Pinterest enabled users to *just* see her image.

Alongside the pins that foregrounded written quotes from Schumer's work, four pins reproduced a photograph of Schumer taken by Annie Leibovitz for the 2016 Pirelli Calendar. Although this calendar has traditionally featured female models and film stars, often semi-nude, the 2016 edition made a bid for cultural distinction by presenting black-and-white images of "women renowned for their work in diverse fields—including comedy, sports, philanthropy, and art" (Whittle 2015). The 12 women included Serena Williams, Patty Smith and Yoko Ono. Each participant is here re-inscribed with significance by the promotion of the calendar and by the cultural status of the photographer and the other selected women.

At the calendar launch event, Leibovitz said that Schumer's image was intended to suggest "that she was the only one who had not got the memo about wearing clothes" (Whittle 2015). In the image of Schumer, we see her body from the side, while her face is turned towards us. She is wearing semi-transparent, white underpants and white, strappy, high-heeled shoes. She is perched on a bar stool, one foot on a wooden platform and the other on the floor. At the edges of the image we see photographic equipment, and there are tape markers on the wooden floor. Schumer's body leans forward a little, supported by her left hand on her left knee. This position creates three folds in the flesh of her stomach. Her blond hair is brushed backwards and flows down her back. Her right arm is bent, concealing her breasts, and she holds a cup of takeout coffee. She looks to the side of the camera, with raised eyebrows and slightly pursed lips, producing a quizzical expression and the impression that she is listening to someone. Presumably, the image is intended to suggest that this person is telling Schumer that she is expected to wear more clothes.

The image draws attention to the unruliness associated with Schumer's comedian-celebrity persona, which is structured by the incongruity between her "innocuously pretty" (Foy 2015: 707) appearance and her "sexually aggressive" comedy (710). This unruliness is here signified by Schumer's participation in the visual joke, which laughs at her *performed* ditzy, white femininity (she didn't think of checking instructions for the shoot) and *performed* slutty, white femininity (she was willing to do nude calendar photos) but also inscribes Schumer-the-comedian with courage and defiance. Her body is not quite thin or toned enough to comply with contemporary ideals of white celebrity femininity, and so she is "making a spectacle out of herself" (Russo 1994: 53). Schumer's display of her "unruly white body" (Redmond 2007: 263) was contextualised in three key ways on Pinterest. Some users focused on the comedic modality of the photograph, including the image on pin boards with titles like "funny folks" or "fun". Some represented her body as a desirable object, pinning the photograph on boards called "sexy" or "curves" alongside images of other scantily clad female bodies. The predominant trend, however, positioned the shot within a discourse of "body positivity", which promotes the valorisation of female bodies that don't comply with dominant ideas of feminine beauty.

As Sastre (2014) observes, this emerging online culture includes "a proliferation of websites dedicated to nurturing bodily acceptance and challenging the normalization of thin, toned bodies" (929). These spaces "claim, in varying ways, to respond to a broader need for alternative images of the body, both exposing the dangers and fallacies of normative constructions of beauty and providing a space for a different performance of self" (930). On Pinterest, users recontextualised Leibovitz's image of Schumer within a body positivity discourse by pinning it on boards that had titles such as "All bodies are beautiful", "positivity" and "body inspo". This was also a recurring orientation towards the 20 pins that quoted Schumer's utterances about her own body. One version of the image made the body positivity discourse explicit by superimposing the text "Thank you Amy Schumer for showing us that all women's bodies are beautiful" over the photograph. This utterance expresses gratitude to Schumer, claiming that her display of her own female body validates "all" female bodies as "beautiful". It implies that Schumer's body challenges dominant ideals of femininity and that its public display therefore has liberating potential. This foregrounds Schumer's unruliness and conceals the ways in which she conforms to such ideals, for example through her whiteness, her able body and her heterosexuality. By suggesting that the photograph's "promise of happiness" (Wilson and Yochim 2015: 242) is universal, the utterance works to reinforce the normativity of such identities.

The purple logo in the bottom right corner identifies the source of the reworked image as Whisper, and the link takes me to whisper.sh. The site describes itself as "a home for every single person who wants to be silly, real, quirky, honest, awkward, raw, less lonely, and most of all... simply loved for who they are". The branding of Whisper tries to align the site with a discourse of authenticity but also, like the body positive sites, present it as a safe space to perform diverse identities. Here, however, this safety is specifically connected to user anonymity, rather than to promises of a tolerant user culture. On Whisper, Schumer's Pirelli image had been "liked" 3.7k times and received 399 replies. In line with Whisper practice, the responses all took the form of images with superimposed text, and they articulated a range of affective responses. Some expressed frustration that Schumer was considered "fat" or disapproval of her perceived failure to discipline her "unhealthy" body. Some inscribed her as a desirable or undesirable sexual object, and some constructed her as a site of identification. This demonstrates that the meanings affixed to pinned Schumer paratexts will be validated, negotiated and challenged across different Pinterest boards and across the different online spaces that Pinterest invites us to visit. As I found in my analysis of responses to Melissa McCarthy's character in *Bridesmaids* (chapter 2) and to Miranda Hart's character in *Miranda* (chapter 6), the reception of Schumer's comedian-celebrity text illustrates the ambivalence of the unruly woman. Schumer "violates the unspoken feminine sanction against 'making a spectacle' of herself" (Rowe 2003: 253), and this transgression was inscribed as inspiring and as abject.

Funny Amy Schumer

The Leibovitz image can be considered an example of Schumer's comedic work, although users often read her nudity through the serious lenses of body inspiration, "thinspiration" (Lewallen and Behm-Morawitz 2016) and desire. Of the 100 pins in my sample, only 30 displayed verbal or visual quotations from Schumer's comedic material. This included three pins that lampooned the "inspirational poster" form by positioning Schumer's aggressively smutty jokes against banal background imagery. For example, one poster combines a close-up photograph of pink meadow flowers with the quote:

I usually feel pretty good about myself.
I know what I look like.
YOU'D BANG ME,

but you wouldn't blog about it.
It's fine...
—Amy Schumer

Like the Leibovitz photograph, the quote draws attention to the patriarchal evaluation of women as desirable bodies and to the broader "identification of women with their bodies rather than their minds" within "Judeo-Christian tradition" (Mizejewski 2014: 14). Schumer's body does not *quite* conform to the patriarchal ideal for the female body, and here she suggests that she is attractive *enough* to be a desirable sexual object but not *so* desirable that a man would consider the encounter worthy of a detailed account. In a way similar to Schumer's blond girl-next-door prettiness, the meadow flowers set up "gender expectations of pleasantness" (93), which facilitate comic surprise at her incongruous smuttiness and her implicit challenge of patriarchal gender norms.

The quote articulates a complex set of affects. Schumer is a little insecure ("I *usually* feel *pretty* good about myself"), positions herself as a sexual object to be "banged", and finally articulates an acceptance of her inscription as a just-about-good-enough body. Simultaneously, her use of irony "exploits and mobilizes a mischievous and messy tension between what is explicit and the intended message" (Goltz 2015: 2017), which I interpret as a critique of the patriarchal authority over women's bodies. This layered utterance can be situated within "a female comedy grounded in the cultural body":

> The politics of this comedy centers on questions of race, sexuality, and power. What female bodies are valued? What bodies count as feminine? As sexy? As visible and legible? Feminist questions of long standing, they are now, for many women comics, the subtext and set-ups for punch lines.
>
> (Mizejewski 2014: 15)

Another example of the mock-inspirational poster features the following quote, centred above a picture of a hand holding three lit sparklers that light up the dark background:

> Tonight I had one goal, and that was
> to just be able to take my underwear off
> at the end of the night and have it not look like
>
> ———
>
> I BLEW MY NOSE IN IT.
>
> ———
>
> —Amy Schumer

Schumer here performs "the female grotesque" (Russo 1994). Her body is unruly, with a leaky vagina and a mouth that voices experiences that are deemed private and shameful. This shame is performed ironically, as she identifies the containment of her vagina as a "goal", but also defiantly *describes* the substance it produces, creating a carnivalesque reversal of the upper and lower regions of her body (Bakhtin 1968). As Pelle (2010) writes in her analysis of Margaret Cho's comedy, using such comic strategies can demonstrate "that there is pleasure to be had in negotiating and then transforming" shame (26). These layered incongruities produce conflicting modality markers and offer audiences multiple ways of engaging with the utterance. First, the joke exploits and ruptures the prettiness that conceals Schumer's unruliness, inviting us to laugh at her abject body. Second, it offers her body as a site of identification, inviting us to laugh at our own unruly bodies. Finally, it confronts patriarchal norms that attempt to prescribe how female bodies can be seen and talked about, inviting us to laugh at the shame and disgust inscribed on our bodies. Drawing on Bakhtin's (1968) work on the carnivalesque, we can think of this laughter as offering relief from the fear of gendered bodily shame: "Laughter demolishes fear and piety before an object, before a world, making of it an object of familiar contact and thus clearing the ground for an absolutely free investigation of it" (23). Such relief is temporary, but it affirms the joke's re-opening of "the body-boundary" (Stallybrass and White 1986: 184) that represses "the lower regions" of women's bodies as "dirty, unmentionable, *unacceptable*" (186). However, it is important to emphasise that irony is co-produced through a dialogue between comedian and audience. Audiences "make irony happen" (Hutcheon 1994/2005: 113), and so their responses "are as much (if not more) about audience investments in power and affinities with systemic oppression as the doings of the performer" (Goltz 2015: 268). So, what can Pinterest tell us about the reception of this joke?

The posters were all from a POPSUGAR article called "9 Amy Schumer Quotes That Are So Beautiful, We Made Them into Posters" (Roschke 2015). This site describes itself as "lifestyle media publisher" that is focused on "Informing, entertaining, and inspiring action through multi-platform content across entertainment, fashion, beauty, fitness, food and parenting" ("About Us"). Like HelloGiggles, this situates Schumer's comedian-celebrity text within a feminised online sphere that foregrounds her appeal to female users. On Pinterest, the mock-inspirational posters were primarily pinned to boards with names such as "Funny shit", "lol" and "quotes and sayings" where the utterances were repositioned among a broad range of humorous quotes. This contrasts sharply with the pinning of the serious quotes and the Leibovitz photograph, which were explicitly marked as inspirational. Examining pinning practices can't tell us how users interpreted the quotes, but curation does put the pinned material under particular interpretive lenses. Here, pinners repeatedly represented the quotes as resources for amusement, while any engagement with their feminist critique was largely rendered invisible. This illustrates the risk associated with Schumer's use of satiric irony as a comic strategy (Goltz 2015), since the slippery critique could be confined to the realm of humour.

My sample included 10 pins that represented Schumer's stand-up performances. These take the form of screenshots with speech in superimposed captions, usually designed to deliver jokes by separating the set up and the punch line within the image or across a series of images. Here, the focus is not on Schumer's appearance. The images are smaller and often quite darkly lit, and they show her *doing* comedy. One of these pins is a vertical set of two images. Each shows a long shot of Schumer on stage, positioned slightly right of centre, against a dark background dotted with tiny lights. She has her hair in a neat up do, she is wearing a short, yellow dress and beige leather boots with heels, and she is holding a microphone to her mouth. Behind her, we can glimpse a table with a drink. In the first image, Schumer is looking into the audience and shielding her eyes from the bright stage lights. The white, superimposed caption is placed in the lower left part of the image, creating an eye line match:

> Audience member:
> Why do you have a small mouth?

In the image below, Schumer is still looking down at the heckler, but she is no longer shielding her eyes. She is smiling. The superimposed caption is in a larger font and the colour matches the yellow of her dress:

> To make dicks
> like yours
> seem big

This image set inscribes Schumer with power over her audience. Her male heckler is only represented through the caption, and his attempt to direct attention to her appearance is met with a tendentious joke that implicates his own body. Schumer reads the heckle as a reference to the fairy tale *Little Red Riding Hood*, adopts the character of a sexually aggressive wolf, and positions the heckler in an ambiguous role as both fellated and emasculated. As Foy (2015) observes in her analysis of Schumer's stand-up act, the tension between audience expectations of gender norms and Schumer's transgressive use of sexual humour "can manifest in the performance space". The comedian "consistently navigates this tension for audiences, negotiating their discomfort by appropriating and dismantling the male gaze" (707). Although Schumer's comedic material frequently explores gendered shame, the heckler's attempt to evaluate her against the norms of ideal femininity is silenced by an aggressive dismissal of his own masculinity. She temporarily adopts the subversive female comic "posture" of "the bitch", which uses disparagement humour as social critique. As Gilbert (2004) notes, "[t]his persona is not interested in pleasing her audience; rather, she frequently insults and offends them or rails out against social mores and cultural norms" (108). Across Schumer's stand up more broadly, however, she "pulls and borrows" from a range of such postures that have been developed by previous female comedians (Goltz 2015: 273).

Along with images from her film *Trainwreck* (2015) and her sketch show *Inside Amy Schumer* (Comedy Central, since 2013), the stand-up pins demonstrate that Schumer's celebrity status has been *achieved* through her affective labour as a comedian, fulfilling the postfeminist requirement for ambition coupled with hard work (McRobbie 2007). Headlines often positioned the images within the feminised discourse of inspiration, presenting them as instances where Schumer "proved that women are f-ing hilarious", "perfectly described being a woman", or provided "ways for you to not give a fuck". This constructs Schumer as a symbolic resource for empowerment, offering women insight and tools for recognising their own funniness, for understanding themselves and for asserting themselves. In contrast, the curation practices of Pinterest users tended to privilege the comedic modality of these quotations by recontextualising them within boards focusing on funny quotes or comedians. This located Schumer's work within a wider quotation culture or within wider comedian fandom. However, some users performed Amy Schumer fandom by adding the stand-up images to boards dedicated specifically to her. This practice was evident across my sample, albeit as a minor pattern, and I´ll now investigate that as an example of "ordinary fandom" (Sandvoss and Kearns 2016).

Amy Schumer Fandom

I examined 20 boards that focused on Amy Schumer, analysing how the combinations of selected images produced specific fan readings of her comedian-celebrity text. I also explored how these Pinterest users' Amy Schumer fandom was situated within their wider pinning practices, as articulated through their other boards. Fourteen of the users in this sample performed fandoms on Pinterest, and this was divided equally into users who devoted boards to specific comedians, comedies and other films and TV programmes and users who focused boards on celebrities more broadly. The remaining six users dedicated most of their boards to lifestyle topics, such as cooking, crafts, travel, fashion, beauty, and so on. This pattern was also evident on the Amy Schumer boards, where I identified two key pinning strategies. Those who focused their Pinterest use on celebrity and lifestyle texts pinned a broad range of paratextual material, including red carpet photographs, magazine shoots, paparazzi shots, celebrity gossip, "inspirational posters", comedic quotes, and so on. The pins here produced a paratextual dialogue characterised by tensions created by Schumer's varied performances as a comedian, as a postfeminist celebrity and as a celebrity feminist. In contrast, those who used boards to perform fandoms of comedy, film and TV texts privileged Schumer's comedian identity by primarily pinning material from or on Schumer's comedic work. This included verbal quotations, screen grabs and videos from *Trainwreck* and *Inside Amy Schumer*, as well as other promotional and critical reception material for those texts. Here, Pinterest was not used to identify "ideas to try" as part of a self-development project, but digital materials to consume. This illustrates the value of fans as consumers and the free digital labour they (and other Pinterest users) undertake by circulating the paratexts, valorising them with pins and comments, promoting Schumer, creating content for Pinterest and driving traffic to host sites.

The Amy Schumer boards might offer the fannish pleasures of collection and curation. Digital paratextual materials tend to be ephemeral, and so their collection "can be viewed as a personal strategy that allows the fan to participate in and embody the contradictions of consumer capitalism" by preserving and valorising "products designed for obsolence" (Tankel and Murphy 1998: 58). However, the practices I observed tended to be distinct from the "completist" collection associated with cult fandom (Mathijs and Sexton 2011: 23). Although one of the 20 users had 513 pins on his or her Amy Schumer board, the average was 70 pins, and most had between 30 and 50 pins. They were also distinct from the Pinterest practices of the *Doctor Who* fans in Fogle's (2015) study, which focused on "conversations and fan-created content", and although Pinterest can be "a host for fans to congregate and aggregate their fan knowledge" (306), I did not observe any interaction between these Amy Schumer fans, and there was no evidence of fan textual production. This might be indicative both of the wider tendency to see Pinterest use as a solitary activity (Linder *et al.* 2014: 5) and of what Sandvoss and Kearns (2016) call "ordinary fandom".

Noting that academic fan studies have tended to focus on "creativity and collectivity", Sandvoss and Kearns (2016) shift attention onto "ordinary, everyday life fandom" and propose that "the quintessential, constitutive condition of fandom is *transitive* rather than collective or creative – and maintained through the affective bond with a given fan object that is constructed through processes of textual selection facilitated by digital media" (91). Similarly, Andò (2015) reflects on the distinction between online "fashion poaching" and fan cosplay, suggesting that Pinterest users poach "the identity traits expressed by [the] fashion and clothing" of celebrities and screen characters, recombine these traits "in ways that are not necessarily related to the fandom frame or to the original media content frame", and seek validation for their appropriation within Pinterest itself, rather than within a fan community.

Although such practices can certainly be characterised by both creativity and collectivity, Andò maintains that they "serve to build a performative identity that is more individual and ordinary than those which are fan produced" (218). Drawing on these studies, I think it's useful to see the pinning of Amy Schumer paratexts as a practice of ordinary fandom.

For Pinterest users, these boards contextualise their Amy Schumer fandom, maintaining and reinforcing the particular readings and meaning making that underlie their affective bond with her as a fan object (Sandvoss and Kearns 2016: 101). My analysis suggests that some located her within a wider celebrity fandom, some within a wider comedy fandom, and some within a discourse of inspiration. However, these reading strategies frequently overlapped, demonstrating that Schumer resonated with her fans in a broad range of ways and functioned as a flexible symbolic resource in the affective economy of Pinterest. Crucially, the construction and expansion of the Amy Schumer boards also contributed to the users' articulation of online identities on Pinterest, displaying this resonance as well as the position of the fan object within the web of their wider digital consumption practices.

Conclusion

This chapter has examined transgressive comedy through a case study of the circulation of Amy Schumer paratexts on Pinterest. Positioning Schumer within a pattern of "women's comedy taking on the contradictions of multiple feminisms registered in popular culture" (Mizejewski 2014: 10), I have explored how her complex comedian-celebrity text has been fractured through the prism of this popular social bookmarking site. My analysis reflected on the resulting mosaic of celebrity discourse and quotations from Schumer's work, arguing that she became a flexible symbolic resource inscribed as desirable, inspirational and funny. Importantly, this resource was often positioned within a dual project of women's self-improvement. One pinning practice focused on the appropriation of her desirable style, while another focused on her "promise" (Wilson and Yochim 2015) of female agency in a patriarchal society.

Considering Schumer as a participant in celebrity feminism, I have problematised this "promise" in three key ways. First, drawing on McRobbie (2008), I have stressed the gendered, regulatory discourse of personal responsibility underlying the project of self-improvement. Second, I have suggested that the foregrounding of Schumer's unruliness obscures the ways in which she complies with ideals for postfeminist celebrities, which reinforces the normativity of female bodies as young, white, middle-class and heterosexual. Third, I have argued that Schumer's multi-layered representations of the gendered negotiations of everyday life were reduced to seductively simple assertions of female agency. This gloss was produced by the filtering of her work through the practices of quotation culture and the inspiration discourse facilitated by Pinterest.

My analysis also identified distinct pinning practices for serious and humorous quotations. Although my sample included examples of Schumer challenging gender conventions through both humorous and serious discursive strategies, comedic quotations tended to be pinned to boards dedicated to humour, while the serious quotations were frequently pinned to boards focusing on feminism and inspiration. Although my investigation can't tell us how Pinterest users interpreted the utterances, it is notable that their pinning practices concealed engagement with the feminist critique in her comedy. Goltz (2015) emphasises that Schumer's ironic comedy is co-created by her audiences, and that contribution was rarely articulated here. This illustrates that one of the challenges of contemporary feminist comedy is the appropriation and recontextualisation of material across different digital contexts.

Quotations from her transgressive comedy tended to be positioned as resources for amusement but were also sometimes valorised as part of Amy Schumer fandom. On Pinterest, this fandom was characterised by the digital consumption, curation and circulation of paratexts that maintained and confirmed fan readings of Schumer and their affective bond with her. I have argued that this might usefully be thought of as what Sandvoss and Kearns (2016) call "ordinary fandom" but would like to stress that more work is needed on developing this approach for comedy fandom. I hope to encourage further debate with this book and now move on to a consideration of cult fandom, unintended comedy and comic failure.

9 Unintentional Comedy and Comic Failure

Tommy Wiseau Fandom on Reddit

Across several of the preceding chapters, I have explored the ways in which audiences discuss whether or not specific comedies are "good". In this final case study, however, I want to look at a cult celebrity whose work has overwhelmingly been positioned as "bad". When audiences laughed at Tommy Wiseau's melodrama *The Room*, he responded by insisting that the film was intended as a dark comedy. Wiseau's claim can be seen as an attempt to reposition him simultaneously as a comedian and as a competent media producer. Audiences had inscribed the film and its creator as laughable, and he tried to reorient this laughter by presenting himself as the joker, rather than the butt of the joke. The intervention largely failed to alter the reception discourse around *The Room*, which simultaneously mocked and celebrated the film (Bonnstetter 2012). However, Wiseau has continued to construct himself as a comedian and finally released the sitcom *The Neighbors* on Hulu in the U.S. in 2015. So, what happened when audiences were explicitly invited to laugh *with*, rather than *at* Wiseau?

In this chapter I want to explore some of the ambiguities and tensions of laughter as an affective response by returning to the idea of comedy fandom, which I explored through chapter 2's analysis of *Parks and Recreation* fans, as well as in the previous chapter on Amy Schumer fans. However, I am here looking at an example of "critical fandom" (Haig 2014) and, in the last part of the chapter, even "anti-fandom" (Gray 2003), rather than the celebration I found on Tumblr and Pinterest. I am going to use data from discussion threads on reddit.com to examine Wiseau as a nexus of discourses around comedy, otherness, authenticity and cultural competency. The analysis argues that, following repeated participatory screenings of *The Room* as a bad film (McCulloch 2011), Wiseau has become "sticky" (Ahmed 2004) with conflicting affective responses that inscribe him as other and as ridiculous but also as unique and authentic. This inscription framed audience expectations of *The Neighbors*, and was evident in three key orientations towards the sitcom. The first orientation developed a narrative of Wiseau's perceived change from "genuine" to "self-aware", which positioned *The Neighbors* as a failed attempt at exploiting *The Room*'s cult success as a bad film. The second orientation maintained Wiseau's authenticity by constructing him as incapable of understanding what audiences want or how comedy "should" be made. Whereas both of these readings can be seen to articulate Wiseau fandom, a third orientation challenged the discourse of "so bad it's good" by rejecting his body of work as "just bad".

Tommy Wiseau and *The Room*

As Durgnat (1969) notes, "a film may become a comedy involuntarily, being built round a greater intensity of dramatic tension than it makes an audience feel" (51). Wiseau's melodrama was promoted as "A film with the passion of Tennessee Williams" (Allen 2009) and is widely considered to be an example of such involuntary or unintentional comedy. In attempting to follow the mode and narrative conventions of the melodrama genre, it offers "the spectacle of a film failing to find a form capable of soliciting in the viewer an intended emotional response" (MacDowell and Zborowski 2013: 14). *The Room*, then, has been variously positioned within the "badfilm" (1) and "so-bad-it's-good" subgenres. As Popescu (2013) observes, films in the latter category are usually associated with "an auteur who is characterised by a passionate and earnest, idiot-savant filmmaking ability" and they involve "really bad acting and effects, elliptical dialogue, characters with unknown motivations and juvenile emotions and reactions to situations, plot lines that are nonsensical, bad editing, and bad sound" (571). He argues that audiences usually watch *The Room* in order "to laugh at the film and to mock the filmmaker", which highlights "mockery and cruel humour as driving factors" in its popularity (572). Such audience engagement appears to offer an example of the smug and malicious laughter that superiority theorists were concerned about: Audiences seem to be amused by Wiseau's "folly" (Morreall 1983: 4) and his "deformed" work (1651: 36), while the popularity of participatory screenings (McCulloch 2011) further suggests that this laughter reinforces boundaries between "us" as audiences and Wiseau as "the other". However, while superiority theory certainly offers a useful lens for this case study, I think some viewers' compound affective responses to Wiseau complicate this reading.

Some reddit contributors could be seen to adopt the "reading protocol" of "paracinematic culture", which Sconce (1995) defines as "a counter-aesthetic turned subcultural sensibility" that seeks "to valorize all forms of cinematic 'trash', whether such films have been explicitly rejected or simply ignored by legitimate film culture" (372). Bonnstetter (2012) defines this fan practice as a form of *"textual production"*, arguing that fans are "re-creating" the films "into new, meaningful experiences" (95). Reflecting on what fans might valorise in *The Room*, MacDowell and Zborowski suggest that the film's "strangely consistent narrational inconsistency" combines with "the many moments which are not only inept, but also intensely unusual" to produce a sense of "global uniqueness" that it is tempting to attribute to Wiseau's "distinct point of view" (21). McCulloch's (2011) study of *The Room* cinema audiences emphasises the significance of communal viewing contexts and participatory screenings, arguing that participants can increase their social capital by making contributions that are "legitimated" by other audience members (213). I want to draw on these ideas of a paracinematic reading protocol and "fan social capital" (Hills 2002: 30) in my analysis of Wiseau's audiences on reddit. I am interested in how contributors valorised and devalorised Wiseau and his work through their affective responses, how their engagement negotiated reddit as an online space and as a community, and how we can use this case study to think about the application of superiority theory to screen comedy audiences.

Researching Reddit

My analysis is based on all reddit discussion threads that included comments about *The Neighbors* at the time of writing. Reddit.com was then the 12th most visited website in the U.S. (SimilarWeb 2016), and Singer *et al.* (2014) describe it as "a community-driven platform for submitting, commenting and rating links and text posts" (518). Reddit users (called "redditors") can submit and vote on content, and each post earns the contributor "karma points", a score calculated from "the number of upvotes minus downvotes an item has received" (Massanari 2015: 3). As suggested by the tagline *"the front page of the Internet"*, reddit was designed "to capture and rank all kinds of diverse content collected from the Web by promoting the best parts via its voting process" (518). However, Singer *et al.* have identified a marked shift towards image- and text-based posts, instead of links to external sites, concluding that the site has *"transformed from a dedicated gateway to the Web ... to an increasingly self-referential community"* (522). This trend was reflected in most of the threads I looked at. My data also included an example of the popular subreddit "I am a... Ask me anything" (IAmA ... AMA), where someone offers to answer questions about a particular topic, and redditors participate by asking questions and discussing answers. At the time of writing, the most popular AMA was that of U.S. president Barack Obama, followed by those of chef Gordon Ramsay and Apple co-founder Steve Wozniak. As Massanari (2015) observes, these rankings "reflect both the general popularity of the individual involved, and the specific appeal the celebrity has for reddit's technology-savvy/geek audience" (52). Wiseau's AMA in March 2015 was intended to promote *The Neighbors,* and it received 4248 comments.

Importantly, reddit users tend to be male, under 50 years old and living in urban or suburban areas in the U.S. In fact, "men are twice as likely as women to be reddit users" (Duggan and Smith 2013), and

Massanari (2015) argues that the site is dominated by a "geek masculinity" that "discursively excludes women and people of color" (16). As a cultural space, then, reddit reproduces the dominance of white masculinity that is also associated with comedy culture and cult fandom (e.g. Klinger 2010). In this chapter, I am interested in exploring the ways in which users "othered" a white, male, heterosexual celebrity within this white, masculine space, while often positioning him and his work as fan objects. I will start by examining how reddit users articulated affective responses to Wiseau and *The Room* in the AMA before moving on to explore audience orientations towards *The Neighbors* across reddit.

Tommy Wiseau as "Other" and Fan Object

Across Wiseau's AMA, redditors frequently performed Wiseau fandom in different ways. Many expressed strong affective responses, such as excitement, amazement, love and laughter, which indicates that audience enjoyment of Wiseau's work can't be reduced to malicious superiority:

> Tommy I can never express my love for you adequately
> I'm crying a little bit and my side's hurt. What a day!

Like this last redditor, contributors often demonstrated fan knowledge by quoting lines from Wiseau's work, both in their questions to him and in their comments, which tended to address fellow fans. "What a day!" is the catchphrase of one of Wiseau's two characters in *The Neighbors*, but users were more likely to reproduce lines from *The Room*. This often involved transcription as reperformance, with fans trying to capture Wiseau's particular speech pattern in writing:

> DAT SONOFABITCH TOOOOOODE ME!!

This approach was also adopted by reddit's then AMA co-ordinator Victoria Taylor (username chooter), who transcribed the responses Wiseau gave her over the telephone. This was Wiseau's answer to a question about whether fans ask him to quote his own lines:

> Neaaaaaaooo.
> I say, you can laugh, you can cry, you can express yourself, but please don't hurt each other. It's up to them what they want me to say, you know? I enjoy, move on next question.

Taylor's transcription was celebrated in a number of posts:

> For real, this AMA may be /u/chooter's best work yet. She captures his voice and cadence perfectly. I'm loving this.

Massanari (2015) argues that redditors value AMAs as an opportunity for users "to access these prominent individuals without relying on gate-keepers", and she identifies "an unstated expectation … that the celebrities will be willing to disclose and will engage with the reddit community in a way that suggests an unfiltered lack of self-consciousness" (53). So, although Taylor clearly did act in a gatekeeping capacity, participants suggested that her transcription style facilitated the desired sense of access and authenticity.

The emphasis on accuracy also reflects the centrality of quoting in comedy fandom, as discussed in chapters 2 and 8. While writing rarely enables fans to give others a sense of how a line was *delivered*, a shared understanding of Wiseau's speech pattern facilitated such reperformance. As the AMA went on, users also started quoting Wiseau's answers back at him and to each other:

> He has sex erryday

This practice incorporated the AMA into Wiseau's celebrity text and inscribed it with otherness. In particular, it drew attention to his limited command of English and his use of non-sequiturs:

> I'm pretty sure he just stroked out mid sentence.

As Montemurro and Benfield (2015) observe, people use disparagement humour if they can distance themselves from the target, even if that target is objectively similar to them. Although Wiseau's white masculinity aligns him with the norm in comedy culture and on reddit, contributors often constructed him as an object of ridicule. As Graefer (2014) argues, "Humour, and the complex and contradictory affects that it can engender, can be seen as one affective-discursive tool through which social norms are made visible, felt in the body and reinforced / re-negotiated" (109). Here, participants used that tool to other Wiseau along the axes of gender, nationality and cultural competence.

Wiseau's masculinity was made strange through a recurring preoccupation with his body. Some participants asked questions about his "fitness regime" and his long hair, some derided his sex scenes in *The Room*, some made fun of his habit of wearing multiple belts, some asked about his girlfriend, and many, many more quoted *The Room* by asking him and each other "so how is your sex life?"

> AMA Request – Tommy Wiseau's special lady
> Yeah. That whole thread: "So how's your sex life?"

Participants also frequently speculated about Wiseau's national origins and about how he made his fortune. They repeatedly asked him about where he was born, what languages he speaks and what his accent is, without success. They brought up various Internet rumours, including fantastical speculations that Wiseau is actually a vampire, an alien or U.S. hijacker D.B. Cooper. And, finally, they invoked Greg Sestero ("Mark" from *The Room*) and Tom Bissell's book *The Disaster Artist: My Life inside The Room, the Greatest Bad Movie Ever Made* as an important paratext. As Sconce (1995) notes in his discussion of Ed Wood fandom, fan knowledge of the director is essential for the "process of 'seeing through' the diegesis", enabling fans to enhance their understanding of a film's "cultural codes" and "production processes" (389). On reddit, contributors shared information from *The Disaster Artist* to support their guesses about Wiseau's background but also to "prove" his incompetence by referencing Sestero's stories from the shooting of *The Room*. The AMA represented another opportunity for fans to gain insight into his production practices, and it was a recurring topic in their questions:

> What kind of cameras did you use on The Neighbors and will we ever meet the ghost character?

This was the opening of Wiseau's answer:

> GOOD QUESTION! We use a red camera, and for your information, we used 2 cameras, actually we had 3 cameras we'd be using.

When some redditors mocked Wiseau's perceived reference to the colour of his camera, others drew on their own industry knowledge to clarify: "RED is a brand of expensive 4k, 5k and 6k resolution cameras. However, being with who were talking to, it might actually just be a red camera". By displaying knowledge of this particular camera, Wiseau destabilised the discourse of the idiot-savant auteur (Popescu 2013: 571) that positioned him as an object of ridicule. One poster expressed disappointment that this information made Wiseau's answer "a lot less hilarious", but others quickly glossed over the discursive fissure by identifying a comic incongruity between Wiseau's professional equipment and the "shitty" image quality of *The Neighbors*. This exchange demonstrates a fan desire to maintain the inscription of Wiseau as culturally incompetent. As MacDowell and Zborowski (2013) observe, badfilm fans value the incompetence and failure of filmmakers, and so this particular moment in the AMA briefly disrupted a narrative that structures fan engagement with Wiseau and his work.

The persistent othering of Wiseau along the axes of gender, nationality and cultural competence reinforces the notion of audiences laughing at him because they feel pleasurably superior, and we can see redditors working to maintain that power relationship. However, I think it also indicates their valorisation of the perceived strangeness of Wiseau and his work. As Corrigan writes of cult films:

> ... audiences seek out not only the unfamiliar in character and story, but the unfamiliar style, frame, and imagistic texture. But once discovered and identified, the cult film and its strange images are then brought home, appropriated by viewers, who make these images privately and personally meaningful ...
>
> (Corrigan 1991: 26)

Although the reception discourse around *The Room* certainly suggests that its unfamiliarity is crucial to its resonance with fans, there is not always evidence to suggest that the film's elements were made meaningful. In fact, reddit users often seemed to relish their *failure* to make sense of *The Room* and of Wiseau's AMA responses:

> What the fuck could that possibly mean? It's so bizarre, god I love it.

The incongruity between Wiseau's utterances and cultural conventions of meaning making were read as comic by redditors and often used as a springboard for play. As McCulloch (2011) writes of his attendance at a participatory cinema screening of *The Room*:

> It was July 2010, and as the film played out in front of me at the Prince Charles Cinema, London, I was relishing the opportunity to launch plastic cutlery and yell at the characters on screen. Others around me were indulging in similar behaviour, filling the cinema with the sound of heckles and chants, and laughing hysterically throughout.
>
> (McCulloch 2010: 189)

Similarly to such participatory screenings, the reddit community platform encourages irreverent and collaborative fan engagement in AMAs. Analysing the patterns of play across the different subcultures of reddit, Massanari (2015) argues that "cleverness and creativity, as in other spaces of geek culture, are prized above all else, along with plenty of crass and base humor" (125). So, user participation in Wiseau's AMA was not limited to asking questions, but involved creative play with his work, his answers and the contributions of other redditors. Exchanges tended to operate within the realm of humour, reinforcing existing conventions within Wiseau fandom that have developed across participatory midnight screenings and conventions (for a further discussion of play at cinema screenings, see Vivar 2016).

This affective-discursive practice highlights a key tension in that fandom: Wiseau was frequently positioned as an object of both ridicule and celebration. Scholars have previously examined such tensions within "snark fandom" (Harman and Jones 2013), Indonesian horror anti-fandom (Downes 2015) and critical *Twilight* fandom (Haig 2014). Haig argues that this particular form of *Twilight* fandom is "humorous and critical", but also "affectionate", and she stresses that the criticism itself is pleasurable (12): "This form of critical fandom does not simply recognise *Twilight* as rubbish and enjoy it *in spite of* that recognition; the recognition *itself* and the analysis, discussion and parody that it permits, provide much of the fans' pleasure" (15). *The Room* fandom and critical *Twilight* fandom clearly differ in important ways. The latter can still entail some of the pleasures traditionally associated with romantic melodramas, while fans of the former certainly don't complain about the film's failings. However, the two fan cultures share conflicting affective responses to their fan objects, and pleasurable critique forms an important part of that engagement.

The tension between ridicule and celebration in the reception discourse around *The Room* on reddit also indicates the circulation of two key viewing strategies, which McCoy and Scarborough (2014) term "ironic consumption" and "camp consumption". In their study of audience responses to "bad" television, they argue that the former viewing style adopts a superior position and a "normative distance" to the "bad" text but plays with this "symbolic boundary" between them by "both watching and condemning" the text, and by talking and laughing about it with other viewers (49). Drawing on Sonntag's (1994/1964) concept of a "camp sensibility", McCoy and Scarborough (2014) then argue that the camp viewing position "reveres the cultural object for how bad it is and admires the vision and passion of the producer". This reading strategy re-evaluates the text using different aesthetic criteria, which "can often mean admiring the creator's vision and, ultimately failed, endeavor to bring this vision to fruition" (51). Across the AMA, posts articulated ironic and camp consumption of *The Room* and of Wiseau's celebrity persona, sometimes quite clearly aligned with one reading strategy and at other times occupying a more ambiguous and shifting ground in between. Such ambiguity was reinforced by the play and humour invited by reddit as a cultural space.

By offering creative, humorous contributions to the AMA, participants were able to reinforce their social capital (made explicit through Karma points) and promote a sense of belonging within the reddit user community and Wiseau fandom. By repeatedly targeting Wiseau, the joking also functioned "as a regulatory technique" (Fine and De Soucey 2005: 11) that maintained the boundary between the fans as "us" and Wiseau as "other". However, the onslaught of ridicule can have a "double function". Writing about banter between male friends, Easthope argues:

> Outwardly banter is aggressive, a form in which the masculine ego asserts itself. Inwardly, however, banter depends on a close, intimate and personal understanding of the person who is the butt of the

attack. It thus works as a way of affirming the bond of love between men while appearing to deny it.

(Easthope 1990: 87–88)

The inscription of Wiseau as enigmatic prevents the particular sense of understanding that Easthope describes. Nevertheless, the aggressive mockery can be read as demonstrations of fan knowledge and fan love, articulated in the masculine manner encouraged by the cultural conventions of reddit.

So, the humorous and playful responses to Wiseau were characterised by a push-pull dynamic that simultaneously distanced fans from him and reinforced their attachment to him as a fan object. Such fan attachment was also explicitly articulated through earnest and more playful wishes to be closer to Wiseau. Some asked him if and how they could work on his next film, some encouraged him to do events in their home cities, some shared anecdotes and pictures of their meetings with him and some discussed their Wiseau-designed underwear. When he suggested that one poster should invite him to his upcoming wedding, redditors posted a rush of invitations to upcoming and imagined nuptials. Contributors shared their excitement about Wiseau's possible attendance at the redditor's wedding, drew on readings of *The Room* in their playful imaginings of how the wedding might play out, and revisited the thread intermittently in the hope of discovering whether Wiseau actually came to the event. So, although a minority of contributors used Wiseau's inscribed difference to dismiss him, most participants exploited it as a comic incongruity while continuing to valorise him as special and intriguing.

The narrative of difference was sometimes anchored by a discourse of authenticity. Reddit users described Wiseau as "unique", "genuine" and "earnest" and constructed his failures as inevitable:

We love him because he doesn't think like any rational human being. He doesn't understand logic or sensibility. Tommy Wiseau essentially IS a joke. He is an accidental comedian, he is trying, in all ways. He sincerely tries. He has a vision, but his serious vision is hilarious to us "normal" folks. Which is why we absolutely eat him up.

This justification of Wiseau fandom pathologised and celebrated him. It emphasised difference, sincerity and failure, echoing Popescu's (2013) distinction between "bad taste" films and "best-worst" movies. While the former self-consciously reference "already established cult, camp, kitsch, and bad-taste aesthetics", the latter appear to be "unintentionally bad" (571). For many reddit users, this notion of authentic failure became key to their expectations of *The Neighbors*, a sitcom that had been in the making for so long that one contributor described it as "an urban legend".

The preview expectations and reception of *The Neighbors* will be the focus of the last part of the chapter, where I will explore the three key audience orientations that emerged from my analysis of discussions about the show across reddit. Before doing so, however, I want to note the absence of discussions about whether or not *The Neighbors* succeeded *as a sitcom*. My discussion so far has highlighted that, although Wiseau had attempted to rebrand *The Room* as a dark comedy, this had very little impact on the film's reception discourse. Wiseau continues to be perceived as someone to be laughed at, rather than with. Therefore, although Wiseau fans had a range of expectations of *The Neighbors*, this did not seem to include the expectation that it would make people laugh in the way Wiseau intended. This structuring absence constructed *The Neighbors* as a comic failure. It also reinforced the reading of *The Room* as failed melodrama and the associated discourse of Wiseau as other and as incompetent media producer. In short, it cemented Wiseau's role within the fandom.

The Neighbors as Inauthentic Comic Failure

The first of these three orientations developed a narrative of increasing self-consciousness that erodes Wiseau's authenticity as an idiot-savant auteur:

> I haven't watched this, and I don't think I want to. I say this as someone who loved The Room. I believe it's almost impossible to make something "so-bad-it's-good" on purpose. The tricky thing is that the filmmakers can't be in on the joke. Ever since Wiseau became self-aware, he lost his charm. Wiseau trying to make a dramatic masterpiece was incredible and hilarious. Wiseau trying to make money off his reputation and try to be funny usually just ends up awkward and forced. He's not a man capable of creating something that ends up how he wants it to be.

This reddit user raised two concerns: First, that *The Neighbors* is primarily a ploy for making money from fans of *The Room* and second, that it is a doomed attempt at funniness. The post inscribed Wiseau with failure, both as a producer of drama and as a producer of comedy. However, whereas it valorised the failure of *The Room*, *The Neighbors* was rejected. The key distinction between these two texts is rooted in the notion that Wiseau, at some point, "became self-aware". This argument drew on the notion of cult film production as catching "lightning in a bottle" to produce something unique and unrepeatable.[1] Moreover, it employed science fiction discourse, dehumanising Wiseau as machine and denying him the possibility of being "in on the joke". Within this recurring narrative, Wiseau can only be a valued fan object if he remains the butt of fan jokes without understanding what anyone is laughing about.

Tyler (2008) argues that, when we are laughing "at the expense of another ... we effectively 'fix' the other, as the object of comedy. Laughter moves us both literally and figuratively, we are averted, moved away from the thing, the object or figure, we laugh at" (23). So although fans often celebrated Wiseau, he had been fixed as an object of laughter, and their wish that he should be oblivious to that laughter indicated a desire to maintain a distance between themselves and their fan object. It seemed almost as if Wiseau had been cast as a comedic *character*, who then broke the fourth wall and made the audience take responsibility for its laughter (Mills 2005). This pretence of oblivion was also suggested by aggressive and hurtful disparagement humour in redditor comments on his AMA responses, made with no evident concern that Wiseau might read them and be upset by them.

So, fans adopting this orientation rejected the possibility that *The Neighbors* could be intentionally funny. However, they didn't expect it to offer the pleasures that they associated with *The Room*, either, because they read it as a self-parody, and this prevented it from being an authentic failure. As MacDowell (2011) argues, "We absolutely *must* assume that *The Room* wasn't intended to be a self-parodic comedy in order to laugh at it in the way that we do". Some redditors refused to watch the sitcom, performing distanced anti-fandom (Gray 2003), rather than "the gleeful, critical pleasure" of critical fandom (Haig 2014: 19). This anti-fandom relied on paratextual material, such as Wiseau interviews and his appearances at conventions, to justify resistance to *The Neighbors*.

This orientation to *The Neighbors* articulated a fundamental opposition to the idea of Wiseau having the power to direct laughter. In response to the cult celebrity's attempts at humour, the fan cited above divested him of his charm and reinscribed him as awkward, attaching the "sign" of their own emotions to Wiseau's body (Ahmed 2004: 13). This response rejected Wiseau's perceived attempt to change his persona from idiot-savant auteur to a self-reflexive badfilm auteur that replicates and exaggerates the aesthetics of his previous work. It demonstrated that he had transgressed his demarcated space and become "understood as out of place and abject" (Graefer 2014: 112).

The discourse of transgression intersected with discourses of fan exploitation and commercialisation, which echoes one of the key responses by the *Ghostbusters* fans discussed in chapter 3. Those tweets positioned the resurrection of the sci-fi comedy franchise within a narrative of greedy, unimaginative Hollywood studios. Here, anti-fans produced a suspicion that Wiseau was taking advantage of his cult status to sell a deliberately bad and underfunded sitcom:

> eh, the room was a hit because he tried so hard to make it something emotional and dramatic, that's what makes it so fun to watch. it was a genuine attempt to make something great, obviously it didn't pan out, the script and acting were awful but unintentionally hilarious which is why it gathered such a massive following. it seems that the neighbours isn't really a genuine attempt at anything, just cashing in on the idea that Tommy is goofy and unpredictable. he's trying to make a comedy now and simply he can't …

In this post, *The Neighbors* was contrasted with *The Room*, which was "fun to watch" because it was read as "a genuine attempt". The value of *The Room*, then, was located in the perceived gap between Wiseau's intentions and what he produced. This pleasurable gap was not provided by *The Neighbors*, because fans assumed Wiseau set out to exploit and fulfil fan expectations and enjoyment of his failure by making a bad sitcom. As Hills (2002) notes, there is "an expressed hostility within cult fandoms towards commercialisation and commodification" that conflicts both with commodity-completist fan practices (4) and with an industry perception of fans "as loyal consumers … to be courted" (11). Writing about "resurrections" of fan objects through new films or TV programmes, Williams (2015) also suggests that "some fans remain ambivalent about openly accepting and embracing the commercial value they possess as target audiences / consumers for new imaginings of dormant fan objects, preferring to reject such new texts as commercial, economically driven and inferior" (175).

This orientation, then, identified and rejected an expectation of fan loyalty, constructing *The Neighbors* as an inauthentic failure and as a comic failure. The anti-fans responded to Wiseau with "unlaughter", described by Billig (2005) as "a display of not laughing when laughter might otherwise be expected, hoped for or demanded" (192). As a form of rhetoric, this unlaughter policed the structure of Wiseau fandom by marking his undesired transgression of the role that had been defined for him. It emphasised Wiseau's exclusion from the privileged group that is "allowed" to attempt humour and highlighted fan investment in their sense of superiority.

The Neighbors as Authentic Comic Failure

The notion of authenticity is also key to the second orientation to *The Neighbors*, but here Wiseau remained firmly in the role as "idiot-savant" auteur:

I saw the premier in NYC. Trust me, he really believes in what he does. He has no idea that this is bad.

This fan adopted a position of authority based on the experience of the premiere for *The Neighbors* and drew on that event to inscribe Wiseau with an erroneous belief in his own work and with an absence of self-awareness. Within this orientation, *The Neighbors* is understood as another authentic failure, which means that, even though it is a "bad" sitcom, it can still offer the pleasures of unintentional comedy:

> And even if it is self-aware, Tommy's weird interpretation of what people think is funny about him is, in itself, kind of interesting and funny. It's definitely not the masterpiece that The Room was, but I think it's worth watching.

This post challenged the possibility of Wiseau's fully comprehending why his fans are laughing. Although he might have recognised that fans were laughing *at* him, his understanding of that laughter would necessarily be shaped by his fundamental otherness. So, similar to the first audience orientation, this approach to *The Neighbors* rejected Wiseau's invitation to laugh *with* him. However, maintaining the "so-bad-it's-good" discourse, it then repositioned him and his work as objects of laughter. Within this confined role, Wiseau could still offer fans pleasure.

As this extract indicates, however, the redditors who saw *The Neighbors* as an authentic comic failure still tended to construct it as inferior to *The Room*. While some praised it as "pretty magical" and "fucking hilariously awful", most wrote that they struggled to sit through the episodes. So, although they marvelled at how bad it was, this spectacle was not always inscribed as enjoyable. This may in part be due to the domestic experience of sitcom viewing, which is less likely to offer the pleasures of playful, rowdy participation and the sense of sharing "the viewing experience with a like-minded community" (Middlemost 2013) of audience members who legitimate our own readings and pleasures. As you might expect, McCulloch's (2011) study of *The Room* fans found that most participants preferred communal viewing to watching the film alone. This preference was also indicated in reddit discussions of *The Neighbors*:

> 5 minutes in to the first episode and it's so bluntly painful I love it already
>
> Me too - it's fully Wiseau-esque improv. I'm going to watch more once I get my Room-crew together.

The first contributor here articulated a compound affective response of pain and love, with the feeling of love being constructed as a response to the pain inscribed on the sitcom. The post valorised the badness of *The Neighbors*, suggesting that the pleasures of *The Room* are also available here. The second contributor supported this evaluation and added that he or she would postpone further viewing until a communal viewing could be organised. This suggested that the encounter with *The Neighbors* was an important event that should be shared with fellow fans. It also indicated that, although the poster enjoyed watching the sitcom alone, this was not the ideal viewing experience. Crucially, the desired participants were the "Room-crew", who would have the fan cultural capital necessary to participate appropriately. This includes "social, collective critiques" (Downes 2015: 9) of the show, but also the identification of moments and elements that can be reperformed, laughed at and celebrated.

The second post connected the value of *The Neighbors* to its "fully Wiseau-esque improv" performances. Writing about comedy improv, Seham (2001) argues that such performances combine two key approaches; "making do and letting go". Drawing on de Certeau (1984), she defines the former as "a conscious creativity within restraints, through the rearrangement of available elements". The latter, on the other hand, is "the surrender of the conscious control that allows the performer to serve as a channel or instrument for artistic or divine inspiration" (xx). However, this fan linked the improvisation to Wiseau, rather than to the performers (although he is also one of them), constructing it as a particular performance style associated with his work. Wexman (1980) has written about improvisation in the films of directors such as Martin Scorsese and Robert Altman, arguing that the director is responsible for understanding the relationships between individual improvised performances and the other elements of the film and for knowing "what particular quality the scene should project in order to arouse an appropriate emotional response to the audience" (32). Wiseau's work, on the other hand, is known for its incoherence and for its persistent failure to achieve "appropriate" affective responses. In this case, the apparent improvisation draws attention to the acting process, to flaws in the performances and to the constructedness of the work.

Like the first orientation to *The Neighbors*, then, the second orientation remained preoccupied by the question of authenticity. The former articulated a concern that Wiseau had made a deliberately bad sitcom to exploit fan expectations of incompetence, which prevented *The Neighbors* from offering the pleasures that fans associated with *The Room* as unintentional comedy and an authentic failure. In contrast, the latter orientation argued that Wiseau's deluded otherness prevented such self-reflexivity and repositioned the sitcom as unintentional comedy and an authentic comic failure. In both cases, fans locate audience pleasure in the perceived gap between Wiseau's intentions and the work he produces. I will now turn to the third and final orientation, which dismissed this idea and focused instead on the negative affective experience of watching *The Neighbors*.

The Neighbors as Too Bad to Be Good

While *The Room* clearly resonates with many fans, some reddit users articulated a strong sense of dissonance in their responses to *The Neighbors*. They complained about the sitcom's messy storylines, the "shittiest" camera work, "terrible" actors and, most of all, the sound quality. They described the viewing experience as "painful", questioned their ability to watch all four episodes, and shared a drinking game that would make the experience more acceptable:

> Definitely one of the more miserable theater experiences I've ever had. It's only thirty or so minutes, but it feels like two hours of nothing but screaming.

This poster watched the pilot in the cinema and identified his or her affective response as misery. Here, *The Neighbors* not only failed to offer the pleasures traditionally associated with sitcom, and the pleasures associated with *The Room* as unintentional comedy, but was constructed as a source of *dis*pleasure. In particular, this dissonance was linked to noise and the perception that characters screamed instead of spoke. Later, the poster elaborated:

The audio is for sure the shittiest part of it; like the worst smelling shit in a pile of shit...

Here, the repetition of "shit" marked *The Neighbors* as abject, a debased sitcom that offends the senses by hurting your ears and smelling foul. This reading was reinforced by another poster:

> That show makes me feel like I'm watching a 30 min porno every time. I immediately feel shameful and stop watching with each attempt.

Again, this articulated an embodied experience of dissonance, identified as feelings of shame and regret. The negative comparison with pornography reinforced the notion of *The Neighbors* as abject, a transgression that the viewer felt compelled to stop by switching the show off. However, he or she also noted making several attempts at watching the programme, which might suggest a wish to find something of value in it or perhaps to endure the entire text to fulfil the criteria of fan completism.

The orientation differs markedly to what we might ordinarily associate with sitcom viewing (see for example chapter 6), and it is clear that the feelings of discomfort did not predispose these viewers to laugh at any jokes or comic situations and that *The Neighbors* failed to combine such discomfort with moments of pleasurable relief. The orientation also differed to the playful audience protocol associated with *The Room*. Earlier in this chapter I identified a distance between fans and fan object, characterised by a tension between ridicule and celebration. Here, the distance was obliterated by the excess of *The Neighbors*, which was seen to invade the viewers' bodies as they responded with discomfort, disgust and shame. *The Neighbors* was deemed too bad to be pleasurable. This challenges the discourse of "so bad it's good" and reinforces MacDowell's (2011) argument that this label really describes a good viewing experience of a bad film that is valued "because it is 'bad' in very special and very strange ways" that remain difficult to pin down.

   The intense affective responses articulated within this orientation resemble one discussed by McCoy and Scarborough (2014) in their study of audience responses to "bad" television. Viewers who avoided watching TV programmes that they deemed to be "bad" tended "to be particularly judgmental and condemnatory" when talking about them: "They tend to not only judge a television show to be inferior or in bad taste, but they are often incensed by these shows; they experience a strong emotional and normative response against them" (47). However, *The Neighbors* anti-fans often identified as fans of *The Room*, and so, unlike the viewers in that study, they did not have a rigid symbolic boundary between "good" and "bad" productions (55). Perhaps, then, the intensity of their responses articulated a sense of disappointment that their investment in Wiseau had not been rewarded by his first substantial production since *The Room*. As Williams (2015) notes:

> [S]econd-rate versions of beloved fan objects can work to undermine fans' self-identities and sense of ontological security since they threaten to dilute and undermine many of the things that the fan was originally attracted to. Inauthentic or inferior copies of a fan object can, therefore, endanger fan attachments both by highlighting the commercial nature of fandom, as well as threatening to "betray" the original characters and narrative worlds. (175)

I have previously discussed such anxiety in relation to the *Ghostbusters* franchise resurrection (chapter 3), and this affective response was also alluded to in reddit posts:

> Everything about it was terrible, but in a much worse kind of terrible then The Room. Like, it was really obvious that no effort whatsoever had been put into this production.

This response is distinct from what Lübecker (2015) calls "the feel-bad experience", where films like *Dogville* (von Trier 2003) and *Elephant* (Van Sant 2003) are "characterised by a very direct disturbance of the spectator" and aim "to get on the[ir] nerves". Whereas these films create "a spectatorial desire" only to frustrate this "desire for catharsis" (2), these viewers of *The Neighbors* only seemed to want to switch the show off. The response was also distinct from an experience of gross-out comedy, which King (2002) defines as "comedy based on crude and deliberate transgressions of the bounds of 'normal' everyday taste", with "a repeated focus on lower regions of the body and the emission of bodily products" (63). Here, the transgression was connected not to representations but to expectations of production values. The accusation that "no effort whatsoever" had been made demonstrated that Wiseau was no longer seen to fit the role of the "passionate and earnest" so-bad-it's-good filmmaker.

Conclusion

This final case study chapter has tried to unpack some of the ambiguities and tensions of laughter by exploring discourses around unintentional comedy and comic failure. In doing so, I have returned to the study of fandom, but I here focused on the *critical* fandom around cult celebrity Tommy Wiseau and examined him as a nexus of discourses of comedy, otherness, authenticity and cultural competency. Wiseau's failed melodrama *The Room* became an object of celebration and ridicule through ironic and camp consumption at participatory cinema screenings, and I wanted to examine the reception of his attempt to reposition himself as a joker, rather than the butt of the joke, through his release of the sitcom *The Neighbors*. My case study focused on reddit, a platform that is dominated by white, geek masculinity and privileges humour and creative play.

The first part of the chapter analysed reddit users' engagement with Wiseau in his IAMA ... AMA, which was intended to promote the release of *The Neighbors*. I explored the ways in which contributors othered Wiseau along the axes of gender and nationality, inscribing him with a fundamental cultural difference that was mocked but also celebrated as unique and authentic. Reflecting on how this indicated fluctuations between ironic and camp reading strategies, I emphasised that fan engagement with Wiseau was characterised by a push-pull dynamic that distanced fans from him while reinforcing their attachment to him.

The second part of the chapter examined discussion of *The Neighbors* across reddit and identified three key orientations to the programme. Two of these orientations were preoccupied with the question of whether the sitcom was an authentic failure, like *The Room*, or whether it was a commercial ploy designed by Wiseau to exploit fan expectations of incompetence. The third orientation articulated intensely negative affective responses to *The Neighbors*, suggesting that the excess of the sitcom had transgressed the distance between fans and fan object and was interpreted as an unwelcome bodily intrusion.

Importantly, I failed to identify any reddit discussions about whether *The Neighbors* worked as comedy. This structuring absence constructed its comic failure as obvious, even if it was sometimes seen to be unintentionally funny, and it reinforced the reading of *The Room* as a failed melodrama, rather than a dark comedy. So, although I have traced some changes in the discourses of authenticity around Wiseau's celebrity text, he remained fixed within the fandom as culturally incompetent and as an object of laughter. Despite inhabiting the privileged space of white, masculine celebrity, he was excluded from the group that is "allowed" to direct laughter. As a fan object, he had become sticky with a specific set of pleasures, and his attempt to manoeuvre into a different space was blocked or marked as transgressive. This draws attention to the rigidity of symbolic boundaries in comedy culture, demonstrating that although unintentional comedy is valued for the pleasures it offers, this value does not necessarily facilitate movement within the structure of this culture.

Note

1 Thank you to Matt Hills, who raised this issue when I presented a paper on *The Neighbors* at the 2016 *Celebrity Studies Conference* in Amsterdam.

10 Conclusion
The Structure of Comedy Culture

This book has attempted to draw attention to a glaring gap in comedy studies: While there is a rich body of work on comedic texts, we still know very little about how audiences respond to those texts. Building on a small body of existing book-length work that explores comedy audiences in relation to taste (e.g. Friedman 2014 and Kuipers 2006) and interpretation (e.g. Coleman 2000 and Jhally and Lewis 1992), this book has taken a broad approach. Engaging with extant debates around the significance of gender, "race", nationality, genre and cultural transgression in comedy, I have also argued for the value of exploring the specificities of comedy fandom and comic failure. My hope is to encourage further investigations of what audiences to with comedy.

I have emphasised the importance of developing theoretical frameworks that enable us to explore the complexities of contemporary audience practices. Here, I have integrated humour and comedy theory with Mills's (2009) notion of cue theory, with the semiotic concept of modality, and with Ahmed's (2004) perspective on affect. This theoretical approach has facilitated the study of how audiences interpret and evaluate comedy in light of its assumed goal (to "be funny"), how they negotiate the push/pull dynamic that invites a broader range of affects, and how they construct cultural identities through their responses. I have been particularly interested in considering what articulations of such engagement can tell us about whom audiences expect to make them laugh, and with whom they want to share that laughter.

I have also stressed the need to consider the cultural contexts of comedy audiences, and I have foregrounded this challenge through a study that is both multi-text and multi-sited. The approach has enabled me to consider how affects and discourses of comedy circulate within and across different audience cultures and online contexts, while reflecting on the affordances and constraints provided by each platform. Studies of online audiences have tended to concentrate on message boards. Drawing on work in computer science and Internet studies, I here tried to demonstrate that it is important to consider activities that are situated in other online spaces. Different sites may attract different demographic groups, while also facilitating different kinds of audience engagement.

This includes the emphasis on quotation culture on Tumblr, promotional discourse on official Facebook pages, consumer discourse on Amazon, inspiration discourse on Pinterest, and humorous play on reddit.

Comedy Fandom

This book has also sought to contribute to the field of fan studies by shedding light on some of the specificities of comedy fandom. In particular, I have stressed the significance of the push/pull dynamic between comic insulation and fan investment. Comedy needs to distance us from characters, so that we feel able to laugh when things go wrong for them. However, it also often invites us to become emotionally invested in characters and their relationships. This push/pull dynamic is facilitated through modality shifts that position the comedy closer to, and further from, reality.

I have looked at two key examples of how fans negotiated this dynamic. The first was comedic quotation in *Parks and Recreation* posts on Tumblr, where fans shared screen grabs and GIFs from the show. This practice enabled fans to perform their love for their fan object, to inscribe particular textual moments with resonance, and to integrate those moments into their own lives. On the other hand, comedic quotations retain humour as a discursive strategy, avoiding the close, analytical discussion so discouraged by the dominant discourse of comedy. The second example I examined was the cult fandom around Tommy Wiseau and his unintentionally funny melodrama *The Room*. My analysis of fans' playful participation in Wiseau's AMA on reddit argued that their mockery of him simultaneously distanced them from him *and* valorised him through demonstrations of fan knowledge. How, then, is this dynamic negotiated in other comedy fandoms?

Comedy remains underexplored in fan studies. The field has been preoccupied with creative and textually productive fandom, as well as cult intensities. The two fan cultures I have discussed here can certainly be positioned within these two traditions, but I would argue that much comedy fandom cannot. This might partly explain comedy's neglect by fan studies, but I think Sandvoss and Kearns's (2016) concept of "ordinary fandom" offers a useful starting point. I began to explore this idea in my discussion of Amy Schumer fandom on Pinterest. With its emphasis on emotional attachment and everyday practices, the concept can help us think about how fans read comedy and focus in on elements that resonate with them, as well as about how they perform fandom in everyday life, for example through repeat viewings and quotation practices. But the concept of "ordinary fandom" requires further development, and we need to learn more about the practices of comedy fans, the affects of their shifting or continuing attachments to comedies and comedians, and their readings of comedic texts. I hope this book will encourage new and diverse approaches.

Comedic Genres, Traditions and Innovations

A key theme in this book's explorations of comedy fans and audiences has been the centre/margin structure of Western comedy culture, and the ways in which it reproduces broader cultural hierarchies and power relations. This discussion has focused on the two interlinked issues of genre and cultural identities, and this final chapter will reflect on these in turn. First, I examined how audience discussions of mainstream comedic genres negotiate discourses established by professional critics, and reflected on emerging tensions between dominant cultural values and pleasures valued by viewers. Second, I explored responses to the marginal genre of web comedy series, considering how viewers drew on expectations developed from their experiences of watching television comedy, and how the online distribution model facilitated an international fan community.

My multi-sited study of three sitcoms examined a recurring desire for "traditional" sitcom. Amazon reviews of *Everybody Hates Chris* valorised the experience of watching and laughing together as a family. *Gavin & Stacey* anti-fans critiqued the trend towards narrative comedy and suggested that this form required less comic skill and offered fewer pleasures than the "classic" sitcoms that foreground jokes and comic situations. And, finally, *Miranda* fans celebrated this sitcom as a "refreshing" alternative to contemporary shows, praising it for offering the silliness and belly laughs they associated with "old-fashioned" sitcoms. I don't wish to gloss over the diversity of responses to these shows. For example, *Gavin & Stacey* fans found pleasure in its "subtle" humour and their emotional investment in characters' development, while *Miranda*'s anti-fans dismissed it as "outdated" and "fake". However, I would argue that the recurring valorisation of pleasures associated with conventional sitcom suggested a resistance to the class-based, dominant critical discourse that privileges "highbrow humour" (Kuipers 2015: 113), stylistic innovation and niche, middle-class audiences.

The circulation of critical reception discourse was also evident in my analysis of IMDb reviews of *(500) Days of Summer*. Examining how reviewers articulated criteria for "good" romcoms, I argued that they remained preoccupied with negotiating criteria that had already been established by professional film critics. In particular, I identified a wish to "rescue" *(500) Days of Summer* from the feminised romantic comedy genre by constructing it as "authentic", "original" and "innovative". This discursive practice reproduced gendered and classed dichotomies of high culture / mass culture. However, these distinctions were also undermined by a recurring desire to feel "swept away" by the on-screen romance, which re-valorised affective responses that are encouraged by romcoms but scorned by critics.

These two chapters on sitcom and romcom demonstrate the privileging of middle-class and masculine pleasures in Western comedy culture, but also the circulation of counter-discourses that claimed and celebrated pleasures associated with working-class and feminine tastes. I think the tendency for scholars to study our own fan objects and fandoms means that we run the risk of reinforcing this cultural hierarchy, and of developing problematic blind spots in our fields. For example, it remains important to study the reception of popular, but critically derided comedies. In what ways do they resonate with audiences? How do fans negotiate the low cultural status of such fan objects? However, as will hopefully become apparent, it is also vital that we study audiences that are underserved by mainstream film and television.

My analysis of YouTube responses to the British web comedy series *Brothers with No Game* reflects on the marginalisation of blackness in comedy culture, and on U.S. and UK television, and suggests that online distribution can provide alternative spaces for the development of black-centred narratives. YouTube users sometimes critiqued *Brothers with No Game* for failing to achieve the production values they associated with television comedy, but they also articulated investment in the show by offering recommendations and praising improvements. Importantly, the online distribution model ensured that all fans had access to new episodes at the same time, which facilitated the development of an international community of fans who discussed the show in the comment threads. Participants used the threads to articulate affective responses to observational comedy and romantic relationships, but also to discuss characters and events in relation to wider cultural issues of race and class. So, as a web comedy, *Brothers with No Game* provided a space for fans to articulate black identities and participate in public debates around the representation of black masculinities and femininities. It has become clear, then, that questions of genre intersected with questions of cultural identity in negotiations of the centre/margin structure of comedy culture. I will now reflect further on the significance of such identities for fan and wider audience engagement with comedy.

Comedy and Cultural Identities

Blog responses to *Bridesmaids* often praised the film's focus on female comedians and female friendship. But this celebration reproduced a critical reception narrative of women comedians and female-driven comedies as isolated instances of success, which ignores previous achievements, constructs women as competitors (Warner and Savigny 2015) and reinforces masculine normativity in comedy culture. In contrast, when Paul Feig tweeted that his *Ghostbusters* film would star "hilarious women", he was met with a wealth of casting suggestions that highlighted and valorised a broad range of female comedians. Such fan casting was often informed by paratextual knowledge of Feig's previous productions, which disrupted the narrative of isolated achievements by drawing connections *between* successful women-centred comedies. The gendered significance of *Ghostbusters*, as a reboot of a franchise structured around male star comedians, was also indicated by the hostile rejection discourse (Williams 2015) that was articulated by mostly male fans. This rejection grew increasingly aggressive, culminating in horrific racist and misogynistic harassment of *Ghostbusters* star Leslie Jones on Twitter in 2016. The vitriol suggests that the film was perceived as a threat to the privileged position of white masculinity in *Ghostbusters* fandom, but the reaction may also be situated within a wider white male supremacist movement that has been associated with Donald Trump's rise to power.

The raced centre/margin structure emerged again in my analysis of responses to the U.S. sitcom *Everybody Hates Chris* and the British web comedy *Brothers With No Game*. Amazon reviews of *Everybody Hates Chris* sometimes situated the show within a very limited history of black-centred sitcom that comprised *The Cosby Show* and *The Fresh Prince of Bel-Air*. This narrative indicated the perceived whiteness of mainstream U.S. sitcom, a view that was made explicit in YouTube responses to *Brothers With No Game*. Here, fans positioned the series outside of white, mainstream television, and within a culture of black web shows. This body of online screen fiction was constructed as offering the black-centred narratives viewers were missing on mainstream television.

Both *Everybody Hates Chris* and *Brothers With No Game* were inscribed with funniness and "authenticity", praised for providing representations of black characters that viewers could recognise, care about and laugh at, rather than the stereotyped blackness viewers associated with white-centred narratives. My analysis reflected on the ways in which *Brothers With No Game* provided an alternative space where YouTube users could experience a pleasurable sense of belonging to a black diasporic audience, but it remains deeply problematic that viewers are marginalised by mainstream television in their own national contexts. In particular, we can identify a failure of British public service broadcasters to adequately serve black British audiences, and this demonstrates the need for further research on opportunities and challenges for addressing this neglect.

My final chapter complicated the narrative of white, masculine privilege in comedy culture, by exploring responses to Wiseau as a white, male celebrity who was inscribed with comic failure. Wiseau is primarily known for his "so bad it's good" film *The Room*, and I was interested in exploring how fans responded to his attempt to reposition himself as a comedian. My analysis of reddit discussons about his sitcom *The Neighbors* identified a structuring absence of talk about whether or not the show succeeded *as a sitcom*. Instead, the debate focused on whether it was possible for this production to be an "authentic" comic failure, and therefore offer the pleasures fans associated with his unintentionally funny melodrama. Across reddit, fans repeatedly othered Wiseau's production practice, as well as his performances of heterosexual masculinity and "Americanness", and this otherness was simultaneously mocked and celebrated as "authentic" and "unique". Excluding him from becoming one of "us" at the centre of comedy culture, this inscribed otherness blocked Wiseau's attempted bid for the power to direct laughter.

Fan engagement with this cult celebrity demonstrated that the centre/margin structure is also nation-based. U.S. screen comedy is exported to numerous territories, while British comedy has had transnational success on a smaller scale. In contrast, *Lilyhammer*'s distribution deals represented a rare opportunity for Norwegian comedy to gain international visibility. For some Norwegian viewers, this exposure seemed risky: If transnational viewers perceived the show to be a comic failure, *Lilyhammer*'s Norwegianness would implicate the domestic audience in "national shame" (Ahmed 2004: 101). This transnational audience was primarily imagined as U.S. based, and the official *Lilyhammer* Facebook page further reinforced the centrality of the U.S. audience. Branding the show as a Netflix Original, the page erased the role of Norwegian public service broadcaster NRK, and repeatedly ignored site users from a range of countries by structuring news and fan activities around the show's release dates in the U.S.

Ain't No Bitches Gonna Hunt No Ghosts

So, then, my analysis suggests that attempts to destabilise the centre/margin structure of comedy culture can be associated with risks. *Bridesmaids*, *Brothers With No Game* and *Lilyhammer* were sometimes inscribed with "the burden of representation" (Tagg 1988), tasked with often contradictory responsibilities that are rarely leveled at comedy originating from the centre. *Bridesmaids* should promote feminism, but also convince a male-dominated movie industry that female comedians could attract and please male cinema-goers. *Brothers With No Game* should provide "positive" representations of black characters, but the characters should also be complex, "authentic" and funny. *Lilyhammer* should not represent Norwegians as fools, but it should make U.S. audiences laugh. Failure to achieve these expectations carried with it the possibility of gendered, raced and national shame.

The continued policing of centre/margin boundaries represents another key risk, as demonstrated by the backlash against *Ghostbusters* and Leslie Jones. The film itself offered one approach to tackling that challenge. Looking through comments on a YouTube video of their encounter with a ghost, Kristen Wiig's character Erin reads one out: "Ain't no bitches gonna hunt no ghosts". Melissa McCarthy's Abbey swiftly dismisses the attack, redirecting Erin's attention to something more important: "You're not supposed to be reading what crazy people write online". This scene confronts and dismisses the misogynist shaming of

Ghostbusters and its cast as abject, using disparagement humour to return the shame to online bullies.

Gendered shame is also addressed and ridiculed in Amy Schumer's
comedy, through the use of ironic performativity (Goltz 2015). Like
Parks and Recreation, Miranda, Bridesmaids and *Ghostbusters*, her
work is part of a comedic space "where feminism speaks, talks back, and
is contested" (Mizejewski 2014: 6). On Pinterest, however, user practices located Schumer's feminism in her "serious" discourse, rather than
in her comedy. Through quotations from her celebrity interviews and
speeches, Schumer was constructed as a symbolic resource in a postfeminist project of self-development, where she demonstrated the possibility
of claiming female agency in a patriarchal society. Engagement with her
transgressive comedy's more complex negotiations of feminism remained
invisible on this platform, where curating practices positioned comedic
quotations as resources for entertainment. This raises questions of how
male and female audiences respond to "women's comedy". How do feminist discourses and feminist affects circulate within such comedy? And
how do they spill over into other contexts, with other affordances? How
are they experienced, negotiated and rejected?

More broadly, comedy studies needs to investigate opportunities and
challenges for destabilising the centre/margin structure of comedy culture. And while we already have a rich tradition of work on films, sitcoms and stars that challenge these boundaries, we should also venture
outside of textual analysis. We need to explore the creativity, labour,
obstacles and achievements of those who make comedy (e.g. Mills and
Horton 2016). And we need to explore the readings, desires, pleasures
and disappointments of marginalised comedy audiences. This argument
intersects with calls to expand academic attention in fan studies beyond
the practices of younger, white fans (e.g. Petersen 2017 and Warner
2015), and I think a dialogue between these two fields could develop
exciting avenues for further research.

First, the tension between comic insulation and fan investment may
offer a way of thinking about the specificities of affective resonance in
comedy fandom. How do different fans negotiate that push/pull dynamic
through their fan practices, and through their affective relationships with
comedies and comedians as fan objects? I wonder if this tension might
sometimes discourage the intensities of cult fandom, as well as creative
fan production. Quoting comedy is a quick and accessible way to appropriate the comedic skills of the comedians we love, and so it offers a way
to rupture the boundary between the text and our own everyday lives,
while being funny. And although comedic re-performance certainly can
be used for interpretation and creative development, fidelity remains
highly valued as a demonstration of fan knowledge and performative
skill. I think, then, that the concept of ordinary fandom might offer
a useful way into thinking about the everyday practices and affects of

comedy fans. However, I would like to emphasise that we should also consider creative fan practices. For example, how does comedy fan fiction engage with humour? And what are the specific pleasures and challenges of writing fan fiction that aims to make readers laugh?

Finally, both comedy and fandom can offer a sense of belonging, and this feeling is reinforced through shared values and pleasures. But such invitations necessarily come with distinctions between what is included and what remains on the outside. Who gets to make fans laugh? Who is met with silence, or "unlaughter" (Billig 2005: 192)? And with whom do fans want to share their laughter? We need to consider where those boundaries are drawn, how they are policed, and how they are challenged.

References

Abbott, D. (2014) "Old Plays, New Narratives: Fan Production of New Media Texts from Broadcast Theatre". Paper presented at the Interactive Narratives, New Media & Social Engagement International Conference, Toronto. http://radar.gsa.ac.uk/3553/1/ntlive-brafftv.pdf.

Abbot, S. and Jermyn, D. (2009) "Introduction – a Lot Like Love: The Romantic Comedy in Contemporary Cinema". In S. Abbot and D. Jermyn (eds.) *Falling in Love Again: Romantic Comedy in Contemporary Cinema*. London and New York: I.B. Tauris, pp. 1–8.

"About". https://about.pinterest.com/en-gb.

"About Us". http://corp.popsugar.com/#about.

Acham, C. (2012) "Blacks in the Future: braving the frontier of the web series". In B. E. Smith-Shomade (ed.) *Watching While Black: centering the television of black audiences*. New Brunswick, NJ: Rutgers University Press, pp. 63–74.

Adams, E. (2012) "Showrunner Michael Schur on Building *Parks and Recreation*'s Fourth Season (Part 1 of 5)". The A.V. Club, 18 June. http://www.avclub.com/article/showrunner-michael-schur-on-building-iparks-and-re-81404.

Adewunmi, B. (2012) "Why Black British Drama is Going Online, Not on TV". *The Guardian* 2 July. https://www.theguardian.com/world/2012/jul/02/black-british-tv-drama-online.

Ahmed, S. (2004) *The Cultural Politics of Emotions*. Edinburgh: Edinburgh University Press.

Ahmed, S. (2010) *The Promise of Happiness*. Durham, NC: Duke University Press.

Allen, N. (2009) "The Room: the 'Citizen Kane' of bad films". *The Daily Telegraph* 1 November. http://www.telegraph.co.uk/culture/film/film-news/6479392/The-Room-the-Citizen-Kane-of-bad-films.html.

Anderson, B. (1991) *Imagined Communities*. London: Verso.

Andò, R. (2015) "Fashion and Fandom on TV and Social Media: Claire Underwood's power dressing". *Critical Studies in Fashion & Beauty* 6(2): 207–231.

Angelo, M. (2011) "Tossing the Bouquet Out of the Genre". *The New York Times* 6 May. http://www.nytimes.com/2011/05/08/movies/bridesmaids-with-kristen-wiig-opens-friday.html.

Associated Press (2005) "Chris Rock Talks on 'Everybody Hates Chris'". http://www.foxnews.com/story/2005/07/22/chris-rock-talks-on-everybody-hates-chris.html.

Austin, T. (2002) *Hollywood Hype and Audiences: selling and watching popular film in the 1990s*. Manchester: Manchester University Press.

Babington, B. and Evans, P.W. (1989) *Affairs to Remember: the Hollywood comedy of the sexes*. Manchester and New York: Manchester University Press.

Bakhtin, M.M. (1968) *Rabelais and His World*. Trans. H. Iswolsky. London: The M.I.T. Press.

Bakhtin, M.M. (1992) "The Problem of Speech Genres". In C. Emerson and M. Holquist (eds.) *Speech Genres and Other Late Essays*. Austin: University of Texas Press, pp. 60–102.

Barker, M. (2008) "The Pleasures of Watching an 'Off-Beat' Film: the case of being John Malkovich". *Scope* (11). http://www.scope.nottingham.ac.uk/article.php?issue=11&id=1020.

Bastiansen, H. and Syvertsen, T. (1996) "Towards a Norwegian Television History". In I. Bondebjerg and F. Bono (eds.) *Television in Scandinavia: history, politics and aesthetics*. Luton: University of Luton Press, pp. 127–155.

BBC (no date) "Brothers with No Game: from web to screen". BBC Academy. http://www.bbc.co.uk/academy/production/article/art20150119163453371.

Becker, C. (2008) "Acting for the Cameras: performance in the multi-camera sitcom", *Mediascape* (Spring). http://www.tft.ucla.edu/mediascape/Spring08_ActingForTheCameras.html.

Bergson, H. (1901/2004) *Laughter: an essay on the meaning of the comic*. C. Brereton and F. Rothwell. Whitefish: Kessinger.

Bergstrom, K. (2011) "Don't Feed the Troll": shutting down debate about community expectations on reddit.com". *First Monday* 16(8). http://firstmonday.org/ojs/index.php/fm/article/viewArticle/3498/3029.

Betz, S. (2014) "Affective Moorings: the online sociality of fandom". Paper presented at the ASAANZ/AAS Conference in Queenstown, Australia, 10–13 November. https://www.academia.edu/9296518/Affective_Moorings_The_Online_Sociality_of_Fandom.

Billig, M. (1995) *Banal Nationalism*. London, Thousand Oaks and New Delhi: Sage.

Billig, M. (2005) *Laughter and Ridicule: towards a social critique of humour*. London, Thousand Oaks and New Delhi: Sage.

Biswas, S. and Choudhury, A. (2016) "Rearticulating Slave Women's History: black feminism in Margaret Walker's *Jubilee*". *Research Journal of English Language and Literature* 4(2): 672–679.

Bonnstetter, B.E. (2012) "The Legacy of Mystery Science Theater 3000: text, textual production, paracinema, and media literacy". *Journal of Popular Film & Television* 40(2): 94–104.

Bore, I.K. (2010) "Undermining Comediennes: audience perceptions of women in TV comedy". *Feminist Media Studies* 10(4): 481–485.

Bore, I.K. (2011a) "The Cultural World of T.V. Comedy Audiences: gender, nationality and humour". Ph.D. thesis. Cardiff University.

Bore, I.K. (2011b) "Transnational TV Comedy Audiences". *Television & New Media* 12(4): 347–369.

Bore, I.K. (2012) "Focus Group Research and TV Comedy Audiences". *Participations* 9(2): 3–22. http://www.participations.org/Volume%209/Issue%20 2/2%20Bore.pdf.

Bore, I.K. and Williams, R. (2010) "Transnational Twilighters: a *Twilight* fan community in Norway". In M. Click, J.S. Aubrey and E. Behm-Morawitz (eds.)

Bitten by Twilight: youth culture, media, and the Twilight saga. New York: Peter Lang, pp. 189–206.

Bourdieu, P. (1984) *Distinction: a social critique of the judgement of taste.* Translated by R. Nice. London: Routledge.

Boyle, K. (2014) "Gender, Comedy and Reviewing Culture on the Internet Movie Database". *Participations* 11(1): 31–49. http://www.participations. org/Volume%2011/Issue%201/3.pdf.

Box Office Mojo (2011) "Bridesmaids". http://www.boxofficemojo.com/movies/ ?id=wiigapatow.htm.

Bradley, R. N. (2015) "Awkwardly Hysterical: theorizing black girl awkwardness and humor in social media". *Comedy Studies* 6(2): 148–153.

Brady, A. (2016) "Taking Time between G-String Changes to Educate Ourselves: Sinéad O'Connor, Miley Cyrus, and celebrity feminism". *Feminist Media Studies* 16(3): 429–444.

Braxton, G. (2014) "On Diversity, Mindy Kaling Finds Herself Held to Higher Standard". *The Los Angeles Times* 29 March. http://articles.latimes. com/2014/mar/29/entertainment/la-et-st-mindy-project-diversity-20140329.

Brunsdon, C. and Spigel, L. (2008) "Introduction to the Second Edition". In C. Brunsdon and L. Spigel (eds.) *Feminist Television Criticism: a reader, Second Edition.* Maidenhead: Open University Press, pp. 1–19.

Burgess, J. and Green, J. (2009) *YouTube.* Cambridge, U.K.: Polity.

Bury, R. (2016) "Technology, Fandom and Community in the Second Media Age". *Convergence*, published online before print: 1–16. http://con.sagepub. com/content/early/2016/05/24/1354856516648084.abstract.

Caldwell, N. (1999) "Spoilers and Cheaters: narrative closure and the cultural dimensions of alternate reading practices". *M/C Journal*, 2(8): http://journal. media-culture.org.au/9912/spoilers.php.

Carby, H. (1982/2005) "White Woman Listen! Black Feminism and the Boundaries of Sisterhood". In K. Owusu (ed.) *Black British Culture and Society: a text reader.* London: Routledge, pp. 86–93.

Carpentier, N. (2014) "'Fuck the Clowns from Grease!!' Fantasies of Participation and Agency in the YouTube Comments on a Cypriot Problem Documentary". *Information, Communication & Society* 17(8): 1001–1016.

de Certeau, M. (1984) *The Practice of Everyday Life.* Trans. S. Rendall. Berkeley: University of California Press.

Chang, Y., Tang, L., Inagaki, Y. and Liu, Y. (2014) "What is Tumblr: A Statistical Overview and Comparison". *ACM SIGKDD Explorations Newsletter* 16(1): 21–29.

Child, B. (2015) "Sony plans *Ghostbusters* 'cinematic universe' with Channing Tatum movie". *The Guardian* 10 March. https://www.theguardian.com/ film/2015/mar/10/ghostbusters-cinematic-universe-channing-tatum-sony.

Chin, B. and Gray, J. (2002) "'One Ring to Rule Them All': pre-viewers and pre-texts of the *Lord of the Rings* films". *Intensities: The Journal of Cult Media* 2: http://web.archive.org/web/20021003033127/www.cult-media.com/issue2/ Achingray.htm.

Christian, A.J. (2011) "Fandom as Industrial Response: producing identity in an independent web series". *Transformative Works and Cultures* 8. http:// testjournal.transformativeworks.org/index.php/twc/article/view/250/237.

Christian, A.J. (2012) "The Web as Television Reimagined? Online Networks and the Pursuit of Legacy Media". *Journal of Communication Inquiry* 36(4): 340–356.

Coates, J. (2003) *Men Talk: stories in the making of masculinities.* Malden: Blackwell.

Coleman, R. R. M. (1998) *African American Viewers and the Black Situation Comedy: situating racial humor.* New York: Garland Publishing.

Collie, H. (2017) "'I've Been Having Fantasies About Regan and Carter Three Times a Week': television, women and desire". In R. Moseley, H. Wheatley and H. Wood (eds.) *Television for Women: new directions.* London: Routledge, pp. 223–240.

Cook, J. (1982) "Narrative, Comedy, Character and Performance". In J. Cook (ed.) *BFI Dossier 17: Television sitcom.* London: BFI, pp. 13–18.

Corrigan, T. (1991) "Film and the Culture of Cult". In J.P. Telotte (ed.) *The Cult Film Experience: beyond all reason.* Austin: University of Texas Press, pp. 26–37.

Creeber, G. (2011) "It's Not TV, It's Online Drama: the return of the intimate screen". *International Journal of Cultural Studies* 14(6): 591–606.

Critchley, S. (2002) *On Humour.* New York: Routledge.

Cunningham, S. and Silver, J. (2012) "On-Line Film Distribution: its history and global complexion". In S. Cunningham and D. Iordanova (eds.) *Digital Disruption: cinema moves on-line.* St Andrews: St Andrews Film Studies, pp. 33–66.

Deleyto, C. (1998) "Love and Other Triangles: *Alice* and the conventions of romantic comedy". In P.W. Evans and C. Deleyto (eds.) *Terms of Endearment: Hollywood romantic comedy of the 1980s and 1990s.* Edinburgh: Edinburgh University Press, pp. 129–147.

Deller, R. (2011) "Twittering On: audience research and participation using Twitter". *Participations* 8(1): 216–245. http://www.participations.org/ Volume%208/Issue%201/PDF/deller.pdf.

Deller, R. (2015) "Simblr Famous and SimSecret Infamous: performance, community norms, and shaming among fans of *The Sims*". *Transformative Works and Cultures* 18: http://journal.transformativeworks.org/index.php/twc/article/view/615/503.

Del Rio, C. (1998) "*Something Wild*: take a walk on the wild side (but be home before midnight)". In P.W. Evans and C. Deleyto (eds.) *Terms of Endearment: Hollywood romantic comedy of the 1980s and 1990s.* Edinburgh: Edinburgh University Press, pp. 75–92.

Dhoest, A. (2007) "The National Everyday in Contemporary European Television Fiction: the Flemish case". *Critical Studies in Television* 2(2): 60–76.

Dockterman, E. (2014) "How Amy Schumer Gets Guys to Think Feminists Are Funny" *Time,* 1 April. http://time.com/45771/how-amy-schumer-got-guys-to-think-feminists-are-funny/.

Downes, M. (2015) "Critical Pleasures: reflections on the Indonesian horror genre and its anti-fans". *Plaridel* 12(2): 1–18 http://www.plarideljournal.org/article/critical-pleasures-reflections-on-the-indonesian-horror-genre-and-its-anti-fans/.

Duggan, M. (2015) "Mobile Messaging and Social Media 2015". *PewResearchCentre.* http://www.pewinternet.org/2015/08/19/mobile-messaging-and-social-media-2015/.

Duggan, M. and Smith, A. (2013) "6% of Online Adults are reddit Users". *Pew Research Centre*. http://www.pewinternet.org/files/old-media/Files/Reports/2013/PIP_reddit_usage_2013.pdf.

Durgnat, R. (1969) *The Crazy Mirror: hollywood comedy and the American image*. London: Faber.

Dyer, R. (1979/1998) *Stars* (New Edition). London: BFI.

Easthope, A. (1990) *What a Man's Gotta Do: the masculine myth in popular culture*. New York and London: Routledge.

Fey, Tina (2011) *Bossypants*. Kindle edition. New York, Boston and London: Reagan Arthur Books / Little, Brown & Company.

Fine, G. A. and De Soucey, M. (2005) "Joking Cultures: humor themes as social regulation in group life". *Humor* 18 (1): 1–22.

Finnegan, R. (2011) *Why Do We Quote? The Culture and History of Quotation*. Cambridge: Open Book Publishers.

Fiske, J. (1992) "The Cultural Economy of Fandom". In L. Lewis (ed.) *The Adoring Audience: fan culture and popular media*. London and New York: Routledge, pp. 30–49.

Fogle, K. (2015) "It's Bigger on the Inside: fandom, social media, and *Doctor Who*". In A.F. Slade, A.J. Narro and D. Givens-Carroll (eds.) *Television, Social Media, and Fan Culture*. Lanham: Lexington Books, pp. 297–318.

Foy, J. (2015) "Fooling Around: female stand-ups and sexual joking". *The Journal of Popular Culture* 48(4): 703–713.

Freeman, H. (2015) "Amy Poehler: 'I see life as being attacked by a bear'". *The Guardian* 11 July. https://www.theguardian.com/culture/2015/jul/11/amy-poehler (last accessed 11 December 2016).

Fretts, B. (2015) "Michael Schur on the *Parks and Recreation* Series Finale". *ArtsBeat*, February 25. http://artsbeat.blogs.nytimes.com/2015/02/25/michael-schur-on-the-parks-and-recreation-series-finale/?_r=0.

Freud, S. (1905/1991) *Jokes and their Relation to the Unconscious*. Translated by J. Strachey. London: Penguin Books.

Freud, S. (1927/1990) "Humour". In A. Dickson (ed.) *Art and Literature: Jensen's Gradiva, Leonardo da Vinci and other works*. 14. Harmondsworth: Penguin, pp. 425–434.

Fricker, K. (2015) "Blogging". *Contemporary Theatre Review* 25(1): 39–45.

Friedman, S. (2014) *Comedy and Distinction: the cultural currency of a "good" sense of humour*. London and New York: Routledge.

Gates, H.L. Jr. (1997/2000) "A Reporter at Large: black London". In K. Owusu (ed.) *Black British Culture and Society: a text reader*. London: Routledge, pp. 183–194.

Genette, G. (1997) *Paratexts: thresholds of interpretation*. Cambridge: Cambridge University Press.

Gennis, S. (2015) "Amy Schumer's *12 Angry Men* Parody is the Best Sketch of the Year". *TV Guide*, 6 May. http://www.tvguide.com/news/amy-schumer-12-angry-men-parody/.

Gilbert, J. (1997) *Performing Marginality: humor, gender, and cultural critique*. Detroit: Wayne State University Press.

Gilbert, E., Bakhshi, S., Chang, S. and Terveen, L. (2013) "I Need to Try This"?: a statistical overview of Pinterest". CHI '13 Proceedings of the SIGCHI Conference on Human Factors in Computing System, pp. 2427–2436.

http://citeseerx.ist.psu.edu/viewdoc/download?doi=10.1.1.658.2983& rep=rep1&type=pdf.

Gilroy, P. (1993) *Small Acts: thoughts on the politics of black cultures.* London: Serpent's Tail.

Goltz, D.B. (2015) "Ironic Performativity: Amy Schumer's big (white) balls". *Text and Performance Quarterly* 35(4): 266–285.

Graefer, A. (2014) "White Stars and Orange Celebrities: the affective production of whiteness in humorous celebrity-gossip blogs". *Celebrity Studies* 5(1–2): 107–122.

Graefer, A. (2016) "The Work of Humour in Affective Capitalism: a case study of celebrity gossip blogs". *Ephemera* 16(4): 143–162. http://www.ephemerajournal.org/sites/default/files/pdfs/contribution/16–4graefer.pdf.

Grant, D. (2013) "David Avery: he's got game". *The Voice* 13 May. http://www.voice-online.co.uk/article/david-avery-hes-got-game.

Gray, J. (2003) "New Audiences, New Textualities: anti-fans and non-fans". *International Journal of Cultural Studies* 6(1): 64–81.

Gray, J. (2007) "Imagining America: *The Simpsons* go global". *Popular Communication* 5(2): 129–148.

Gray, J. (2010) *Show Sold Separately: promos, spoilers, and other media paratexts.* New York: New York University Press.

Gray, J. and Mittell, J. (2007) "Speculation on Spoilers: *lost* fandom, narrative consumption and rethinking textuality". *Participations* 4(1): http://www.participations.org/Volume%204/Issue%201/4_01_graymittell.htm.

Griffin, D. (1994) *Satire: a critical reintroduction.* Lexington: The University Press of Kentucky.

Gripsrud, J. (1995) *The Dynasty Years: Hollywood television and critical media studies.* New York: Routledge.

Gullestad, M. (2002) "Invisible Fences: egalitarianism, nationalism and racism". *The Journal of the Royal Anthropological Institute* 8(1): 45–63.

Gundelach, P. (2000) "Joking Relationships and National Identity in Scandinavia". *Acta Sociologica* 43(2): 113–122.

Guo, L. and Lee, L. (2013) "The Critique of YouTube-based Vernacular. Discourse: a case study of YouTube's Asian community". *Critical Studies in Media Communication* 30(5): 391–406.

Haig, F. (2014) "Guilty Pleasures: *Twilight, snark and critical fandom*". In W. Clayton and S. Harman (eds.) *Screening Twilight: critical approaches to a cinematic phenomenon.* London and New York: I.B. Tauris, pp. 11–25.

Hall, S. (1990) "Cultural Identity and Diaspora". In J. Rutherford (ed.) *Identity: culture, difference, community.* London: Lawrence and Wishart, pp. 222–237.

Hamad, H. and Taylor, A. (2015) "Introduction: feminism and contemporary celebrity culture". *Celebrity Studies* 6(1): 124–127.

Hansen, W. (2015) "10 Amy Schumer Quotes that Prove How Awesome She Really Is". *Hello Giggles,* 19 May. http://hellogiggles.com/10-amy-schumer-quotes-prove-awesome-really/.

Harbidge, L. (2009) "A New Direction in Comedian Comedy?: *eternal sunshine of the spotless mind, punch-drunk love* and the post-comedian rom-com". In S. Abbot and D. Jermyn (eds.) *Falling in Love Again: Romantic Comedy in Contemporary Cinema.* London: I.B. Tauris, pp. 176–189.

Harman, S. and Jones, B. (2013) "Fifty Shades of Ghey: snark fandom and the figure of the anti-fan". *Sexualities* 16(8): 951–968.

Hay, J. (2000) "Functions of Humor in the Conversations of Men and Women". *Journal of Pragmatics* 32: 709–742.

Herring, S.C., Kouper, I., Paolillo, J.C., Scheidt, L.A., Tyworth, M., Welsch, P., Wright, E. and Yu, N. (2005) "Conversations in the Blogosphere: an analysis 'from the bottom up'". Paper presented to the Thirty-Eighth Hawai'i International Conference on System Sciences (HICSS-38). Big Island. http://cns. iu.edu/docs/publications/2005-herring-blogosph.pdf.

Hervik, P. (2004) "The Danish Cultural World of Unbridgeable Differences". *Ethnos* 69 (2): 247–267.

Hillman, S., Procyk, J. and Neustaedter, C. (2014) "'alksjdf;lksfd': Tumblr and the fandom user experience". Paper presented to DIS'14, Vancouver. http://www.drinkthecoolaid.com/wp-content/uploads/tumblr-dis-paper-V8.pdf.

Hills, M. (2002) *Fan Cultures*. London and New York: Routledge.

Hills, M. (2015) "*Doctor Who's* 50th Anniversary as an Unfolding Media Event: rethinking narratives of hype and their paratextual arrays". *BCMCR Research Seminar Series*, Birmingham City University, 4th of March.

Hine, C. (2011) "Towards Ethnography of Television on the Internet: a mobile strategy for exploring mundane interpretive activities". *Media, Culture & Society* 33(4): 567–582.

Hobbes, T. (1651) *Leviathan, or the Matter, Forme, & Power of a Common-Wealth Ecclesiasticall and Civil.* London: Andrew Crooke. http://socserv2. socsci.mcmaster.ca/econ/ugcm/3ll3/hobbes/Leviathan.pdf.

Hodge, R. and Tripp, D. (1986) *Children and Television: a semiotic approach.* Cambridge: Polity Press.

Holland, D., Lachicotte Jr., W., Skinner, D. and Cain, C. (1998) *Identity and Agency in Cultural Worlds.* Cambridge, MA: Harvard University Press.

Holquist, M. (2002) *Dialogism: Bakhtin and his world.* New York: Routledge.

hooks, b. (1992) *Black Looks: race and representation.* Boston, MA: South End Press.

Hutcheon, L. (1994/2005) *Irony's Edge: the theory and politics of irony.* London: Routledge.

Ihlebæk, K.A., Syvertsen, T. and Ytreberg, E. (2014) "Keeping Them and Moving. Them: TV scheduling in the phase of channel and platform proliferation". *Television & New Media* 15(5): 470–486.

Indigogo (no date) "Brothers with No Game: - The Web Series - Season 2". https://www.indiegogo.com/projects/brothers-with-no-game-the-web-series-season-2#/.

Isaksson, M. (2013) "Telling New Stories? *Twilight* Fan Fiction Pairing Bella and Alice". In D. Holmes, D. Platten, L. Artiaga and J. Migozzi (eds.) *Finding the Plot: storytelling in popular fictions.* Newcastle upon Tyne: Cambridge Scholars Publishing, pp. 292–305.

Jeffers Mcdonald, T. (2007) *Romantic Comedy: boy meets girl meets genre.* London: Wallflower.

Jeffers Mcdonald, T. (2009) "Homme-Com: engendering change in contemporary romantic comedy". In S. Abbot and D. Jermyn (eds.) *Falling in Love Again: romantic comedy in contemporary cinema.* London: I.B. Tauris, pp. 146–159.

Jenkins, H. (1992) *Textual Poachers: television fans and participatory culture.* New York: Routledge.

Jenkins, H., Ford, S. and Green, J. (2013) *Spreadable Media: creating value and meaning in a networked culture.* New York: New York University Press.

Jenkins, H. and Karnick, K.B. (1995) "Introduction: acting funny". In H. Jenkins and K.B. Karnick (eds.) *Classical Hollywood Comedy.* New York: Routledge, pp. 149–167.

Jenner, M. (2014) "Is This TVIV? On Netflix, TVIII and binge-watching". *New Media & Society* Online: 1–17. http://nms.sagepub.com/content/early/2014/07/03/1461444814541523.

Jenner, M. (2015) "Binge-Watching: video-on-demand, quality TV and mainstreaming fandom". *International Journal of Cultural Studies*, published online before print: 1–17. http://ics.sagepub.com/content/early/2015/09/16/1367877915606485.full.pdf+html.

Jhally, S. and Lewis, J. (1992) *Enlightened Racism*: The Cosby Show, *audiences, and the myth of the American dream.* Boulder, San Francisco: Westview Press.

Jurca, R. and Faltings, B. (2007) "Reporting Incentives in Online Feedback Forums: the influence of effort". Ecole Polytechnique Federale de Lausanne. http://liawww.epfl.ch/Publications/Archive/Jurca2007f.pdf.

Kaling, M. (2012) *Is Everybody Hanging out without Me? (And Other Concerns).* New York: Three Rivers Press.

Kanai, A. (2015) "Jennifer Lawrence, Remixed: approaching celebrity through DIY digital culture". *Celebrity Studies*, published online. http://dx.doi.org/10.1080/19392397.2015.1062644.

Kehily, M.J. and Nayak, A. (1997) "'Lads and Laughter': humour and the production of heterosexual hierarchies". *Gender and Education* 9 (1): 69–88.

Keller, J. and Ringrose, J. (2015) "But Then Feminism Goes out the Window!": exploring teenage girls' critical response to celebrity feminism". *Celebrity Studies* 6(1): 132–135.

Kendall, E. (1990) *The Runaway Bride: Hollywood romantic comedy of the 1930s.* New York: Knopf.

Kim, S.-M., Pantel, P., Chklovski, T. and Pennacchiotti, M. (2006) "Automatically Assessing Review Helpfulness". *Proceedings of the 2006 Conference on Empirical Methods in Natural Language Processing.* Sydney: Association for Computational Linguistics, pp. 423–430.

Kim, Y. (2012) "The Institutionalization of YouTube: from user-generated content to professionally generated content". *Media, Culture & Society* 34(1): 53–67.

King, G. (2002) *Film Comedy.* London: Wallflower.

Klinger, B. (2006) *Beyond the Multiplex: cinema, new technologies, and the home.* London, Berkeley and Los Angeles: University of California Press.

Klinger, B. (2008) "'Say It Again, Sam': movie quotation, performance and masculinity". *Participations* 5(2): http://www.participations.org/Volume%205/Issue%202/5_02_klinger.htm.

Klinger, B. (2010) "Becoming Cult: *The Big Lebowski*, replay culture and male fans". *Screen* 51(1): 1–20.

Kotthoff, H. (2006) "Gender and Humor: the state of the art". *Journal of Pragmatics* 38: 4–25.

Kristine (2015) "Reddit in 2015". http://www.redditblog.com/2015/12/reddit-in-2015.html.

Kuhn, M. (2014) "Web Series between User Generated Aesthetics and Self-Reflexive Narration: on the diversification of audiovisual narration on the Internet". In J. Alber and P.K. Hansen (eds.) *Beyond Classical Narration: transmedial and unnatural challenges*. Berlin: De Gruyter, pp. 137–160.

Kuipers, G. (2006) "Television and Taste Hierarchy: The case of Dutch television comedy". *Media, Culture and Society* 28 (3): 359–378.

Kuipers, G. (2015) *Good Humor, Bad Taste: a sociology of the joke*. Berlin and Boston: De Gruyter.

Lauzen, M. (2014) "The Funny Business of Being Tina Fey: constructing a (feminist) comedy icon". *Feminist Media Studies* 14(1): 106–117.

Leal, S. (2015) "Amy Schumer Gets Real about Feminism: 'I don't think people know what the word means'". *Marie Claire* March 17. http://www.marieclaire.com/celebrity/news/a13731/amy-schumer-feminism-sxsw/.

Lehtinen, J. (2017) "'True to the End'?: fan responses to the final season and series finale of HBO's *True Blood*". *Journal of Fandom Studies* 5(1).

Lent, T.O. (1995) "Romantic Love and Friendship: the redefinition of gender relations in screwball comedy". In K.B. Karnick and H. Jenkins (eds.) *Classical Hollywood Comedy*. London: Routledge, pp. 314–331.

Lewallen, J. and Behm-Morawitz, E. (2016) "Pinterest or Thinterest?: social comparison and body image on social media". *Social Media + Society* 2(1): 1–9.

Linder, R., Snodgrass, C. and Kerne, A. (2014) *CHI '14 Proceedings of the SIGCHI Conference on Human Factors in Computing Systems*, pp. 1–10. http://www.w.ecologylab.net/research/publications/everyday_ideation_pinterest.pdf.

Lockyer, S. (2011) "From Toothpick Legs to Dropping Vaginas: gender and sexuality in Joan Rivers' stand-up comedy performance". *Comedy Studies* 2(2): 113–123.

Lopez, L.K. (2014) "Blogging while Angry: the sustainability of emotional labor in the Asian American blogosphere". *Media, Culture & Society* 36(4): 421–436.

Lübecker, N. (2015) *The Feel-Bad Film*. Edinburgh: Edinburgh University Press.

MacDowell, J. (2011) "Thoughts on 'So Bad It's Good': the pleasures of *The Room*". *Alternate Takes*. http://www.alternatetakes.co.uk/?2011,5,293.

MacDowell, J. and Zborowski, J. (2013) "The Aesthetics of 'So Bad It's Good': value, intention, and *The Room*". *Intensities* 6: 1–30. https://intensitiescultmedia.files.wordpress.com/2014/01/j-macdowell-j-zborowski-the-aesthetics-of-so-bad-its-good1.pdf.

Malik, S. (2002) *Representing Black Britain: a history of black and Asian images on British television*. London: Sage.

Malik, S. (2010) "How *Little Britain* Does 'Race'". In S. Lockyer (ed.) *Reading Little Britain: comedy matters on contemporary television*. London: I.B. Tauris, pp. 75–94.

Malik, S. (2013) "The Indian Family on UK Reality Television: convivial culture in salient contexts". *Television & New Media* 14(6): 510–528.

Marwick, A. and boyd, d. (2011) "I Tweet Honestly, I Tweet Passionately: Twitter users, context collapse, and the imagined audience". *New Media & Society* 13(1): 114–133.

Massanari, A.L. (2015) *Participatory Culture, Community, and Play: learning from reddit*. New York: Peter Lang.

Mathijs, E. and Sexton, J. (2011) *Cult Cinema: an introduction*. Oxford: Wiley-Blackwell.

McCabe, J. (2009) "Lost in Transition: problems of modern (heterosexual) romance and the catatonic male hero in the post-feminist age". In S. Abbot and D. Jermyn (eds.) *Falling in Love Again: romantic comedy in contemporary cinema*. London: I.B. Tauris, pp. 160–175.

McClintock, P. (2011) "'Bridesmaids' Rocks Weekend Box Office With $24.6 Million Opening". *The Hollywood Reporter* 15 May: http://www.hollywoodreporter.com/news/bridesmaids-rocks-weekend-box-office-188509.

McCoy, C.A. and Scarborough, R.C. (2014) "Watching 'Bad' Television: ironic consumption, camp, and guilty pleasures". *Poetics* 47: 41–59.

McCulloch, R. (2011) "'Most People Bring Their Own Spoons': The Room's participatory audiences as comedy mediators". *Participations* 8(2): 189–218. http://www.participations.org/Volume%208/Issue%202/2d%20McCulloch.pdf.

McRobbie, A. (2004) "Post-Feminism and Popular Culture". *Feminist Media Studies* 4(3): 255–264.

McRobbie, A. (2007) "Top Girls?". *Cultural Studies* 21(4–5): 718–737.

Medhurst, A. (2007) *A National Joke: popular comedy and English cultural identities*. New York: Routledge.

Mellencamp, P. (2003) "Situation Comedy, Feminism, and Freud: discourses of Gracie and Lucy". In J. Morreale (ed.) *Critiquing the Sitcom: a reader*. Syracuse: Syracuse University Press, pp. 41–55.

Mercer, K. (1994) *Welcome to the Jungle: new positions in black cultural studies*. London: Routledge.

Meyers, E.A. (2010) "Gossip Talk and Online Community: celebrity gossip blogs and their audiences". Ph.D. Thesis. University of Massachusetts – Amherst. http://scholarworks.umass.edu/cgi/viewcontent.cgi?article=1296&context=open_access_dissertations.

Middlemost, R.M. (2013) "Amongst Friends: the Australian cult film experience". Ph.D. thesis. University of Wollongong.

Mills, B. (2004) "Comedy Verité: contemporary sitcom form". *Screen* 45(1): 63–78.

Mills, B. (2005) *Television sitcom*. London: BFI.

Mills, B. (2009) *The Sitcom*. Edinburgh: Edinburgh University Press.

Mills, B. (2011) "'A Pleasure Working With You': humour theory and Joan Rivers". *Comedy Studies* 2(2): 151–160.

Mills, B. (2016) "Schrödinger Projects: indeterminacy in television comedy production". Paper presented at the BCMCR research seminar, Birmingham City University, Birmingham, U.K., 10 February.

Mills, B. and Horton, E. (2016) *Creativity in the British Television Comedy Industry*. London: Routledge.

Mizejewski, L. (2012) "Feminism, Postfeminism, Liz Lemonism: comedy and gender politics on *30 Rock*". *Genders* 55 (spring). http://www.genders.org.proxy.lib.ohio-state.edu.

Mizejewski, L. (2014) *Pretty/Funny: women comedians and body politics*. Austin: University of Texas Press.

Montemurro, B. and Benfield, J.A. (2015) "Hung out to Dry: use and consequences of disparagement humor on American Idol". *HUMOR* 28(2): 229–251.

Morreall, J. (1983) *Taking Laughter Seriously*. Albany: State University of New York.

Morreale, J. (2008) "Do Bitches Get Stuff Done?" *Flow* 9: http://flowjournal. org/wp-content/uploads/2008/09/morreale-position-paper.pdf.

Mulkay, M. (1988) *On Humour*. Cambridge: Polity Press.

Neale, S. and Krutnik, F. (1990) *Popular Film and Television Comedy*. London: Routledge.

Newman, M.Z. (2014) "Say 'Pulp Fiction' One More Goddamn Time: quotation culture and an Internet-age classic", *New Review of Film and Television Studies* 12(2): 125–142.

Nicholson, A. (2014a) "The Classification of Black Celebrity Women in Cyberspace". In *Black Women and Popular Culture: the conversation continues*. Lanham, MD: Lexington Books, pp. 273–292.

Nicholson, R. (2014b) "Lena Dunham Tackles Diversity and Sexism in Girls on Heated Panel Debate". *The Guardian* 10 January. https://www.theguardian. com/tv-and-radio/2014/jan/10/lena-dunham-girls-hbo-panel-judd-apatow.

O'Regan, T. (2000) "The International Circulation of British Television". In E. Buscombe (ed.) *British Television: a reader*. Oxford: Clarendon Press, pp. 303–321.

Osborne, D. with Bourne, S. (2016) "Black British Comedy: *Desmond's* and the changing face of television". In J. Kamm and B. Neumann (eds.) *British TV Comedies: cultural concepts, contexts and controversies*. Basingstoke: Macmillan, pp. 167–182.

Otterbacher, J. (2011) "Being Heard in Review Communities: communication tactics and review prominence". *Journal of Computer-Mediated Communication* (16): pp. 424–444.

Ottoni, R., Pesce, J.P., Las Casas, D., Franciscani Jr., G., Meira Jr., W., Kumaraguru, P. and Almeida, V. (2013) "Ladies First: analyzing gender roles and behaviors in Pinterest". *Proceedings of the Seventh International AAAI Conference on Weblogs and Social Media*. https://www.semanticscholar.org/paper/ Ladies-First-Analyzing-Gender-Roles-and-Behaviors-Ottoni-Pesce/94f52b9e 42d80a9dfa614a750fb7579050ad9144/pdf.

Paasonen, S. (2011) *Carnal Resonance: affect and online pornography*. Cambridge, MA: MIT Press.

Palmer, J. (1987) *The Logic of the Absurd: on film and television comedy*. London: BFI.

Palmer, J. (1994) *Taking Humour Seriously*. London: Routledge.

Parker, R. Jr. (1984) "Ghostbusters". Arista.

Patterson, E. (2012) "Fracturing Tina Fey: a critical analysis of postfeminist television comedy stardom". *The Communication Review* 15(3): 232–251.

Patton, S. and Leonard, D.J. (2015) "Don't Believe Her Defenders. Amy Schumer's Jokes are Racist". *The Washington Post* July 26. https:// www.washingtonpost.com/posteverything/wp/2015/07/06/dont-believe- her-defenders-amy-schumers-jokes-are-racist/.

Pelle, S. (2010) "The 'Grotesque' Pussy: 'transformational shame' in Margaret Cho's stand-up performances". *Text and Performance Quarterly* 30(1): 21–37.

Petersen, L.N. (2017) "'The Florals': female fans over 50 in the *Sherlock* fandom". *Transformative Works & Cultures* 23. http://journal.transformativeworks. org/index.php/twc/article/view/956/760.

Phillips, T. (2011) "When Film Fans Become Fan Family: Kevin Smith fandom and communal experience". *Participations* 8(2): 478–496. http://www. participations.org/Volume%208/Issue%202/3i%20Phillips.pdf.

Phillips, T. (2012) "Too Fat to Fly: a case study of unsuccessful fan mobilization". *Transformative Works and Cultures* 10. http://testjournal.transformativeworks. org/index.php/twc/article/view/330/268.

Pinch, T. and Kesler, F. (2011) "How Aunt Ammy Gets Her Free Lunch: a study of the top-thousand customer reviewers at amazon.com". http://www. freelunch.me/filecabinet.

Pittman, M. and Sheehan, K. (2015) "Sprinting a Media Marathon: uses and gratifications of binge-watching television through Netflix". *First Monday* 20(10): http://uncommonculture.org/ojs/index.php/fm/article/ view/6138/4999#p4.

Poehler, A. (2014) *Yes, Please.* New York: Dey Street.

Popescu, S.O. (2013) "Hyper-real Narratives: the emergence of contemporary film subgenres". *Journal of Literature and Art Studies* 3(9): 568–575.

Proctor, W. (2012) "Beginning Again: The reboot phenomenon in comic books and film". *Scan: Journal of Media Arts Culture* 9(1).

Proctor, W. (2013) "'Holy Crap, More *Star Wars*! More *Star Wars*? What If They're Crap?': Disney, Lucasfilm and Star Wars online fandom in the 21st century". *Participations* 10(1): 198–224. http://www.participations.org/ Volume%2010/Issue%201/12%20Proctor%2010.1.pdf.

Pujolar, J. (2000) *Gender, Heteroglossia and Power: a sociolinguistic study of youth culture.* Berlin: Mouton de Gruyter.

Purdie, S. (1993) *Comedy: the mastery of discourse.* New York: Harvester Wheatsheaf.

Ratvik, E.H. (2012) "Nordmenn Får Se Lilyhammer Først Likevel". *NRK*, 17 January. https://www.nrk.no/kultur/endelig-norsk-lilyhammer-premiere- 1.7955761.

Redmond, S. (2007) "The Whiteness of Stars: looking at Kate Winslet's unruly white body". In S. Redmond and S. Holmes (eds.) *Stardom and Celebrity: a reader.* Los Angeles: Sage, pp. 263–274.

Redmond, S. (2009) "The Healing Power of Romantic Love in Popular Indian Romantic Comedies: Raja Hindustani". In S. Abbot and D. Jermyn (eds.) *Falling in Love Again: romantic comedy in contemporary cinema.* London: I.B. Tauris, pp. 65–78.

Rettberg, J.W. (2013) *Blogging, the 2nd Edition.* Cambridge: Polity.

Roschke, R. (2015) "9 Amy Schumer Quotes That Are So Beautiful, We Made Them Into Posters". *POPSUGAR*, 10 August. http://www.popsugar.co.uk/ celebrity/9-Amy-Schumer-Quotes-So-Beautiful-We-Made-Them-Posters- 38062827#photo-38062823.

Ross, K. (1996) *Black and White Media: black images in popular film and television.* Cambridge: Polity Press.

Ross, S.M. (2005) "Talking Sex: comparison shopping through female conversation in HBO's *Sex and the City*". In M.M. Dalton and L.R. Linder (eds.) *The Sitcom Reader: America viewed and skewed*. Albany: State University of New York Press, pp. 111–122.

Rowe, K. (2003) "Roseanne: unruly woman as domestic goddess". In J. Morrealle (ed.) *Critiquing the Sitcom: a reader*. Syracuse: Syracuse University Press, pp. 251–261.

Rowe, K. (1995) "Comedy, Melodrama and Gender: theorizing the genres of laughter". In K.B. Karnick and H. Jenkins (eds.) *Classical Hollywood Comedy*. London: Routledge, pp. 265–281.

Rowe, K. (1995) *The Unruly Woman: gender and the genres of laughter*. Austin: University of Texas Press.

Russo, M. (1988) "Female Grotesques: carnival and theory". In T. De Lauretis (ed.) *Feminist Studies/Critical Studies*. Basingstoke: Macmillan Press, pp. 213–229.

Russo, M. J. (1994) *The Female Grotesque: risk, excess and modernity*. New York: Routledge.

Sandvoss, C. and Kearns, L. (2016) "From Interpretive Communities to Interpretative Fairs: ordinary fandom, textual selection and digital media". In L. Duits, K. Zwaan and S. Reijnders (eds.) *The Ashgate Research Companion to Fan Cultures*. New York: Routledge, pp. 91–106.

Sastre, A. (2014) "Towards a Radical Body Positive". *Feminist Media Studies* 14(6): 929–943. http://dx.doi.org/10.1080/14680777.2014.883420.

Saukko, P. (2003) *Doing Research in Cultural Studies: an introduction to classical and new methodological approaches*. London: Sage.

Savorelli, A. (2010) *Beyond Sitcom: new directions in American television comedy*. Jefferson, NC: McFarland.

Schumer, A. (2016) *The Girl with the Lower Back Tattoo*. New York: Gallery Books.

Scodari, C. and Felder, J. (2000) "Creating a Pocket Universe: 'shippers,' fan fiction, and *The X-Files* online. *Communication Studies* 51(3): 238–257.

Sconce, J. (1995) "'Trashing' the Academy: taste, excess, and an emerging politics of cinematic style". *Screen* 36(4): 371–393.

Scott, S. (2015) "The Moral Economy of Crowdfunding and the Transformative Capacity of Fan-ancing". *New Media & Society* 17(2): 167–182.

Seham, A. (2001) *Whose Improv Is It Anyway? Beyond Second City*. Jackson: University Press of Mississippi.

Sestero, G. and Bissell, T. (2013) *The Disaster Artist: my life inside The Room, the Greatest Bad Movie Ever Made*. New York: Simon & Schuster.

Shrum, W. (1996) *Fringe and Fortune: the role of critics in high and popular art*. Princeton, NJ: Princeton University Press.

SimilarWeb (2016) "Reddit.com". https://www.similarweb.com/website/reddit.com.

Singer, P., Flöck, F., Meinhart, C., Zeitfogel, E. and Strohmaier, M. (2014) "Evolution of Reddit: from the front page of the Internet to a self-referential community?" *WWW '14 Companion, Proceedings of the 23rd International Conference on World Wide Web*, pp. 517–522. http://arxiv.org/pdf/1402.1386.pdf.

Smith, G. M. (1999) "'To Waste More Time, Please Click Here Again': Monty Python and the quest for film / CD-ROM adaptation". In G.M. Smith (ed.)

On a Silver Platter: CD-ROMs and the promises of a new technology. New York and London: New York University Press, pp. 58–86.

Smith, J. (2005) "The Frenzy of the Audible: pleasure, authenticity, and recorded laughter". *Television & New Media* 6(1): 23–47.

Smith, M. (1995) *Engaging Characters: fiction, emotion, and the cinema.* Oxford: Clarendon Press.

Smith-Shomade, B.E. (2012) "Introduction: I see black people". In B.E. Smith-Shomade (ed.) *Watching While Black: centering the television of black audiences.* New Brunswick, NJ: Rutgers University Press, pp. 1–15.

Sonntag, S. (1994/1964) "Notes on Camp". In F. Cleto (ed.) *Camp, Queer Aesthetics and the Performing Subject: a reader.* Ann Arbor, MI: University of Michigan Press, pp. 53–62.

Sørenes, A. (2014) "Svært Stolt av 'Lilyhammer'". *NRK,* 6 April. https://www.nrk.no/ho/svaert-stolt-av-_lilyhammer_-1.11652403.

Stallybrass, P. and White, A. (1986) *The Politics and Poetics of Transgression.* Ithaca, NY: Cornell University Press.

Stilwell, R.J. (2009) "Music, Ritual and Genre in Edward Burns' Indie Romantic Comedies". In S. Abbot and D. Jermyn (eds.) *Falling in Love Again: romantic comedy in contemporary cinema.* London: I.B. Tauris, pp. 25–37.

Sundet, V.S. (2016) "Still 'Desperately Seeking the Audience'? Audience Making in the Age of Media Convergence" (The *Lilyhammer* Experience)". *Northern Lights* 14: 11–27.

Sutherland, H. (2013) "'Trousered' and 'Sexless' at the BBC: women light entertainment makers in the 1970s and 1980s". *Journal of British Cinema and Television* 10(3): 650–663.

Sutton, P.l (2009) "Après Le Coup De Foudre: narrative, love and spectatorship in Groundhog Day". In S. Abbot and D. Jermyn (eds.) *Falling in Love Again: romantic comedy in contemporary cinema.* London: I.B. Tauris, pp. 38–51.

Syvertsen, T. (1992) "Public Television in Transition". Ph.D. thesis. University of Leicester. https://lra.le.ac.uk/bitstream/2381/27779/1/1992Syvertsen TPhD.pdf.

Syvertsen, T. (2004) "Citizens, Audiences, Customers and Players: a conceptual discussion of the relationship between broadcasters and their publics". *European Journal of Cultural Studies* 7(3): 363–380.

Tagg, J. (1988) *The Burden of Representation: essays on photographies and histories.* Basingstoke: Macmillan.

Tankel, J.D. and Murphy, K. (1998) "Collecting Comic Books: a study of the fan and curatorial consumption". In C. Harris and A. Alexander (eds.) *Theorizing Fandom: fans, subculture, and identity.* Cresskill, NJ: Hampton Press, pp. 55–68.

Taylor, A. (2014) "'Blockbuster' Celebrity Feminism". *Celebrity Studies* 5(1–2): 75–78.

Taylor, S. (2015) "Arrested Development: can funny female characters survive script development processes?" *Philament* 20: https://philamentjournal.files. wordpress.com/2016/01/20_taylor_150204.pdf.

Thelwall, M., Sud, P. and Vis, F. (2012) "Commenting on YouTube videos: from Guatemalan rock to El Big Bang". *Journal of the American Society for Information Science and Technology* 63(3): 616–629.

Thielman, S. (2014) "Fox Cancels Us & Them Before Airing a Single Episode. The romantic sitcom had been slated to launch this summer". *Adweek*. http://www.adweek.com/news/television/fox-wont-even-burn-its-last-episodes-us-them-158239.

Thomas, J.M. (2015) *Working to Laugh: assembling difference in American stand-up comedy venues*. Lanham: Lexington Books.

Thornton, S. (1995) *Club Cultures: music, media and subcultural capital*. Cambridge: Polity.

Todd, A.M. (2011) "Saying Goodbye to *Friends*: fan culture as lived experience". *The Journal of Popular Culture* 44(4): 854–871.

Toffoletti, K. and Mewett, P. (2012) "Oh Yes, He is Hot: female football fans and the sexual objectification of sportsmen's bodies". In K. Toffoletti and P. Mewett (eds.) *Sport and Its Female Fans*. New York: Routledge, pp. 99–114.

Tryon, C. (2009) *Reinventing Cinema: movies in the age of media convergence*. New Brunswick, NJ: Rutgers University Press.

Tryon, C. (2013) "Reboot Cinema". *Convergence* 19(4): 432–437.

Tsagarousianou, R. (2004) "Rethinking the Concept of Diaspora: mobility, connectivity and communication in a globalised world". *Westminster Papers in Communication and Culture* 1(1): 52–65.

Tueth, M.V. (2005) *Laughter in the Living Room: television comedy and the American home audience*. New York: Peter Lang.

Tyler, I. (2008) "Chav Mum Chav Scum". *Feminist Media Studies* 8(1): 17–34.

Verdery, K. (1996) "Whither 'Nation' and 'Nationalism'?" In G. Balakrishnan (ed.) *Mapping the Nation*. London: Verso, pp. 226–234.

Vineyard, J. (2014) "Read Amy Schumer's Powerful Speech About Confidence". *Vulture*, 2 May. http://www.vulture.com/2014/05/read-amy-schumers-ms-gala-speech.html.

Vivar, R. (2016) "A Film Bacchanal: playfulness and audience sovereignty in San Sebastian Horror and Fantasy Film Festival". *Participations* 13(1): 234–251. http://www.participations.org/Volume%2013/Issue%201/S1/6.pdf.

Vološinov, V. N. (1973) *Marxism and the Philosophy of Language*. L. Matejka and I.R. Titunik. New York: Seminar Press.

Wanzo, R. (2015) "African American Acafandom and Other Strangers: new genealogies of fan studies". *Transformative Works and Cultures* 20. http://journal.transformativeworks.org/index.php/twc/article/view/699/538.

Warner, H. (2013) "'A New Feminist Revolution in Hollywood Comedy'?: post-feminist discourses and the critical reception of *Bridesmaids*". In J. Gwynne and N. Muller (eds.) *Postfeminism and Contemporary Hollywood Cinema*. Basingstoke: Palgrave Macmillan, pp. 222–237.

Warner, H. and Savigny, H. (2015) "'Where Do You Go After *Bridesmaids*?': the politics of being a woman in Hollywood". In H. Savigny and H. Warner (eds.) *The Politics of Being a Woman: feminism, media and 21st century popular culture*. Houndsmills, Basingstoke: Palgrave Macmillan, pp. 112–134.

Warner, K.J. (2015) "ABC's *Scandal* and Black Women's Fandom". In E. Levine (ed.) *Cupcakes, Pinterest and Ladyporn: feminized popular culture in the early twenty-first century*. Urbana: University of Illinois Press, pp. 32–50.

Wexman, V.W. (1980) "The Rhetoric of Cinematic Improvisation". *Cinema Journal.* 20(1): 29–41.

Whalley, J. (2010) *Saturday Night Live, Hollywood Comedy, and American Culture.* Basingstoke: Palgrave Macmillan.

Wheatley, H. (2016) *Spectacular Television: Exploring Televisual Pleasure.* London: I.B. Tauris.

Whisper (no date) "Press". https://whisper.sh/press.

White, R. (2010) "Funny Women". *Feminist Media Studies* 10(3): 355–358.

Whittle, A. (2015) "The 2016 Pirelli Calendar Breaks Tradition and Stereotypes". *Vanity Fair,* 2 December. http://www.vanityfair.com/culture/2015/12/2016-pirelli-calendar-amy-schumer-annie-leibovitz.

Williams, R. (2011a), "'Wandering off into Soap Land': fandom, genre and 'shipping' *The West Wing*". *Participations* 8(1): http://www.participations.org/Volume%208/Issue%201/williams.htm.

Williams, R. (2011b) "'This Is the Night TV Died': television post-object fandom and the demise of *The West Wing. Popular Communication* 8(4): 266–279.

Williams, R. (2015) *Post-Object Fandom: television, identity and self-narrative.* London: Bloomsbury.

Wilson, J. and Yochim, E.C. (2015) "Pinning Happiness: affect, social media and the work of mothers". In E. Levine (ed.) *Cupcakes, Pinterest, and Ladyporn: feminized popular culture in the early twenty-first century.* Champaign, IL: University of Illinois Press, pp. 232–248.

Worsley, S. M. (2010) *Audience, Agency and Identity in Black Popular Culture.* New York: Routledge.

Wright, M.M. (2004) *Becoming Black: creating identity in the African diaspora.* Durham: Duke University Press.

York, A.E. (2010) "From Chick Flicks to Millennial Blockbusters: spinning female-driven narratives into franchises". *The Journal of Popular Culture* 43(1): 3–25.

Ytreberg, E. (1996) "Textual Strategies in Recent Norwegian Television: public service television's reactions to the challenge from commercial channels". In I. Bondebjerg and F. Bono (eds.) *Television in Scandinavia: history, politics and aesthetics.* Luton: University of Luton Press, pp. 156–181.

Index

For Product Safety Concerns and Information please contact our EU
representative GPSR@taylorandfrancis.com
Taylor & Francis Verlag GmbH, Kaufingerstraße 24, 80331 München, Germany

www.ingramcontent.com/pod-product-compliance
Ingram Content Group UK Ltd.
Pitfield, Milton Keynes, MK11 3LW, UK
UKHW020944180425
457613UK00019B/515